THE FORGOTTEN LEGENDS

MANCHESTER UNITED'S GREATS OF A BYGONE ERA

BY CHARBEL BOUJAOUDE,
IAIN McCARTNEY & FRANK COLBERT

EMPIRE
PUBLICATIONS

EMPIRE PUBLICATIONS
1 Newton Street, Manchester M1 1HW
© Charbel Boujaoude, Iain McCartney and Frank Colbert 2013

ISBN 1901746 291 – 9781901746297

Printed and bound by CPI Group (UK) Ltd, Croydon, CR0 4YY

Cover by Tim Ashmore.

CONTENTS

Acknowledgments

Charbel Boujaoude would like to thank Iain and Frank for their collaboration on this project; Ted Roberts, Mary Stafford, Matt Johnson, and Mike and Diane Roberts for their contribution of personal information and memorabilia pertaining to their ancestors; Mark Wylie, Tom Clare and Ray Adler for their knowledge of Manchester United; my lovely assistant Gisele for all her help with research; Paul Nagel for setting up the book's website; Alex Paul for contact information; Ashley Shaw for the original idea and the final product; and my dear wife for her love, patience and unwavering tolerance.

Frank Colbert - It was a true labour of love to try to pen the biography of such a great fellow-Irishman as "Gentleman" Johnny Carey. My thanks to Arthur Fitzsimons and Eamonn D'arcy for their recollections of him. My gratitude for the great support and encouragement to Iain McCartney, my brother Maurice and especially my editor and mentor, Charbel Boujaoude. David Meek's highly recommended "Legends of United" was my inspiration. In particular, the forbearance and patience of my wife Kay helped to make it all possible.

Introduction

CHARLIE ROBERTS

After so many years we now have a written story of the exploits of the great Charlie Roberts, my grandfather. Captain of Manchester United for eight of the nine years that he played for our great club, he was the man who set the tenor for future generations. He set the bar high with the club's first league championship, first FA Cup victory, first foray into Europe and Charlie was the first player from United to gain England honours. Not only was he a force to be reckoned with on the field of play but he was also instrumental in setting up the Players' Union. He was fearless in his approach to bettering the lot of the footballers of the day – days when the bosses were all powerful and the players subservient to their whims. Charlie would have none of that and we, the family, firmly believe that this forceful man had his international career curtailed as a result of his struggle on behalf of his fellow football players.

Later Charlie was disillusioned with United when they sold him to Oldham Athletic in 1913 for the then huge fee of £1500, as he had thought that he would end his playing career with his beloved United. Nevertheless he continued to believe in United and made himself available to manage the club during the crisis years in the early thirties if called upon.. This did not endear him to the then directors who believed him to be responsible for the unrest amongst the fans and, to this day, I believe he is the only former player to be banned from using the Directors' box at Old Trafford. Charlie was fearless and not afraid of grasping the political hot potato as you will read in Charbel's splendid account.

The Company he started in 1907 prospered greatly after the Second World War and the forty or so delivery vehicles bearing his name, exhorting everyone to 'Have a nice day', were a common sight around the Greater Manchester area. The arson attacks on his factory in Manchester in 1992 gave rise to the building of the City of Manchester Stadium, first the venue for the Commonwealth Games and now rented by Manchester City FC. As Charbel records in his story, Charlie's ghost will roam there until such time as the perpetrators of the arson attacks are brought to justice...

The principal legacy left by this formidable man is, of course, the Players Union or PFA as it is now known. The riches heaped upon the modern day football stars owe much to the hardships suffered by those long gone pioneers in the first decade of the last century. I, together with all my many cousins, take enormous pride in the achievements of our illustrious grandfather, and we applaud Charbel and the team at Empire Publications for bringing to life the tales of these, no longer, 'Forgotten Legends'.

Thank-you,

Ted Roberts.

Foreword

JOE SPENCE

I feel extremely privileged to have the opportunity to write a few words by way of introduction to the life story of my Grandad, Joe Spence, of Manchester United.

It came as a total surprise when out of the blue I was approached by Charbel. I'm indebted to his fine prose in recalling the life and times of my Grandad's long association with Old Trafford for the United supporters. His story is certainly worth telling as he was the 'star' of his time at United and would probably be worth many millions if he was playing today. By all accounts he was in the mould of Steve Coppell with a big helping of Wayne Rooney thrown in!

Over the years, whenever we had new visitors to our house, the conversation would inevitably turn to football and particularly my Grandad's Manchester United days. My father, also a Joe, on such occasions would bring out a host of memorabilia, including newspaper cuttings, photographs, cartoon strips, and the like, all about his dad Joe. The mere mention of him having played for Manchester United invoked intrigue. Many would be amazed of how good Joe must have been, even if they were not necessarily football followers, as they had all heard of Manchester United Football Club.

Interest was usually raised when discovering Joe was, for a long period of time, the club's all time highest goalscorer and holder of the club's league appearance record. The appearance of Joe's England caps always drew admiring comments and the fact that Joe scored more league goals for United than a certain George Best would give rise to appreciative raised eye brows! My dad used to love telling tales of his dad's story, in particular his United days. He was a very proud son.

One particular tale which always raised a smile was when Joe was picked for England. He received the travel arrangements by letter from the Football Association and the letter also required Joe to bring a pair of navy blue shorts to wear for the match! The same instructions also suggested that Joe was to bring his own toothbrush and toothpaste.

Unfortunately I was very young when Joe passed away but I feel he has been a big part of my life and an even bigger part of the lives of the United supporters throughout his 14 year association with the club. Whenever they were struggling on the pitch and the team needed a lift, which, due to their topsy turvey league form, was quite frequent, the United supporters used to shout 'Give it to Joe', to let him take charge of the game.

I am really pleased that Joe's story is now being told along with other Manchester United greats. Up until now my dad has told just a lucky few listeners but, thanks to Charbel, my Grandad's exploits are here for the pleasure of all United supporters. I'm sure that many of the United supporters have wondered who Joe was, particularly as there are frequent references to him in the newspapers when the top ten goalscorers/appearance record holders for the club are published.

Even though I was a girl it was not surprising that I became a fully fledged football fan, though not of United but of my home town club, Chesterfield FC, where Joe ended his playing career in 1939. My interest was further aided by my dad who also played league football for York City in the early 1950's. I have been a football fan to this day and, to keep his name alive in the family, we named our son Joe after his great Grandad and my dad.

I also have to thank Charbel for unearthing a Pathé News film clip that shows Joe running out from a tunnel onto the pitch at the start of a game. I had given up any hope of seeing him in action but the brief five seconds were special to the family.

Enjoy the story.

Diane Spence

HARRY STAFFORD

As I write this foreword, Manchester United have just won their 20th league title! When my Great Grandfather, Harry Stafford, a hundred and eleven years ago took to the field as United's first captain, he could never have imagined how successful the club would become. His loyalty, dedication, sacrifice and love for this team assured its survival to become the world's richest and most supported sports institution!

Much folklore and mystery exists about Harry's life on and off the field! My thanks to Charbel in telling my Great Grandfather's amazing story, a true Manchester United Legend!

Matt Johnson, son of Mary Stafford, Harry's Granddaughter

Preface

There comes the time every now and then for one of those surveys to determine the greatest players in Manchester United's history. Now, for Reds fans, these are always enjoyable to read mainly because we have been spoiled over the years with a plethora of fine footballers. There is the Holy Trinity of Charlton, Law and Best, or the quartet of Beckham, Keane, Scholes, and Giggs. We can choose Eric the King, or Duncan 'Boom Boom' Edwards, as the blitzed Germans took to calling him. Robson, Schmeichel, Taylor… the illustrious names are endless. Yet there is one thing that irritates whenever these lists are compiled. Sure enough, the names of Ruud, Rooney and Ronaldo are near the top, and the likes of Coppell, Whelan, and Stiles are deservedly up there too. But where is Billy Meredith? Where is Charlie Roberts? Mitten, Pearson, Rowley and Carey? So many distinguished figures from the club's long, long history… they are all missing. You could scroll down the list looking for Joe Spence, Sandy Turnbull, or Frank Barson. You would reach the end of the list, but there is no mention of their names.

Yet in their time these were the biggest stars that Manchester United had! Much like we chant for our heroes today, the Old Trafford masses sang their names back in the day. Heck, they even wrote poems about Turnbull and put Meredith in motion pictures. So, how come they have lost their exalted status with the passage of time? A spurious excuse often heard is that players from the past, talented as they were, simply would not have been able to live with the more athletic type that dwells in the faster game of today. Well, that is pure nonsense. If all that a star from the past needed to do to match his modern day equivalent was to get fit, then that is a much easier task than, say, acquiring the necessary talent.

Which leaves us with one plausible reason for their exclusion – the passage of decades has ensured that a new, younger breed of fans has evolved, some that have never heard of the legends of a century ago, or others who might have briefly read about them but have never seen their brilliance to believe in them. That is the only acceptable explanation as to why modern-day journeymen spring readily to mind whereas legends of the past have been left behind by history. So, let us take a nostalgic trip back in time to the age of Harry Stafford, Charlie Roberts, Sandy Turnbull, Joe Spence, Johnny Carey and Jack Rowley. These were the greats who made Manchester United great. They could lick creation then have a laugh about it. They were real men who could fight in wars for their country and even die if they had to. And they had two more things in common: all made their United debuts before the start of the Second World War and none of them have had their story told. If poor Ralph Milne could make the Top 100 Manchester United players' list by default, then these legends really ought to make it on merit.

Iain McCartney
Frank Colbert
Charbel Boujaoude
To read more United articles from Charbel please visit his website www.munitedhistory.com

THE SAVIOUR OF
MANCHESTER UNITED

"Everything I have done has been
in the interests of the club"

HARRY STAFFORD

HARRY STAFFORD BY CHARBEL BOUJAOUDE

Saint Harry

Were it not for Harry Stafford, there would be no Manchester United. Do you understand what I am saying? Were it not for Harry Stafford, Manchester United would not exist, the name would never have been uttered, and all of us would instead be supporting some other club that we really do not care much about. Fortunately, miraculously, Harry was present at the moment of reckoning to fulfill his destiny as the saviour of the club and the empire that followed. On talent alone Harry perhaps does not belong in this book, for the only way you can compare him to Manchester United greats is by stating that he dribbled like Beckham, tackled like Scholes, and passed like Ronaldo. In reality, he was an average fullback of second tier standard, yet he ought to rank among the club's legends purely because, were it not for him, there would be no greats to talk about. His claim to eternal fame comes not from any deeds on the field of play but, as we shall see from his life story, his role as captain of Manchester United starting back when they were still called Newton Heath. What he did a hundred years ago is not something that has been replicated by any other Red in history. In fact, his actions and influence have no documented match by another footballer anywhere in the world at any time. Accordingly, for anyone for whom Manchester United is *the* religion, it would be considered blasphemous if Harry was not the first name in a book about the club's past legends. Forget a knighthood – a sainthood is a more appropriate title to bestow upon Harry Stafford, the Saviour of Manchester United.

The Boilermaker

The way I have introduced Harry Stafford makes it seem like a surprise that he was not born in a manger. Mind, the modest home through which he entered the world could not have been much better. Crewe was a railway town and his parents were railway folks - the hardworking type, to be exact, who cared not for the luxury of a home as long as their sweat and toil were rewarded with a roof for the family. The father, George, had travelled from Leicestershire looking for a job as an engine-fitter in the railway company. The mother, Eliza, not to be outdone, came all the way from France to infuse some Gallic flair into Manchester United a whole century before Eric Le Roi.

Harry was born in late 1869. Or was it early 1870? Like a lot of relevant issues later in Harry's life, mystery surrounds the exact date. Either way, what is clear is that his arrival preceded his ultimate calling, for it would be another eight years before a group of workers on the Newton Heath end of the railway line decided to form a future empire, and a further 24 years before they required his intervention to prevent its extinction. But he was not going to simply wait around until that moment came, opting instead to live out half a lifetime. Harry grew up at 26 Crofts Street in nearby Nantwich, located southwest of Crewe. He was the youngest child in his family following his sister, Mary, and his brother, Walter. Times were tough for the Staffords, like most families of the era, but young Harry concentrated on school during the day and football in the afternoons.

It was the time of the Industrial Revolution, of railways and emerging electricity. Bowler hats were all the rage, complimented by a waistcoat and a jacket. And you were not a man unless you sported a coiffured moustache – the 'walrus' was as rugged as they come but the 'handlebar' would do. Yet Harry was ahead of his time on this particular subject, eschewing any facial hair for the refined, clean-shaven look which heralded the age of the modern, civilized man. But hats and waistcoats were firmly within his trendsetting tastes… provided they fit specific criteria: the hat had to be white and, as for the waistcoat, the brighter the better!

By his late teenage years Harry had begun a career in football, though that was not the only career he pursued. Of course, times back then were far removed from today. Chronologically, the eras may be just over a century apart but, financially, the gap was perhaps about a million years wide. These days top pros can make a killing making a living. For Harry, however, his football gig merely provided him with just some bonus pocket money, if any. The bulk of his meagre wages instead came from his day job. For people in the area, day jobs were aplenty, though they were mostly concentrated at the Crewe Works, which was part of the London and North Western Railway. At any given time, thousands of the town's inhabitants were employed by the company, and the Staffords were no different. They were working class folk, hard-working class, even. His father toiled there for years and it was inevitable that Harry would eventually get absorbed into the harsh reality of a nineteenth-century teenager with a job of his own. Occupation: boilermaker. Job description: welding metal into large containers inside which water could be boiled to searing temperatures to provide energy. What's not to love about it? Apparently, so thought Harry for he performed this task for years.

Of Optimal Talent

Although he was born in Crewe and was now employed there, Harry did not begin his football career with the town's team. Crewe Alexandra had been around since 1877 alright, but there was a little drawback: they did not entertain thoughts of turning professional until 1893. In the meantime, Harry had heard about some interesting developments emanating from across Lancashire by the seashore. A team newly renamed Southport Central was enticing footballers from everywhere by paying them wages. This was indeed interesting because, before the summer of 1888, the team consisted entirely of local men. In fact, the one time they had attempted to field 'foreign' imports, several of the local players refused to play! Consequently, this turnaround was designed to raise the club's profile, especially as the Football League had just been launched and football was about to take off in a big way. But Central's renaissance was not without some labour pains – when they asked a team called Lytham FC for a friendly match, they were rejected with the message: "We do not know this club"!

By 1889-90, however, Central's name was known enough to get them accepted as founding members of the regional Lancashire League. More outsiders flocked to Sussex Road, lured by competitive action and a wage packet. Young Harry became one of those outsiders when he first set about on his ultimately eventful career. As Central plugged away in that inaugural season to finish sixth out of 13 teams, Harry did his bit at right-back. However, as a relative novice, he was not an ever-present member of the side.

In truth, Harry never developed into a top class footballer such as, for instance, the outstanding Charlie Roberts who inherited his symbolic standing as Manchester United's defensive lynchpin and guiding light. There is a revealing story in Percy Young's 1960 book, 'Manchester United', that was passed down by an actual eyewitness. Not too impressed with Harry's constructive play, or lack of, one terrace pedant taunted him by saying "Harry, you can't play football", though he probably did not use such nice language. Yet Stafford instantly quipped: "No, but I can stop those that can!" The irony, if you think about it, is that it was indeed Harry's superhuman efforts that allowed hundreds of future Manchester United footballers to play.

In fairness, he was fast and full of energy and enthusiasm for the game. Reliable and resolute described his play. For the times, he was physically imposing – 5'9" in height and 12st 9lbs in weight – and that is probably why he was asked to play at the back to block or tackle anything that came his way. Additionally, he was very vocal that you could tell he would one day make a fine captain for some team. But that was about it. And not much else was expected of him. Running up and down the flanks *a la* Patrice Evra was not in the job description for a nineteenth century fullback. Harry may have been ahead of his time in his grooming habits and overall mentality, but on the field of play he was rigidly cemented to his defensive duties. He played football the way God originally intended, without the fancy fanfare or finesse. Consequently, he never attained the highest – or even lofty – standards of footballing excellence.

Yet this was a good thing. A great thing, in fact. Had Harry been any better, he might never have signed for lowly Second Division side Newton Heath. And even if he did, a top flight team would have whisked him away sooner rather than later. Either way, he would not have been around when the Heathens needed him during their darkest days of 1901 and 1902. Consequently, the club would in all probability have folded for, chances are, no equivalent replacement could have been present within the club to perform the same rescue mission when the whole football world lacked one.

Weekend Railwayman

A waste of time is not worth your dime. If that is not already a proverb then it should be. It did not take long for Harry to come to the conclusion that his first stab at professionalism was not all that it was cracked up to be. Sure, he earned a bit more money, but all that trekking across the county for an occasional game was simply not worth it. This was especially more so given that his mates at the works were always excitedly talking about the exploits of the town's own team. Crewe Alexandra were not formed by the railway company but the majority of their players worked there. As a result, there was a sense of attachment by most employees to the football team, who someone quickly dubbed the 'Railwaymen'. Whether they liked it or not, it didn't matter – the name stuck.

The 'excitement' in question centered on Crewe's involvement in the Football Alliance. There is something you have to understand about the game in 1890. Already the Football League was up and around, but it consisted of one division with twelve clubs. That was it. And that was great as far as the Alliance was concerned because *it* was now generally considered as the next best thing. Several big teams of the time, the likes of Sheffield Wednesday and Nottingham Forest, were in it, though I suppose it suffices to say that so were Newton Heath. Perhaps not surprisingly, an enchanted young Harry now wanted in too. He was a Crewe man by birth and a railway man all week long - it felt the natural thing to do was to become a Railwayman on weekends as well. So he left the riches of Southport behind and returned home. Although it seems strange that Harry had originally headed west for the money only to give it all up for better prospects of career advancement, this turn of events would become a recurring theme in his life. You could even argue that every time Harry put himself in a situation where money came first, it was so that the next time he would not have to.

And so Harry headed to Gresty Road for his own long-term good, for the subsequent good of Manchester United, and, hence, for the good of the whole world. Crewe's home, Alexandra Recreational Ground, backed up against the railway tracks. Accordingly, by virtue of good positioning, Harry could simultaneously protect both his goal and his livelihood. Crewe had not set the Football Alliance alight in the inaugural season. And, at the risk of spoiling the intrigue, even for the subsequent campaigns, about the only thing they set alight was perhaps the fire back at the works. Two months into the second season of 1890-91, you could see where the problem was: the defence had shipped 23 goals in seven matches. The main culprit was deemed to be Bayman, a fullback so incompetent, if he fell in the sea, he wouldn't know how to drown. As destiny would have it, this was the cue for new signing Harry Stafford to make the Crewe cut. Only it was not in his more commonly known position of right-back. That was the property of the reliable George Swift, so Harry took over incompetent Bayman's left-back slot instead.

November 22nd, 1890, was the date when Birmingham St. George came to town for Harry's Alliance debut and proceeded to batter the home team 4-1. As far as Stafford debuts go, this was not so bad – wait to see his Football League bow! As a matter of fact, he performed well enough to keep his place for the rest of the season, missing only two matches. One of those was an embarrassing 0-7 loss to Nottingham Forest. However, lest he feel left out, the Railwaymen re-enacted their humiliation when he was present in the side a month later at Sunderland Albion. He was also present on February 14th for a first meeting with Newton Heath. Whether he got a good first impression of his future employers is not clear, but he did receive the mandatory Heathen 'treatment' that left him too battered and bruised to turn out in the following fixture.

By the end of the season, Harry had appeared in 13 matches as Crewe finished eighth in the table. Perhaps I should not mention this as it does not reflect well on Harry, but the Railwaymen contrived to concede the most goals in the Alliance. Apparently, the management did not seem to mind. Instead, he had shown himself to be as adept at making tackles as he was at making boilers, and he was earmarked as a permanent fixture in the first team from now on.

Alliance Days

By the start of the 1891-92 Alliance campaign, not only was Harry a staple of the defence, he was also the senior figure. George Swift had made a swift exit to Wolverhampton Wanderers to be replaced by Alf Cope. Alf and Harry now constituted Crewe's entire defence. You have to remember that, way before all this 4-4-2 nonsense, those were still the days of the original formation with just the two fullbacks. Then there was the halfback line which is known today as midfield. The remaining five players all went on endless attacking forays totally oblivious to such mundane tasks as tracking back or defending in numbers. The result was entertaining matches with goals galore. This was the way football was played back then and a similar format existed at Crewe where most of the team hared forward leaving behind just Stafford and Cope to, er, cope.

And so the pair filled in at fullback, right or left, it changed every weekend. In fact, they swapped positions so frequently it is as if they randomly decided who was playing where with their own coin toss before kickoff. Having said that, Harry did turn out in midfield at left halfback on one occasion on

November 28th… and it proved to be a masterstroke. Up until that afternoon, Crewe had yet to pick up a single point in the Alliance, sitting comfortably four points adrift at the bottom of the table and a mere twenty off leaders Nottingham Forest. But Harry's presence in midfield helped boot Bootle 4-3 to finally kick-start Crewe's season.

A typically high-scoring encounter took place in January 1892 in the battle of the railway teams: Newton Heath 5 – Crewe Alexandra 3. It was Harry's first and solitary visit to the Heathens' then home of North Road. Just over a year later, the Mancunian club would move to Bank Street. Consequently, Harry remains the only outfield footballer to have played at North Road then represented Manchester United after the name change of 1902. Apparently, Harry was so bent on joining the Mancunians that in the home Alliance fixture, he inadvertently helped Newton Heath win by scoring an own goal as a brief glimpse of the future services he would render. He truly had United's best interests at heart all along.

The Railwaymen improved as the season wore on to commendably finish in the top half of the table. Harry appeared in 21 of the 22 Alliance games and he added half a dozen fixtures in the FA Cup. These days you need six matches to win this competition but, during that season, Crewe contested that many just to be knocked out in Round One after having negotiated endless qualifying rounds.

Bottom and Out

Something fantastic happened in the summer of 1892: Harry Stafford became a Football League player. And he did not have to switch clubs to achieve that, nor did he need to help his team get promoted. The good people of the Football League, they of the big beards and bigger waistcoats, had decided to expand into an even bigger money-spinning behemoth. Eventually the League would come to constitute 92 clubs, but the first step was for the Original Twelve to absorb the Football Alliance in one whole piece then chew it into two parts. A lucky select - Newton Heath included – became First Division fodder. The rest, of which one was Crewe, made up the new Second Division.

Harry was still playing footy for kicks, the Railwaymen having resisted the urge to accept professionalism for one more year. Which was fine by Harry, who had kept his day job and had gone back to living in Crewe around this time. Thus, he was already building a sound financial basis as he made his league debut on September 3rd, 1892. It was the very same day that Newton Heath played their first ever league match, losing 3-4 to Blackburn Rovers in Division One. Crewe Alexandra's inaugural Division Two clash was an even more high-scoring affair, Burton Swifts 'edging' an eight-goal thriller by seven goals to one!

If that gave you the impression that Crewe were a useless crew then you were correct. About the only decent quality that could be labeled to them in their introductory phase to League football was that they were at least consistent – they let in 44 goals in the first 11 matches, having apparently upset the God Defence somewhere along their short existence. I can only imagine how hectic a spell that must have been for Harry. All season long, in match after match (he missed only one), there he was pluckily putting away fires all across and around the penalty area; wholeheartedly tackling and blocking as a bevy of opposition forwards swarmed around him like a horde of savage wolves; frantically calling his teammates to track back while urging them to hold the fort. All to no avail.

Obviously, Crewe had to file away any promotion plans… for seventy years. However, come the season's end, they did keep themselves busy filling the re-election application, courtesy of a bottom-but-two placement influenced by a winless away record. 1892-93 was just one season but it would be the template for pretty much the remainder of Harry's stay at the Recreation Ground. The best they could do was finish twelfth out of 16 teams in 1893-94, and you can blame that on an improved professional approach after the club started paying Harry and his teammates at long last.

Once the novelty of money had worn off, however, Crewe plummeted to bottom spot in 1895. Harry was earning a salary both at the works and with the club now, but prosperity had to wait – he did not collect a single win bonus away from home all campaign. He had also developed the habit of picking up injuries as a result of his tenacious, all-action style. As the league program was expanded to 30 matches, the number of times he preferred to be fit was in the low twenties. Also in 1894-95, he did something that was totally unlike him: he scored a league goal. If you had not been keeping count, after two Alliance campaigns and a further three in Division Two, this was his first league goal ever. And then he went on to add another goal to make it a prolific season that was possibly talked about for years in the Stafford household!

1895-96 was an outstanding campaign for Harry, at least in the FA Cup. The record books indicate that Crewe were trounced 0-4 by Bolton Wanderers in the very first round. But to get there the Railwaymen, and Harry especially, had starred in seven qualifying matches. Conveniently, this extended cup run came in handy as an excuse for their abysmal league form which consisted of another winless away campaign and a last place ending. You see, while Crewe's day crew specialized in railway matters, the footballing side concentrated instead on applying for re-election. This was the third application in four years and by now the re-election committee had read their application one too many times. It was catastrophic for the Railwaymen - they were expelled from the Football League for the next 25 years! Only by the time their fate was sealed, Harry was no longer around…

On a Whim

You may never have heard of him but Walter Cartwright was a valuable player for both Newton Heath and Manchester United. From the time he joined in the summer of 1895 and for nearly a decade afterwards, he catered to the team's every need. If there was a tackle to be made in the mud, he would get muddy. If any running, clearing or covering were required, he would put his heart into it. Positions? He filled virtually every one of them: all across the midfield on a normal basis; both fullback spots and most forward slots when needed; and even in goal on a couple of occasions. The only position he was never selected for was out on the right wing, though he probably ventured there once or twice during each match. Yet Walter's lasting contribution to Manchester United was not for any activity on the field.

In the spring of 1896, Newton Heath were short of a right-back. When the club manager casually asked Walter for his opinion, the few words he spoke right then and there changed my life and yours. If that does not make the hairs on the back of your neck stand up then you have probably shaved them. You see, Walter was born in Nantwich, not far from Harry Stafford's birthplace. The year was 1871, which was shortly after Harry's naissance. And when Heath signed Walter in 1895, his previous club had been Crewe Alexandra. It should not come as a surprise then that, when a fullback vacancy came up at Heath, Walter recommended his ex-teammate and good friend Harry. Of course, little did he know that, in doing so, he was altering the history of English football.

In how it significantly influenced the story of the club we love and know today, this moment ranks as arguably the most important in Manchester United's history. The only other event that might be considered of equal magnitude is when United official Louis Rocca sounded out a certain Matt Busby about a managerial job in 1944. Because in bringing Stafford to Newton Heath, by divine intervention or simply on a Cartwright whim, it ensured that, at the moment of reckoning a few years on, a commanding captain would be present to single-mindedly perform whichever daunting task it took to save the club from extinction. As you will see later, were it not for Stafford, it is plausible the term 'Manchester United' would never have been uttered.

But couldn't Harry have performed such heroic deeds at his previous club? Crewe, after all, was the place he was born, dwelled, and made a living. By the end of 1895-96, the Railwaymen would be ejected from the Football League and doomed to eke out a nomadic existence for a quarter of a century. In fairness, Harry did not know in advance the fate that awaited his hometown team. Although they were rock bottom when the transfer to Manchester was proposed, there were still six league matches to go. Crewe might have pulled themselves out of trouble or they might have negotiated another successful re-election, as it had become their habit.

Perhaps Harry had had enough of Alexandra's all-out defence style of play. Since 1890 he had been part of a back line that was habitually at sixes or at sevens, quite often at both. He had toiled wholeheartedly in 142 matches in the League, Alliance, and FA Cup, scoring four goals. He had even helped Crewe to what still constitutes to this day their highest ever ranking: 26th best team in the land in 1892-93! Yet through all those years he had craned his neck while continuously looking at the other clubs up the table. One of these clubs, a previous Division One inhabitant, no less, was now offering him a way out of his footballing misery. He took it and, to be frank, so would you. A case in point: If you were driving on the road and found yourself stuck behind someone moving slowly, you would not wait there endlessly. You would change lanes and move on with your life. Harry would have been in his right to move on with his career.

Perhaps, too, he really did want to help; he cared to prevent Crewe from drifting out of the League. But he was too young, too inexperienced, not enough of a senior voice at the club yet. We should be thankful then that such an episode shaped Harry for the bigger role that awaited him at his next stop. He may have sought to help, it is just that it was not his time yet. He was born to lead, but forced to wait.

HARRY IN TRAINING
From left to right: Stafford, Hayes, Read, Bacon (trainer), Cartwright.

New Old World

When Harry got off the train in Clayton in March 1896, he was stepping into a whole new world… which was much like his old world. On the one hand, there he was in a much bigger city, one of the foremost temples of the Industrial Revolution. There is a short newsreel film in existence today, titled 'Manchester Street Scene', that shows a busy crossroad in the city around the turn of the century, when Harry was with the club. The sidewalks are packed with hundreds of Mancunians, immaculately clad in suits or fancy dresses to the very last one of them. The road is jammed with moving vehicles: horse-ridden carriages transporting barrels, boxes and such, or trams taking passengers to places like Burlington or Brooke's Bar. It is the perfect snapshot of a breathing, thriving modern city that seemed to fit perfectly with Harry's own forward-thinking, metropolitan approach to life. Even back then the lure of Manchester was impossible to resist.

On the other hand, when it came down to actual substance, Harry's life would very much be the same. For a start, he would continue living in Crewe, preferring to take the train to Manchester on a daily basis – on the new company's expense, it must be added. Also, whereas he used to be a boilermaker at Crewe Works, he would remain a boilermaker only at the Lancashire & Yorkshire Railway (LYR) in Manchester now. And, finally, he would continue to operate at fullback, though now he belonged to the superior outfit of Newton Heath.

'Superior' is a relative term here. The Heathens were originally put together in 1878 by the more athletic employees of the Carriage and Wagon Works department of the railway company based in Newton Heath. In the subsequent 18 years their development was mostly on an upward curve: from best side in the LYR, to top team in Manchester, likewise in the Football Alliance, until they reached the First Division of the Football League. Once among the elite, however, the Heathens took a mostly agrophobic view of the division – the lowest spot was good enough for them. After two years of this, they were relegated to Division Two, and now they were in the second of umpteen seasons of trying to bounce back up.

Their pitch at Bank Street was notable for having no grass, and the coffers equally contained no brass. If anything, they were rich in poverty. This was the stark reality of Manchester United when Harry Stafford arrived at the club. It was much like the first time Matt Busby surveyed a derelict Old Trafford, complete with German bomb; or when Alex Ferguson came down from Aberdeen and gathered his player assortment of alcoholics and has-beens who had not been for a long time. This, right here, was Square One for Harry. At least the Heathens were superior to Crewe Alexandra, so thought the newcomer as he was immediately pitched into a glamorous friendly against the reigning champions of England, Sunderland, when he "played capitally" - to quote the

Manchester Guardian – in front of 6,000 spectators. The most incredible journey of his life was about to begin.

There is a reason April 3rd, 1896, was called Good Friday: Harry made his league debut for Newton Heath, who marked the historic occasion with a 4-0 pasting that put a dampener on Darwen's evolution. Harry was selected at right-back for the first of 200 competitive fixtures for his new club. His left-back partner for the afternoon – and the subsequent half a dozen years – was Fred Erentz. Behind them in goal was local lad Ridgway. The midfield consisted of Fitzsimmons, McNaught, and Harry's old mate, Walter Cartwright. And the forward line comprised Clarkin, hat-trick hero for the afternoon Kennedy, old stalwart Bob Donaldson, youngster Vance to balance him out, and Smith, because every side needs to have one. Despite the victory over Darwen, the chance for promotion was gone, but Harry kept his place for the remaining three matches of the season as the Heathens claimed sixth place in the table.

A Decent Defender

Before Harry could embark on his momentous salvation job so that future generations can cherish a Wayne Rooney overhead winner or a John Terry slip, he had to become captain of Newton Heath. And before he could be handed the Heathens' figurative armband, he had to prove himself as one of the leading players on the pitch. And in 1896-97, his first full season with Heath, he did just that. I may have mentioned that he was not the greatest footballer, but I did not say that he was inept either.

On the contrary, once Harry settled at Clayton, he quickly formed part of a formidable defensive trio that can be considered Newton Heath's answer to Manchester United's own protective triangle of Schmeichel, Pallister and Bruce – minus the 'motivational' obscenities. Left-back Erentz, we already met, while the goalkeeper was Scottish international Frank Barrett, signed in late September. Frank would sadly pass away a decade later but not before creating a legacy in Manchester. Stafford, Erentz and Barrett immediately converted the penalty box into a restricted area. To get past them and score against Newton Heath, you had to ask permission individually from all three of them. And they did not give it to just anybody. The proof is in the numbers, whether you choose to believe them or not: over the next five years, Heath boasted the best defensive record of all the teams in the Football League. And, yes, that includes perennial giants of the era, Aston Villa, Sunderland and the likes.

The contrast with statistics from his time with Crewe proved another thing: Harry Stafford was a decent defender. It is just that his efforts with the hopeless Railwaymen were all in vain whereas, in the right setup at Bank Street, he was able to flourish. And so was the whole team. 1896-97 turned out to be Newton Heath's finest season ever. Take the FA Cup, for instance. The Heathens made it all the way to the Last Eight. 'Newton Heath, FA Cup quarter-finalists' is a term you will not find anywhere else in history. They were eventually defeated by First Division highflyers Derby County after working their way through endless qualifying and proper rounds. This meant that in two seasons, first with Crewe then with Heath, Harry had incredibly contested 16 FA Cup ties.

It was a similar story in Division Two. Newton Heath won the first four outings and led the table for the first twelve weeks. They maintained the momentum throughout the campaign, founded on the meanest backline in the division, and earned runners-up spot behind Notts County. This was Heath's best ever finish in the Football League. Unfortunately, much like space rockets and the internet, automatic promotion did not exist at the time. Instead, both County and Heath had to first contest a mini-league with Division One's bottom two sides.

More unfortunate was the fact that the Mancunians would be missing their tenacious right-back, Harry Stafford himself, a victim of a bad tackle in a tussle with Bury in a local competition called the Manchester Senior Cup. Harry had been ever-present since the day he signed but this injury forced him to miss six matches in the run-in. He was so determined to repay the Heathens' faith in signing him and to help them win promotion that he turned out in the ultimate league fixture at Loughborough Town. Alas, he could not prove his fitness for the playoff matches ahead.

And most unfortunately of all, Newton Heath fluffed their promotion hopes, as it had become their habit. This was the third occasion in four years that they failed at the playoff stage. The story was getting so dull and repetitive, it was like watching Groundhog Day... every single day. With impeccable timing Harry's injury healed once the playoff series ended, just in time for a small consolation: his first piece of silverware with Newton Heath. It was not much to brag about, and Harry most probably didn't. Called the Healey Cup after a club director (remember the name), it required one win for the Heathens to reach the final of this friendly tournament. At least it afforded Harry and his teammates a quick opportunity to vent their frustrations on an unsuspecting Manchester City with a 5-2 drubbing. You see, at the time, the two Mancunian neighbours fairly divided derby victories using the following method: City won once in a blue moon, Heath won once in a white moon. Accordingly, the victory count after this match read: Newton Heath 20, City 6.

Love, Loyalty and Confidence

When he lined up against Manchester City in the Healey Cup final at the end of April, it was the last time he would be known as plain old Harry Stafford. The next time he took to the field in September 1897, the boilermaker from Crewe had a new title: Harry Stafford, Captain of Newton Heath. If there was one decision that the club's management got right around the turn of the century, it was to make this appointment. For Harry would proceed to prove without a shadow of a doubt that he was the greatest captain Newton Heath ever had, and arguably Manchester United as well. Sure, sure, there was Charlie Roberts and Frank Barson. There was Johnny Carey and Roger Byrne; Martin Buchan, Bryan Robson, Roy Keane. They were figures who led either by example, deeds, or simply fear. But Stafford was a man whose words were loud and his actions even louder.

So, what made Harry such a commanding skipper? There was a variety of qualities that fatefully blended together to establish his authority. First off was his confidence. You could easily tell he was not short of it from his insistence on strutting around in flashy apparel and that *risqué* clean-shaven look. And just wait to see all the glitz he came up with for his testimonial match. Flamboyant he may have been but, in truth, that is exactly how we love our United captains to be: possessing a certain degree of charisma or pizzazz, an upturned collar even. And Harry needed that confidence, not only to lead the mere mortals among his playing staff, but also to deal with the rich, upper crust of British society and sell them the idea of investing their money into a struggling professional football club to save it.

Another abundant quality was Harry's loyalty – you could practically smell it on him. Before you argue that he never held back from leaving his hometown club, Crewe Alexandra, it is worth considering the difficulty in resisting what seemed like the predestined work of celestial forces, not to mention the lure of Manchester United. Besides, Crewe's demise was an experience that he learned from and that strengthened his sense of responsibility. When the time came, there he was leading his men, organizing a bazaar to raise funds, acting as a liaison in the takeover of the club. There is no doubting Harry's sense of duty, and not just to his club. Indeed, here was a man ready to fight for his country, for he was on 24-hour standby when the Boer War broke out in 1899. Had the call to arms come he would have been gone by the next day. And this was a serious matter. Two other Heathens actually went to battle in South Africa:

An Advertisement for Harry's Ancoats pub

Gilbert Godsmark was sadly killed in action and Joe Clark was never heard from again. In view of Harry's future role in the creation of Manchester United, the club itself could very easily have been one of the casualties of the Boer War. Luckily the call never came, thus allowing Harry instead to walk alongside Newton Heath all the way through their own critical times ahead.

Of course it significantly helped that Harry was now enjoying a comfortable life. It was another case of fate conspiring to aid Heath's survival. By this time, Harry had become the proprietor of a pub in Ancoats, Manchester, called the Bridge Inn, located on the corner of Mill St and Beswick St. Between this, his gig at the works, and his football wages, he was doing quite well for himself. Had Heath's skipper been someone who was struggling to make ends meet, he would have been less prone to abandon personal welfare and financial prudence. As it was, Harry was able to disregard any worries about salary and devote all his time and energy on preserving the club.

Finally, an immense characteristic that shone through was Harry's love for Newton Heath. You could see it with your eyes closed. He may not have been a native Mancunian but nobody could have performed as passionately on the field of play, done what he did for the club in its darkest hour, captained it and led it to a more stable future, unless he loved Manchester United and infinitely cared about all that it stood for. For all of the above, Harry Stafford was the mightiest captain.

The Benefit of Light

Pick a Newton Heath game from the last half of the 1890s and read its match report. Any game. It would probably be one where Harry Stafford led the Heathens onto the field then proceeded to perform with customary gusto, or a certain degree of roughness, if that was his want. These were the Stafford Years. It was the period in which he established his authority and built his reputation as a great servant for the club.

There were good days and there were bad ones. And the worst – from a personal point of view – probably came on March 26th, 1898. This was the day the club won the Lancashire Senior Cup for the first time. It may be a forgotten competition these days but back then it was arguably the next best knockout tournament after the FA Cup, what with all the celebrated teams from the county contesting it annually. Heath's success that season would not be repeated until 1913, and the eleven players who took part were presented with shiny gold medals. Yet Harry was not one of them. After leading the side in all the previous rounds, he received an imperfectly-timed bad kick just days before the final and missed out on Heath's brightest day.

He vowed to make amends. In the following campaign he appeared in all the matches bar one. And by 'all the matches' I mean the League, all three competitions of the FA, Lancashire and Manchester Cups, as well as six friendly outings. And the solitary game he missed? On doctor's orders – he had a severe cold.

Then 1899-00 came along and it was perhaps his best season at the club, or in football as a whole. Newton Heath finished fourth in the Second Division for a third year running and again missed out on promotion, but take a quick glance at the 'Goals Against' column: a mere 27 were conceded. It was the club's best defensive record, and it would be bettered only once in the subsequent 97 years! If the origins of the expression 'parsimonious defence' have been lost in time then Stafford, Erentz and Barrett could lay claim to it.

By 1901, Newton Heath's skipper was due a testimonial. Back then, these were awarded after only five years of service, and Harry was not one to object. These benefit matches tended to fall into one of two categories. Most players would look at the fixture list, identify a game where a large crowd was expected – a local derby, say, or the visit of a top team – and keep a fixed chunk of the proceeds. In the other category belonged players called 'Harry Stafford'! Low-key affairs were not for him. In fairness, whatever he lacked in unfussiness, he more than made up for in flamboyance. A team called New Brighton Tower was summoned for a specially-arranged midweek match on March 6th. Kickoff time: 6:45pm! This, remember, was not at Old Trafford in 2001 but at Bank Street in 1901. Floodlights not yet invented? No problem – special Wells' Lights would be used to illuminate the ground and dazzle the crowd and the opposition. Newton Heath had played under a similar set up before, Harry argued, on one occasion a dozen years earlier, he did not hasten to add. As for the ball, it would be gilded to shine brightly. These were the sort of cutting-edge special effects that would have had a young Steven Spielberg scraping his jaw off the floor.

Too bad Harry did not have a retractable roof installed, for his special evening turned out to be a typically windy one. As soon as the game kicked off, the wind blew off one light, and that was not part of the special effects. The crew rushed to get it lit again. Suddenly another one blew on the other side. Off they scrambled again to fix it. After enough relay racing to merit a gold medal at the Olympics, the exasperated workers chucked in the towel. There was only one light still flickering and the referee – former Heathen Herbert Dale – used it to find his whistle and prematurely blow for time.

Harry's glitzy night was ruined but, first and foremost, he was an honourable and loyal fellow. All he was really worried about was the convenience – or lack of – of the paying fans. So he decided to grant them free entry into a rearranged match on April 22nd. For this occasion Harry had learned his lesson and opted instead to use the tried and trusted light source from the sun. Yet if the event lacked the novelty of artificial lighting, Harry compensated for it by putting together a combined eleven playing under a name you might have heard of –

Manchester United! It was the first ever occasion that the name was used but, despite including former Heath star, Joe Cassidy, and future United legend, Billy Meredith, the team lost 2-4 to New Brighton and folded after one match.

Yet if Harry's testimonial turned out to be farcical, spare a thought for his mate, Walter Cartwright. He unwisely elected to stage his benefit match in the middle of Newton Heath's annual financial crisis. As soon as the game ended, the waiting bailiff seized most of the earnings and Walter famously spent his take on one night out back home in Crewe.

A Goal in a Game

On January 5th, 1901, in an FA Cup tie against Portsmouth at Bank Street, Harry got his name on the scoresheet in a 3-0 victory for Newton Heath. There were around 5,000 spectators in the stands and most of them agreed that this was the best goal Harry had scored for the club. Albeit, this was greatly influenced by the fact that it was also his only ever Heath goal! Indeed, in 200 competitive outings for the club from 1896 to 1903, this was his solitary successful strike. At least that is what the record books say. But was it *really* his goal?

A contemporary match report tells a different story, and I will relay it to you. Heath were already leading 1-0 when they were awarded a free-kick in the opposition half. Captain Harry, full of intent and purpose, stepped up and took it. Portsmouth did not know what hit them. Or *who* hit them, to be precise. Apparently, Harry's intent was to put the ball in the mixer, from where "it was rushed through the goal". In other words, Harry *scored* that day much like Ryan Giggs was credited with a goal on his Manchester derby debut simply for being in the vicinity of the ball when it crossed the line. Harry was not even inside the penalty box but he was the last confirmed player to touch the ball before it briefly disappeared into a whirlwind of bodies then emerged in the net. Nonetheless, it went down in the annals of history as a Stafford goal, and who am I to re-write history?

A Major Event

Compare and contrast. In 2000, Manchester United were the reigning champions of the world. Having won the Intercontinental Club Cup, they were indisputably the best team you could find. A century earlier, in 1900, you could not even find them. The name, that is, had not yet been coined. Still, their predecessors – in Newton Heath guise – were doing their best trying to go extinct. When Harry Stafford joined the team in 1896, the deal was done with the avid intention of taking the Heathens back up to the First Division. And for years they tried. However, they could manage neither promotion nor their finances.

Indeed, when it came to money, the Heath directors had mastered one principle: how to lose it. Through means of misfortune or mismanagement down the years, it did not matter. Now they had reached a point where, to be blunt, if they were any poorer they would be poorest. The prized assets had been sold off to maintain the club: star striker Joe Cassidy grudgingly went to Manchester City while Frank Barrett took to diving under New Brighton's goalposts. Subsequently Heath's quality of play suffered. Harry had been groomed on a swashbuckling style of attacking football but, by 1900-01, the Heathens had abandoned the 'swash' and were mostly focusing on buckling in nearly every match.

The situation was bad and clearly it was continuously getting worse. It was time for Harry to commence the saving of our beloved club. Quite why would a club captain have to undergo such a momentous task may seem odd today but, at the time, it was common for the man with the armband to possess certain superior powers, such as an input into team selection, for instance. So, there was a sense of duty that moved Harry to take action, obviously coupled to his undoubted love for Newton Heath. Plan A had failed – the player sales barely touched the debts. Now it was time for Harry to come up with Plan B.

For this he was not alone, involving instead some of the more willing figures around the club. One was George Lawton, who started out as a big Heath fan, became close friends with Harry, and ended up as a director at Clayton. Another was the gaffer, James West. Now managers are known to complain about the referee, claiming they could do a better job than the man in the middle. With West it was the opposite. He was a referee who reckoned he could do better in the hot seat, so he became the first manager of Manchester United.

Their fundraising idea, and this was obviously something more common back then, was to throw a bazaar! Brass bands, exotic exhibits, celebrity politicians – you name it, they were all on display at St. James' Hall for four days, starting February 27th, 1901. The modest aim was to raise about £1,000. The outcome was that the club was saved! Only it was not like Harry originally intended.

The bazaar itself proved to be a flop, the club apparently not counting on rain (in Manchester in February!) keeping the masses away. Indeed, for several months afterwards, the whole hullabaloo was deemed as nothing but a unique diversion. However, a totally separate development had inadvertently sprouted out of the event and, in time, would ensure that the club would continue to rotate along with the earth.

This, of course, is the famous story about the dog that saved Manchester United. His name was Major and he belonged to Harry Stafford. As far-fetched as this tale might sound, Major's part should never be buried in the dirt. It is said that some pets tend to look like their owners; Major acted on Harry's behalf. For it was when the dog went digging that he struck gold...

Stafford had come up with an idea to bring in more money from the bazaar.

He tied a collection box around Major's neck and sent him to wander around the hall to fetch donations. Late in the third evening of the event, Harry went to check on his beloved dog but there was no sign of it. Nobody had seen this huge St. Bernard. However, one security guard admitted he had heard a ruckus at one of the stalls and went to inspect, only to spot two eyes glaring at him in the dark. Setting the attribute of bravery to the side, he took off through the nearest exit. It was subsequently presumed that Major had followed him out the same door.

Distraught, Harry went on an extensive canine search. And when that proved fruitless, he started handing out leaflets about the missing dog. A few days later there was some good news – his pet had been found and he was summoned over to a particular address to pick it up. From the moment he arrived at his destination, Harry realized he was entering a world totally different to the one he was used to. Major, that lucky dog, had led him to the house of one John Henry Davies after wandering into a pub he owned. *One* of the pubs he owned, in addition to the whole Manchester Breweries, one of the city's leading beer companies. If that was not swanky enough, Mr. Davies was married to the daughter of Sir Henry Tate, the sugar mogul. Put simply, it was a pure case of money marrying into even more money.

"This is the type of man," Harry must have though to himself, "that Newton Heath need to be associated with. Someone with the financial muscle to pick the club up from its terminal state and set it up for a rosier future". Harry grasped the opportunity. He struck up conversation with his host, explaining the chain of events that led to their encounter. Heath's problems, the players' efforts to solve them – Stafford disclosed them all. Davies was fascinated.

"This is the type of man," Davies must have thought to himself, "that I need to have working for me. Someone with the integrity and sense of loyalty who can be trusted to be the right-hand man, who would put in whatever effort required to get things done." They may have existed in separate spheres up to this moment but, due to a common interest, an unlikely union was forged between the two that in due course would change the face of English football.

A Hero Emerges

The cold could be described as bitterly and the rain miserly as Manchester entered into 1902. Even worse was Newton Heath's position in the standings: they were tenth. In the Second Division! Regardless, the Heathens fans resolutely looked forward to the upcoming League fixture with Middlesbrough on January 10th. On the day of the match, however, they could not get into the ground. Not just the fans but the players and officials as well – they were all locked out of Bank Street... by court order.

The main culprit was one William Healey: formerly a Heath director, now a disgruntled creditor who wanted his money back. The club owed him the princely sum of... £242, which they were not in a financial position to repay, so he took the logical step and sued! When the judge delved into the case, he discovered that Mr. Healey's portion was just the tip of the iceberg: the Heathens were in debt to the tune of £2670. Unimpressed, the judge immediately initiated bankruptcy proceedings for the winding up of the famous Newton Heath! If that was not drastic enough, he also ordered that the club's office fixtures be seized and that the ground be locked and surrendered to its rightful owner so he could convert it to grazing land for his cattle should he wish to. Ironically, the afternoon of that match turned out to be a bright, sunny one. They had picked a beautiful day for an eviction.

This was the glum, stark reality facing our beloved Manchester United in January 1902. As the administrator delved deeper into the club's affairs, it seemed only a short matter of time before the inevitable end. Bankruptcy meant the players' wages could not be paid, yet there was a bigger concern. The Middlesbrough fixture had already been called off and now lack of funds to cover travel expenses was threatening the next match away at Bristol City. Should Newton Heath fail to fulfill two obligations in a row, that would very likely bring their final demise. And this was no wild exaggeration. Already several clubs – such as Bootle, Darwen, and Loughborough – had disappeared off the League map, destined never to return. Would Newton Heath become another long-forgotten name that was once a Football League outfit?

It is at times like these that men either are transformed into legendary heroes or fade into the obscure past. Harry Stafford, Newton Heath Captain, stepped forth to face his destiny. This was the precise moment for which fate brought him to Clayton. There is something they say about football, that it is only a game. So what if a football club ceased to play sports? It is a good thing Harry did not conform to this way of thinking. For him it was not simply a game but a profession. You could argue that he was already doing well for himself outside the game through being a publican, but his teammates were not. Football was their only means of livelihood and they were his men; his responsibility. The whole club was. At least that is how he felt and he took it upon himself to rescue it. For that we are forever grateful.

Newton Heath may have hit rock bottom but there is one advantage to lying down on the floor. If you face up you get a clear view of the world above and a better idea of how to climb back up there. Harry figured out what was required and he was ready to act. Ready? He was conceived ready. Of utmost importance was finding quick cash to go to Bristol for the Saturday match. So he printed out hundreds of subscriptions and went around from house to house asking people for donations. Everyone who had given before or anyone who may have never heard of Newton Heath – he begged them all.

It worked. His efforts were rewarded with a collection of almost £100, enough for the train fare to Bristol though not for the hotel bill. The Heathens had to travel on the day of the encounter, arriving there barely in time and getting drubbed 0-4. But it didn't matter. The club had fulfilled its League obligation and the heartbeat was maintained. It is no exaggeration to say that Newton Heath were this one match away from extinction.

Next, Harry turned his attentions to Bank Street's chained gates. The reserve team had a home game scheduled soon, so he met the officials of nearby Berry football club and sweet-talked them into lending him their Harpurhey field for the day. The reserves' problem was temporarily resolved, but what about the first team? Bank Street's owner was seriously considering shelling £230 to demolish the stands. Again, the captain rode to the rescue. With all this talk about Harry's heroics it makes you wonder what the other ten players were for! To be fair, they had a role to play in the next mission. Harry marshaled his men and asked them to dig deep into their pockets. How much they contributed is not clear but what is certain is that the loyal Walter Cartwright joined his friend Harry in chucking in their own money. Even the nice directors chipped in and the club was therefore able to raise £100 to satisfy the ground's owner and convince him to keep it intact.

Throughout all this Harry was shuttling back and forth between Crewe and Manchester knowing the club would probably not be able to reimburse most of his expenses. In fact, he even asked to be reinstated as an amateur to save them more expenses. These were little gestures that showed what additional personal sacrifices Harry was willing to make in the name of Newton Heath. Still, it was not enough.

Heath's existence was one administrator's word away from coming to an end. Veritably, he could declare lights out with the same simplicity as blowing out a candle. For Manchester United to be born, Heath needed a huge injection of cash unlike they had ever been privy to before. And they needed to find such a source very soon. Harry had kept himself busy with his little tricks here and there but now it was time he pulled off the big one.

I Know of Five Men

As far as momentous dates in the history of Manchester United go, few, if any, compare to March 19th, 1902. A meeting was called at the New Islington Hall in Ancoats, open to anyone. The players, supporters who cared about Newton Heath, or directors who might have been partially responsible for the whole mess – they were all welcome. The meeting began in a gloomy fashion as the club suits disclosed to the audience the depressing figures such as the massive debts and the wages owed. Then a question came from a gentleman sat among the crowd. It was club captain, Harry Stafford, casually enquiring about how much dough was needed to make Newton Heath financially stable. All heads turned towards the chairman as he calculated a figure of roughly £1,000. At that very moment, in what was a small bounce for man but a giant leap for Manchester United, Harry rose and declared that there were five men who were prepared to place £200 each in Heath's bank account! It was a statement that brought the house down and left the chairman more bewildered than a deaf man at a gum-chewing competition.

Who were these men? And where did this money come from? Harry was swiftly summoned to the podium. Ever the showman, he gladly took centre stage before commencing a historic roll of names: Mr. Davies of Old Trafford; Mr. Taylor of Sale; Mr. Bown of Denton; Mr. Jones of Manchester; and... Harry himself! A mighty roar, the like of which is usually reserved to greet a last-minute United winning goal, filled the hall, though it is a good thing Gary Neville was not around at that instant, for Edwardian Britain was not yet ready for the full-on, wet snog. Harry was in his element here – the hero rising to the rescue - but, to the directors, this was too much excitement for one evening and they brought the meeting to a halt until he could present the gentlemen in question.

Who were these men indeed, and where did all this money come from? There was one answer to these two questions: these were very rich local men. Newton Heath needed investment; the directors were not providing it. Harry Stafford, a fullback by trade, took it upon himself to find sources. It is not a mere footballer's job to take care of his club's financial business, but Harry boasted a unique connection. At the moment of need – desperation even – he sought the richest person he knew. And to do that, he followed the path that his dog, Major, had traced for him... which led to his old acquaintance, Mr. John Davies.

It was time to hold Mr. Davies to his promise. In other words, it was time for Harry to do some convincing, begging, or whatever it took to sell the idea of a football club to a wealthy businessman whose area of expertise had largely centered on breweries and pubs. As Manchester United fans we love to knock the likes of Manchester City and Chelsea down nowadays for having required a mega-rich oligarch or oil baron to lavish fortunes to turn them into *nouveau riche* contenders at the summit of English football. In truth, however, our own history was originally defined by a near identical development involving Mr. Davies. And if Harry's name should be sullied by having had to use such measures then this is a sacrifice he was willing to make to save his club. It was his last resort. I would call it his ultimate sacrifice but that, in fact, still lay ahead...

Not that Mr. Davies needed much convincing. As Harry nobly pleaded Newton Heath's case, Davies' mind was swayed, not only because of the captain's devotion but also because he himself cherished little more than to see the fortunes of his hometown flying high. A successful football team reflected well on Manchester, in image and in prosperity. And herein lay the bigger picture, one that a shrewd businessman like Davies could see: a mighty club, a mighty institution... a mighty stadium! With such a vision in mind, Davies mobilized his squadron of rich friends and signaled to Harry to attend the New Islington Hall meeting and set in motion the plan for a takeover of Newton Heath.

It was not long after the meeting that Stafford's true intentions emerged. The directors did not like it one bit that they were being ousted, but what could they do? It was ultimately their inability to manage Heath's finances that left them with two straightforward options: bankrupt the club and lose their investments or cut their losses and sell to Davies. There was only one way Newton Heath were going to survive. Mr. Davies came in, paid off the old board, the debts, and the wages, and the club was his. More importantly, Newton Heath were saved.

Spoils For Foils

It would be naïve to assume that Harry Stafford and John Davies just met one day and decided to buy up Newton Heath. After all, it had been a full year since they were first set up on a blind date by Major. By the time the takeover had become public, the two figures had built up a budding relationship. How close it was at the time remains a mystery to this day, although there was already proof of its development. Davies, of course, was the leading beer seer around and it was suspiciously more than a coincidence that Harry was spreading his roots into the same industry.

An ad from the day, for instance, promotes a pub Harry was the proprietor of: Bridge Inn, in Ancoats, Manchester. They served cigars and the finest Burton Ale but, if you wished to visit, it is best you do so on Mondays or Saturdays because that is when they held a concert twice a week. Yet in the 1901 UK Census, which would have been taken around the same time, Harry is listed as being a publican in Wrexham. In fact, one of his nearest competitors was a pub owned by an earlier Heathen hero, Jack Doughty. A modest Second Division footballer in charge of two pubs? It did not require the contemporary Sherlock Holmes' services to conclude that this was in some way influenced by an association between Stafford and Davies. And it was this association that Harry tapped into to lure Davies in and create Manchester United.

This was actually a symbiotic connection. Mr. Davies needed Harry too once he decided to delve into this unfamiliar football world. It was like when you tune in to a Hard Rock song towards the end. It merely sounds like total chaos. Davies needed Harry to explain the lyrics so he could understand the song and make sense of it all. Indeed, it is safe to say that, without Harry's presence in the picture, Davies would never have envisaged nor been confident enough to dump his money onto the club. And if the trust he had in him was at the trial stage before the takeover, what followed was the opening of the floodgates on Davies' munificence. There is no doubt that Mr. Davies was a generous man. When Manchester United's future captain Charlie Roberts' first-born son passed away in infancy, Mr. Davies personally donated the casket. It helped of course that he was made from cash, proverbially speaking. Consequently, Harry's reward for all the sacrifices he had undertaken to salvage the club was becoming the direct beneficiary of Mr. Davies' largesse.

The moment Newton Heath became Davies' property late in April 1902 and the new Manchester United was declared, Harry's life was transformed. Now equipped with friends in high places, he acquired powers that are seldom bestowed on a footballer. James West had been in charge at Newton Heath and he would diligently continue as the first manager of Manchester United, but now Harry was deemed to be of nearly equal status. And you could not say he did not deserve this after all he had done. To start with, Davies placed £3,000 at his disposal and entrusted him to find quality players for the club. It was quite the turnaround: only a couple of months earlier, Harry was running from door to door in the hope of collecting enough money for the train fare to Bristol; now he could afford to sign anyone he might have met *en route*.

This was a shrewd move by the new owner. He knew nothing about this game of football and he did not pretend to. Who better then to scout for talent than someone who knew it inside out and who had already proven his genuine love for this club? This was not the only indulgence allowed to Harry. Soon he became the licensee of the Imperial Hotel on London Road in Piccadilly. And if that was not swanky enough, within one year he would earn himself a seat on the Manchester United board. The life of Harry Stafford had undergone a proper makeover.

Adventures In Recruitment

When the story is all told of how a fullback saved Manchester United, it is worth remembering that, deep down, he was still a fullback. Harry may have occupied himself making epic speeches and rubbing shoulders with the rich and noble, but he still had some unfinished business on the football field. His defensive services were required for Newton Heath's last ever match. And it was a vital one too: the Manchester Cup final on April 26th, 1902. Now in this day and age, this is an often overlooked competition, contested by up-and-coming reserves and viewed by select MUTV subscribers. At the turn of the 20th century, however, the final saw Newton Heath's first team face Manchester City's first team to determine the 'first' team in the city.

The Sky Blues came down from the First Division bringing their Billy

Meredith with them, but Heath countered with a talisman of their own: their captain, Harry Stafford, who seemed to be in the midst of a magical spell where everything he touched turned into gold. Or silver, in this particular instance. The Heathens triumphed 2-1 to raise that piece of silverware for the first time in nine years. Harry himself lifted the trophy to seal the final chapter in the story of Newton Heath.

Spring forward to September 1st. On a sunny Monday afternoon Harry led out a team no one had ever heard of. On closer inspection, it was the old Newton Heath outfit now majestically re-branded as Manchester United. Not only was the name new but so were the club colours – Harry and his men were smartly clad in red for the first time – and there were six debutants as well trotting out as the club embarked on a new era. They lost to Preston 1-5! But that was only a friendly. Over the next few months, as the new name became a more familiar sound, it gradually became clear that the team was heading in the right direction. The ailing club that Harry saved was going to be alright.

Accordingly, it was time for him to wind down. During 1902-03, Harry appeared in just 10 league matches for United, dispersed over a period of six months. His last competitive outing was on March 7th in a 1-2 defeat to Lincoln City in Division Two. Harry had not lost his place. On the contrary, after he had been first choice for seven years, the club could not find a suitable replacement to take over, and a total of seven other players were tried at right-back during the season. But Harry was 33 now, he had more than fulfilled his duties on the field, and now he could concentrate more on the administrative side of the club. And so a competitive career dating back to 1890 with Crewe Alexandra came to an end, Harry having amassed 342 matches in the FA Cup, the League, and the Football Alliance.

What had not come to an end though was his overall involvement in football, for in the summer of 1903 he became a Manchester United director, suitably enough. In the subsequent 100-plus years only three ex-United players have followed in his footsteps: Harold Hardman, Les Olive, and, of course, Sir Bobby Charlton. Yet Harry found a way to trump them. Take a look at the 1903-04 team photo and you will see Harry seated in the middle of the front row with the ball in is lap. There is a reason he was all kitted out even after retirement. If you happened to have followed United's reserve team during 1903-04, there would have been the odd occasion when you could have spotted the director at right-back! There were similar sightings in Crewe where he lived and made the occasional appearance for Alexandra in the Birmingham League around that time.

Yet when Harry was not busy sliding in the mud, he put just as much effort into his position on the board. He handled tasks big or small: erecting terracing at the ground; overseeing the club's match day alcohol sales; obtaining the players' outfits; repairing the damaged hose piping; and let's not forget collecting the ice cream vendors rent.

It seems there was nothing he would not have done for his beloved club. While the aforementioned chores may seem trivial compared to preventing the club's extinction, there was another major task that Harry was especially suited – and suited up – for. Per owner orders, he had taken to scouring the land immaculately dressed in trademark waistcoat and hat to handpick the players that were going to lift Manchester United towards the pinnacle of English football. After all, the last thing he wanted was for Mr. Davies' £3,000 to burn a hole in his smartly pressed pocket. And Manchester United, incidentally, needed a tweak or two: in goal, both fullback positions, all along midfield, and the entire forward line, to be precise.

The first player Harry signed for Manchester United? A youngster named Wood, described as a 'dashing back' from Altrincham. He never made the first team. Better players soon followed, however, like Jock Peddie, Bert Read, and Daniel Hurst, the scorer of the first ever Manchester United goal in that friendly at Preston. International footballers were spotted at Bank Street in the shape of Morrison (Ireland), Richards, and Sutcliffe (both England). It was less the muddy pitch that enticed them and more the greasy money Harry was offering. Apparently the 'nothing he would not have done' at times became 'something he should not have done', but he was willing to cross the legal restrictions of the time for United's sake. A case in point was when he acquired the services of Alec Bell.

There was a former Newton Heath player called Will Davidson who ran a pub in Oldham Road, not too far from Harry's Bridge Inn. And it was Davidson who tipped him about this talented lad up in Ayrshire, Scotland. Legend had it that when Harry, sharply suited as ever, stepped into Alec's parents' humble home, he 'accidentally' dropped a gold coin on the floor. The mother rushed to hand it back to him but he disdainfully remarked: "Oh, don't mind, give it to the baby". Flashy? Grandiose? Quite possibly so, but this was simply an act that Harry put up to wow the Bells. It worked – Alec soon took his place in the Duckworth-Roberts-Bell halfback line which, believe me, would go down as one of the greatest midfield combinations in United's history, even if you have to take my word for it.

The 'Roberts' in that immortal trio belonged to the legendary Charlie Roberts, by far Harry's most important acquisition for Manchester United. It is not certain whether Harry originally intended to find a man in his own image, who would lead the club from then on, but in Roberts he found just that captain. Here was a footballer so talented that a horde of First Division sides were chasing him, but they were gazumped by the *suave* recruiter in the snappy, brilliant waistcoat. With all the footballing eyes fixated on the FA Cup final,

Harry headed straight to Roberts' home in Grimsby. By the time Harry had finished telling him about the vision, the potential, and, ahem, the inducements, Charlie was ready to give his much-sought-after signature to Second Division Manchester United.

Perhaps it was the devil inside that made Harry cross the legal barriers to secure players but the same fellow eventually landed him in trouble. For it was in the line of recruitment that he made his last selfless act for the club. At the time, the FA enforced maximum wages, something that did not sit well with Mr. JH Davies' vision of a superior outfit. So he opened his palm and turned a blind eye as United participated in under-the-table payments. Other clubs used similar underhanded methods too to entice decent players, one being Manchester City. Then one day the FA decided to crack down on City, caught them red-handed, and nearly destroyed the club. Directors were punished and players were banned.

United actually benefitted from City's misfortune, signing Billy Meredith among others. But the only reason they were able to do so was due to Harry's sacrifice. When the FA came sniffing around at Bank Street, Harry stepped forward and took the blame. No harm was to blemish the club. And cynics might add that no embarrassment was to inconvenience club president JJ Bentley, who coincidentally was also the chairman of the Football League. On December 13th, 1904, the FA's verdict was announced by their top auditor, Mr. T. Hindle, as far as our story is concerned, a man so evil he was banned from Hell for fears Satan might lose his job. It basically said: "We find H. Stafford was cognizant of illegal payments having been made to players of Manchester United, and that proper accounts were not kept. For these reasons we recommend that H. Stafford be suspended from football until May 1st, 1907".

With these cold words the man who created Manchester United was spliced away from his creation. I could say that *this* was his ultimate sacrifice but, again, that still lay ahead. As he was being crucified for the forgiveness of United's sins, he defended himself thus: "Everything I have done has been in the interests of the club". That was Harry Stafford.

Looking For Harry

When I was nearly finished writing "The Story of the Green & Gold" about Newton Heath with Harry emerging as the leading character in the book, I decided it was worth it to find out whatever happened to him in his later days. How did his life pan out? How did he disappear without a trace from Manchester United's consciousness? After all, the club has made it their duty to show their timeless appreciation of their loved ones: Sir Matt, for instance, has his statue, Sir Alex his stand, and Sir Bobby his seat on the board. Yet Harry spent the whole second half of his life walking the streets among common folks who were totally oblivious that here was the man who a long time ago prevented the extinction of the mighty Manchester United. The mystery of it all was intriguing enough to get me searching.

There was a specific place where the search began. After Harry was banned from football, he passed his seat on the board to his old friend George Lawton, but he kept himself close to Manchester United for years afterwards. In fact, no one celebrated more feverishly when United won their first championship in 1908 and added the FA Cup a year later. He was generally not making the news anymore, but he did make an exception in late September 1908 during an unemployment crisis. Hundreds of men had been forced to the streets beseeching the authorities for a solution to their problems. In an act that further reveals his true generosity, Harry went to Albert Street on a daily basis and took to handing out tickets again, this time for 30 hungry men to have a free supper at his Imperial Hotel on Piccadilly. However, there was an alarming entry in the board's minutes book for September 19th, 1911:

"The secretary reported that Mr. H. Stafford saw him and informed him that he was going to Australia for his health and asked for a donation in consideration of his past services. It was unanimously resolved to grant Mr. Stafford the sum of £50."

Two startling questions immediately spring to mind from reading this entry: First of all, how could the board deem a paltry fifty pound note ample compensation to Harry for saving Manchester United? And, secondly, exactly what sort of 'health' issues could have necessitated him moving the furthest possible from Manchester without blasting off into space? Mystery surrounds the whole episode even to this day.

In the event, Harry did not linger too long in the land down under as, by 1922, he had traced a diagonal path to Montreal, Canada! Somewhere along the way – either in Manchester, Australia, or the New World – he had struck gold. The ill man who had to solicit £50 from United's board so he could embark on his voyage was now the proprietor of a large hotel in Montreal, located at the intersection of the Ottawa and St. Lawrence rivers. By 'large' it meant that the land encompassed twelve acres, with enough space for football, cricket, lacrosse, and baseball pitches, in addition to a few tennis courts and a dog track. Speaking of canines, they were still present in Harry's background, only for Major read a £900 bull terrier that had never disappointed its owner in a dog show.

Obviously, then, my quest for Harry had one specific starting point: Montreal. And, since my hometown of Houston, Texas, is a good 1,600 miles away, said quest was mostly conducted through the internet and the telephone. So I searched... and searched... for months. But Harry had apparently covered his tracks too well. For instance, the spot where the Ottawa and St. Lawrence rivers

The birth certificate of Harry's son – Harry junior.

meet (and where the hotel was supposed to have been located) is a mishmash of canals and islets, originally formed for natural irrigation but primarily existent to complicate my query. And to say that I called every Stafford resident in the Montreal directory is by no means an exaggeration. However, although the good Staffords of Canada's second largest city seemed genuinely interested in my story, none of them could claim Harry as an ancestor. In the end, I was left with no choice but to release the Newton Heath book just as it was.

A few months after publication, however, there was an extraordinary message in my inbox. It was a short, concise email that filled me with jubilation in a flash as I read through it. The feeling is hard to explain. It was like discovering a treasure chest, not any treasure, but a Manchester United treasure – a box full of old United memorabilia or the like. A gentleman identifying himself as Harry Stafford's great grandson had read my book, noticed how complimentary I had been of the club's great captain, and sought to get in touch! For so long I had been looking for Harry's descendant only for him to come looking for me. Better than that, Matt actually lived in Virginia, in the northeast USA. And best still, he quickly informed me that his mother, Mary Stafford – Harry Stafford's sole surviving grandchild - lived in my very own hometown of Houston! Of all the cities in all the world! Good old Harry had not covered his tracks but rather stretched them all the way to my doorstep. It was enough excitement for one email and several telephone exchanges followed until we decided to meet when Matt came down to visit his mother during the Christmas holidays.

The Ultimate Sacrifice

The rain was dripping as I ran into PF Chang's, a trendy restaurant in Uptown Houston. First to welcome me was Tom Clare's friendly face. Manchester-born, Tom had grown up with the Busby Babes and written a book about them

The Meeting. Your author on the left, then Mary Stafford, Matt, and Tom Clare.

called 'Forever A Babe'. Now living in Texas, he had come along to this lunch meeting to provide the United history and knowledge while I provided the good looks if not the humility! We swiftly obtained a table with room enough for all the excitement that was building up. To say that I was nervous is an understatement but that soon dissipated as, once the Staffords arrived, Matt admitted that his mother was actually nervous to meet *us*!

So there we were, sat in a noisy restaurant, face to face with the Staffords themselves. It felt like a meeting with royalty – Manchester United royalty. Right here in front of me was the long lost heiress to the Old Trafford throne, who I had finally discovered. At the same time I sensed a little feeling that I too was being discovered. Mary Stafford was the quintessential English lady: very polite, mild mannered and soft spoken – I found myself drawn forward while hanging on her every word. She seemed so fragile, obviously a legacy of gracefully growing old – she never divulged her exact age but my best estimation placed her in her late 70s. On the contrary, Matt was a picture of health. He may have been gray-haired and would be considered middle-aged now were he to live to be a hundred, but he was still showing them Virginians how to play football. Evidently he had inherited his great grandfather's sporting genes, particularly the tackling ones. He is also doing quite well for himself: he is a high-ranking executive in an upscale furniture company called Bassett which, as Matt is always eager to inform anyone who cares, was formed in 1902, i.e. the same year his famous ancestor did so much to form Manchester United.

And his famous ancestor would inevitably soon become the main topic of conversation… and the source of a shocking surprise. Harry Stafford's mystery was about to be revealed. I had taken along with me a list of questions that I had meticulously prepared to ask the Staffords about. I might as well have torn the paper up – they knew as much as I did. In fact, they were meeting us in the hope *we* could provide the missing link. But aren't *they* the descendants? Shouldn't they be shedding a light on said link? Harry's revelations were about to become mysterious again.

Apparently, when Harry was busy running around in 1902 looking for ways to save Newton Heath, making stirring public speeches, and finding players for the new Manchester United, all this time he had a pregnant wife at home. The original Mary Stafford – née Evans – hailed from Rhyl in Flintshire. She was 23 when she said "I do" to Harry in 1899 in St. Paul's Church, Crewe. In June 1902, as Manchester United were born, so was Harry's first – and what proved to be only – child. It was a baby boy, and what better name to give him than Harry Jr.? His middle name, incidentally, was 'Bown' which, coincidentally or not, was the surname of one of the directors who took over Newton Heath along with JH Davies. The birth certificate exists to this day and it reveals that the Staffords shacked up at 178 Mill Street in Ancoats.

Just how much time Harry spent in that house is open to debate. The words coming to me across the table were spicier than the chicken entrée I had ordered. Apparently, his heart did not ultimately belong in that place. We have championed for a century Harry's devotion and loyalty to the club, and without all the effort he exhausted in its name there would not be a Manchester United today. But something had to give, and Harry's devotion to our club came at the expense of his family at home. And, whisper it softly, with all the fancy clothing and the facial grooming, there was a hint of philandering about. Either way, the distractions chipped away at the harmony of his home. And, if history puts him down as the man who saved Manchester United, the harsher truth is that his acts in the end left him with a broken marriage. Amid all his tribulations in the football world, this, I believe, was his ultimate sacrifice.

So when Harry boarded the boat bound for Australia in 1911, he was not just putting Manchester United behind, he was also leaving his wife and only son behind. They were never to see him again. The great grandson, Matt, shed a light on their subsequent story:

"When Harry Sr. left, Mary moved in with her sister, Emma, who became like a stepmom to Harry Junior. Harry Jr. himself left home at an early age of 14. On January 25th, 1917, he became a fitter apprentice at the Royal Arsenal in Woolwich. In January 1924 he joined the army in the 4th Royal Sussex Engineers but, shortly after, he was transferred to the Royal Signal Corps. In 1941 he was made 2nd lieutenant in the Home Guard during the war. He was discharged and relinquished of his commission in 1956. After that he was employed at Dartford Southern Hospital".

Matt's mother, soft-spoken of course, concurred: "I was born in Welling and moved to Dartford when my father got a job in Southern Hospital. Matt was born in Dartford. I had a brother who passed away at 22 in a plane crash while on a training mission". From then on she became Harry Stafford's sole surviving grandchild. Only she did not know it!

Abandoned by his father, Harry Jr. understandably never, ever, talked about Harry Senior. As a result, Mary went through the first three decades of her life totally unaware of her 'royal' blood: "I never knew about the connections until the 1960s. Then one day my friend phoned when we were living in Indonesia. She told me to see this upcoming documentary on the BBC about Harry Stafford, and that he might be my grandfather. That is how I found out".

Mary, her husband, and their three sons were living in Indonesia at the time. Then it was New York and the final stop, Houston. Yet she has never been to Manchester, obviously an upshot of a deeply scarred father. However, ever since they re-discovered their ancestor's role in the creation of the club, the Staffords became avid Manchester United fans. It is as if it took an entire generation to cleanse the hurt. Nowadays, Matt's work takes him to the corners of the globe but every trip is another opportunity to spread the Manchester United gospel. Boy, does he have a story to tell! And his teenaged sons love nothing more than absorbing United knowledge faster than it is generated. Meanwhile, Mary may be advancing in years but she keeps herself busy. She volunteers at the local school and library during the week, just to pass the time, she hastens to add. Sundays she goes to church while afternoons are usually spent in the garden but not, I imagine, for the odd kick-about.

You get the satisfying feeling Mary Stafford is at peace with life, a turbulent road had successfully been navigated. And though it was a fascinating tale to absorb, we did not sit there throughout and just listen – Tom and I had a lot of information to relay to the Staffords. For instance, they were not previously aware that Harry had ended up in Canada after initially migrating to Australia, nor were they mindful of the extent of his relationship with JH Davies. Needless to say, this once-in-a-lifetime *rendezvous* was an eye-opener for all involved. Even the waitress was an appropriate match. After noticing the football memorabilia lying around on the table and finding out the significance of the persons involved, she came up with a surprising revelation of her own: she was a professional footballer herself! Her name was Carol Tognetti and she played for Buffalo Flash. It tells you something about the state of women's professional soccer when a player has to supplement her wages on the side as she chases an alternative career in law. In keeping with the spirit of the event, it was a state of affairs that Harry Stafford himself could have related to.

It was unfortunate that the meeting came to an end. I was now more excited than at the start, simply because of what I had just experienced. But it was time for everyone to go their own way. Because I had stayed behind for a moment to jot down some notes, I was the last person from our party to leave. However, as soon as I drove out into the rain, there was no more room to move - traffic had completely stopped. In my excitement upon initially arriving at the restaurant, I had not noticed that there were railroad tracks running alongside the building, and now there was a cargo train crossing. In Uptown Houston! Space City! And then an outlandish but fitting thought occurred to me as I waited there in the rain: did the Staffords just depart by rail?

Folk Hero

In the late 1930s there was a yearly entry in Montreal people's directory. It listed a Harry Stafford living at 1968 Dorchester East, occupation: boiler inspector. The listing was no longer present in 1940. Coincidentally, on November 15th of that year, news reached Manchester that our Harry had passed away. But people were busy looking elsewhere. And you cannot blame them, really. The world was at war and, as a matter of fact, Prime Minister Neville Chamberlain had died that same week. As a result, Harry did not even get an obituary, just a small section in the newspaper. It was hardly befitting of the man.

Former United player's death

Harry Stafford, who was captain of Manchester United when the club changed from Newton Heath, has died aged 62 in Montreal, Canada, where he was in the hotel business.

It is said that Harry Stafford discovered and signed the great Charlie Roberts.

Harry's obituary from the Manchester Evening Chronicle 15th November 1940. Harry is listed as having been 62. He was actually 69.

In truth though – metaphorically, at least - Harry never died that day. He is still present in our lives to this day. Every time a player dons the Manchester United jersey and runs onto the field, he embodies the spirit of Harry Stafford. Every run down the wing, every cross that is turned into a goal, and every trophy we lift – it is all thanks to Harry.

From the moment he saved the club right at the brink, he instilled in it the ethos that Manchester United will never die. This club we love will always bounce back no matter the predicament. When another financial crisis hit in the early 1930s; when United were one match away from relegation to the Third Division on the final afternoon of the 1933-34 season; when Munich occurred; when Eusebio broke free one-on-one with Alex Stepney in the last minute of normal time in the 1968 European Cup final; when Kevin Moran was sent off against rampant champions Everton in the 1985 FA Cup final; when Bergkamp stepped up to take a last-minute penalty in the 1999 semi-final; when that year's Champions League final entered stoppage time with United trailing Bayern Munich; when John Terry stepped up for a spot-kick in Moscow in 2008. We are thankful for Stafford's effect in all these instances.

Old Trafford? Our gratitude goes to him for that too. After all, he brought in JH Davies, who had a vision… and you should know that particular chain of events by now. In the final assessment of Manchester United's history, Harry Stafford should go down as a folk hero. Britain's culture is famous for the type, and Harry fits perfectly in: much like Robin Hood, taking money from the rich (Mr. Davies and his men) to give it to the poor at Newton Heath; or like Sir Lancelot, an outsider from fallen Crewe fighting off the evil bailiffs to prevent the same fate from befalling the Kingdom of Mancunia. There is only one suitable way to remember Harry, and he said it best himself, lest future generations forget: "Everything I have done has been in the interests of the club".

Harry Stafford Statistics

Born: 11.1869 in Crewe
MU debut: 3.4.96

Season	Club	LEAGUE		FA CUP	
		Apps	Goals	Apps	Goals
1890-91	CREWE ALEXANDRA			1	-
1891-92	CREWE ALEXANDRA			6	-
1892-93	CREWE ALEXANDRA	21	-	-	-
1893-94	CREWE ALEXANDRA	25	1	4	1
1894-95	CREWE ALEXANDRA	21	2	1	-
1895-96	NEWTON HEATH	4	-	-	-
1896-97	NEWTON HEATH	24	8	-	-
1897-98	NEWTON HEATH	25			
1898-99	NEWTON HEATH	33	2		
1899-1900	NEWTON HEATH	31	1	2	-
1900-01	NEWTON HEATH	30	-	3	-
1901-02	NEWTON HEATH	26	-	1	-
1902-03	MANCHESTER UNITED	10	-	2	-
	TOTAL	271	3	37	2

THE GREATEST CENTRE-HALF

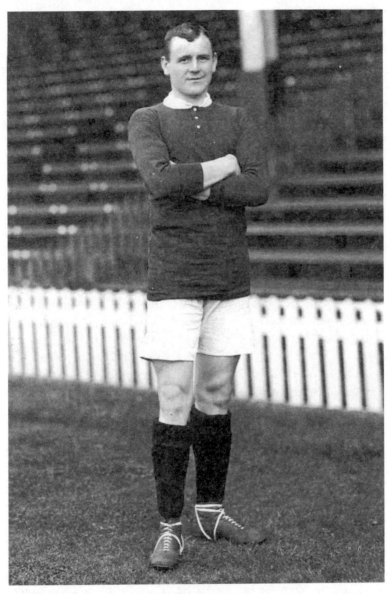

"I know of no class of workers who are less able to look after themselves than footballers. They are a lot like sheep. A representative from the Union could speak to them and they would immediately decide to join. Two minutes after, a manager could go and say a few words, and then they decide not to join."

CHARLIE ROBERTS

CHARLIE ROBERTS BY CHARBEL BOUJAOUDE

The Greatest Centre-half

Imagine a scene unfolding one day in Manchester United Utopia. The club's greatest minds have gathered around a big table. Sir Matt reverently sits at one end, Sir Alex at the other. Knowledgeable figures from the club's present and past are there. Also present are select fans from across the decades who have seen it all and are always eager to reminisce about it. There is one question everyone is seeking to answer: Who was the greatest central defender in Manchester United's history?

Jaap Stam comes readily to mind – so fast, so powerful, so dominant. Martin Buchan, what a great and respected leader! Or Rio Ferdinand, perhaps? He could read the game as easily as a newspaper. What about the Chilton/Foulkes/Vidic school of no-nonsense power and endurance, if that is your preferred type? Let's not forget Paul McGrath, who added exemplary ball skills to his cultured defending. And, if you were searching for a stopper who could score, then look no further than Steve Bruce, defending from the front, where by 'front' it meant all the way up in the opposition's penalty box.

If all these are the combined characteristics demanded of the ultimate United central defender, then none of the aforementioned legends fulfills all the requirements. No one can offer the complete package, each missing at least one ingredient. However, there is one player who has not been mentioned yet, a centre-half – as his position was known back then – who donned the Reds' shirt a century ago and was blessed with it all. He had the speed of Stam, the leadership of Buchan, the fitness of Foulkes, and the skills of McGrath. He could read the game like Ferdinand and could score like Bruce. And his name was Charlie Roberts.

A footballer who played a hundred years ago is the greatest defender in United's history! How is that possible? Well, first, let us look into the future. Will United fans of a century from now be making similar quizzical remarks about, say, some player called Ryan Giggs? Most probably, yes. Now, let us look at the past, and specifically at the testaments given by observers of the day, to unravel the greatness of Roberts. As we have not seen him, we will cede the spotlight to those who have.

"In my opinion", Scottish international Peter McWilliam once wrote, "Charlie Roberts is the greatest centre-half in the United Kingdom. In intelligence, physique and height, he has been well endowed by nature. He stands fully six feet and weighs over thirteen stone. He is the master key, the pivot of Manchester United's team. He shines equally in offensive as in defensive tactics, and he is a source of trouble to goalkeepers as well as centre-forwards".

The 'Pilot', writing a newspaper report once under the headline 'The

Genius of Roberts', said: "As for Roberts, a finer exhibition I have never seen from any halfback. His judgment was supreme, and there was no player on the field who could either get the ball under control so quickly or beat an opponent with such ease".

It was handy, to start with, that Charlie Roberts had the proper ingredients for football, whether in terms of height, speed or stamina. He was perfect for the centre-half role of the early 1900s, or better than perfect, even. At the time, a defender stayed in defence, and a forward's idea of tracking back was to cross the halfway line at the interval. Charlie was one of the first footballers to break those restraints. The physical, regimented role was not the thing for him. Not with the footballing brain he carried around. Half his game, in fact, was played out in his mind – how to intercept; how to create. Here was a man who redefined the position.

He achieved that by possessing almost all the qualities required of an elegant all-rounder, like a Rolls Royce with all the options. Distribution and passing? That was what made him prominent. You could be standing all the way out on the wing minding your own business while well covered by the opposition fullback, and then a deep pass from Charlie would land right on your big toe. Speed? He sure could run, at a rate of 100 yards in 11 seconds if he wanted to. It was not a world record. That stood at 9.6 seconds at the time and belonged to Daniel Kelly, though he never hacked it at soccer. Charlie, meanwhile, certainly did, in a way never seen before. When he arrived in Manchester, it was as if United had installed a motion detector in the team. As soon as an intruder approached their area, Charlie would elegantly race over – like a Rolls Royce, naturally – and snuff the danger out. And then he would launch an attack of his own, by passing or dribbling (did I mention he was also a master dribbler?) sometimes providing the finish himself. Indeed, for a pure defender, his scoring rate was unmatched until the early 1980s. Charlie performed like this in game after game, never tiring, for he had apparently also obtained the limitless endurance option.

About the only attribute lacking from his repertoire was physicality. He simply was not your typical rock hard bruiser, preferring instead to sport a pale, even frail, look. An esteemed journalist of the day summed him best in an early article:

"You see him on the street and you are told it is the famous Roberts. You are disappointed. He doesn't wear the healthy, lusty, muscular habit of the average ball manipulator. You would hint that he was delicate; his very sparseness puts activity out of your mind, and a lack of beam suggests a restful holiday trip as the best means of rescuing him from permanent illness.

"But see him on the field! There you are presented with bottled essence of agility, the personification of unending activity, and a veritable spring-heeled jack. Acrobatics would appear to have been the particular study of this slim youth; and we imagine that, should football fail him, he might readily acquire fame on the music hall stage as an expert in leg-mania."

So Charlie perhaps did not look like your typical footballer but, then again, a tomato does not look like a fruit. Charlie looked like more than just a footballer. Not only does he bid to be considered the greatest defender in Manchester United's history, but he also presents a solid claim to being the club's greatest captain as well. Obviously that is a more challenging task considering it is an area where, luckily, United have been strongly represented down the years. Just a brief glance at the names reveals men like the industrious Stafford, the cerebral Carey (you should see the size of his head!), and the inspirational Robson. Charlie fits right in: the first man to skipper Manchester United to the title, to the FA Cup, and to a host of other accolades, playing in the immortal halfback line of Duckworth, Roberts and Bell that was still recalled fondly by fans in the 1960s.

Yet, more than that, Charlie was a captain who led by principle. As far as he was concerned, only dead fish went with the flow. Thus, he stood up to the authorities with the courage to defy any edict he deemed unjust. The PFA, for instance, exists today largely because of his rebelliousness. Whatever sacrifices Harry Stafford made in the name of Newton Heath, Charlie replicated in the name of Manchester United. He even got into trouble for insisting on wearing short, comfortable shorts! God knows what would have happened had he inadvertently flashed an elbow. Yet his teammates followed him regardless because that's the type of leader he was – larger than life. And not just with the players. When Charlie spoke, people listened, and if you happened to be a journalist, you didn't just listen. You also hurriedly jotted down anything he said. That is why so many 'Charlie Quotes' have been recorded for the ages. It seems common today to gauge a player's value based on his media profile. One hundred years ago, when most players seemingly had no value let alone a profile, Charlie had both substance and a profile. Bigger than life, like I said, and always the first name on the teamsheet, though knowing Charlie, he probably wrote that himself.

There are rare times when Manchester United fall short of achieving success. A loss, or even a draw when a draw is not enough, can send us fans into sadness. The players did not give their all, we think to ourselves, or some are not of the desired standard. In rare times like these, it is good to read about great stars from the club's past who could never be associated with failure. So let me attempt to regale you with the tale of one such man who brought joy, pride, and prestige to Manchester United fans of his time, and should continue to do so today.

Roberts of Darlington

Some people are already grandparents by the age of fifty. Others would have opted long before to shut up shop when it came to having kids. Jacob Roberts was already the father of five children by the time he completed half a century on this earth. Yet an entire generation of Manchester United fans and every player to benefit from the PFA should be grateful Jacob decided to give it one more try. And, thus, Charlie Roberts was born on April 6th, 1883. Four weeks later, he was baptized at St. Paul's Church and sent on his way to a life of greatness.

The setting was at 12 Fry Street in the Rise Carr area of Darlington. It may be located in the North East, but it exhibits none of the area's industrial gloom. Instead, the view is of lush greenery and authentic architecture. It was an attractive destination for Charlie's parents, Jacob and Elizabeth, who hailed originally from Staffordshire. From Tipton, to be precise, on the doorstep of Dudley, which a century later gave us the incomparable Duncan Edwards. It was a long way from Darlington, for sure, but the family headed north in 1866 along with some 200 other experienced men to help start a new ironworks, the like of which was abundant at the time in the nearby regions. This was, after all, the hub of the mining industry and, indeed, the very first railway line the world ever saw was the one that connected Darlington with Stockton to the east.

It was here that Jacob Roberts found employment as a puddler in the ironworks, puddling away all day. It sounds like a fun job to do until you discover that it mainly consisted of transforming the intermediate pig iron into a more refined wrought iron, such as the steel used to make tools, for instance. Meanwhile, Elizabeth handled all domestic matters, including raising her children: William, Hannah, Isaac, Sarah, Christopher, and lest we forget, little Charlie. As old-timers are fond of recalling, old times were so much harsher than the present. Accordingly, I am sure that every day, in sleet or snow, Charlie had to walk uphill to his school... and then walk uphill back home!

The school in question was St. Paul's in Darlington. The academic knowledge Charlie obtained there has not been greatly bragged about in the annals of history, but what is definitely clear is that he gradually emerged as the best pupil in school... at football. The skills he had picked up playing in the streets were now being harnessed at a competitive team level. This meant that, until his very last day in that school, Charlie had to develop his ability in the glare of the spotlight that being a sporting celebrity attracted. If there was one lesson he gleaned from his time at St. Paul's, it was how to handle the pressure of being a leader while excelling day to day in his craft.

The Furnaceman in Boots

Charlie left St. Paul's at the age of thirteen. In retrospect, it is a blessing he did

– Manchester United would have had no use for an engineer, an accountant, or the like when they went looking for a centre-half. Instead, Charlie found a job at the Rise Carr Rolling Mill. It was an ironworks founded by Sir Theodore Fry and Joseph I'Anson, who aptly named it 'Fry, I'Anson, and Co'. Charlie's position was a furnaceman, which meant he had followed in his father's footsteps. Literally; for he was indeed one step behind his old man. Jacob Roberts worked with pig iron whereas Charlie's job description was to convert iron ore into pig iron. This consisted of three steps: 1) He would pour the iron ore at the top of the ventilating furnace. 2) Add oxygen. And 3) Collect the product at the bottom end of the sloped furnace. It was a simple chemical reaction, really. Physically, however, it was a lot of hard labour and Charlie did it for six years, during which he built his body and his character. It was as if he had consumed the steel through the fumes.

What is the point of an ironworks if it did not have a football team? Fortunately for Charlie, the mill came equipped with its very own side – Rise Carr Rangers. They were never destined for the big time (like Thames Ironworks, for instance, who evolved into West Ham United) but their one season in the sun coincided with Charlie's time there. This happened in 1897-98 when the Northern League, which comprised some of the main clubs in the area, such as Middlesbrough and the famous Bishop Auckland, decided to create a Division Two for the smaller clubs. Up until then, Rise Carr Rangers had been participating in a league for even smaller outfits – the Teeside League. Rangers now found themselves competing with a whopping six teams! Luckily, one of them soon resigned to bring the division more in line with a modern day summer tournament qualification group. The boys from Rise Carr actually did well in that inaugural campaign finishing as runners-up, a mere one point behind Howden-Le-Wear. However, there was no promotion or relegation agreed between the two divisions so Rangers decided instead to revert to the serenity of the Darlington District League.

It is not known whether Charlie saw much action in that competition for his name did not first make the local papers until 1899. The fact he would have only been 14 years old in 1897-98 suggests not but Charlie was already a prodigy and, with his imposing physique, he may well have been the original prototype of Norman Whiteside.

A Saint Before a Devil

Charlie represented Rise Carr on the field until the age of eighteen. His service by the furnace lasted longer, but he was now in demand by higher level teams in Darlington. Darlington FC obviously is the club most commonly associated with the town, though this was not always the case. They did not join the Football League until 1921. A short while earlier, a temporary outfit called

Darlington Forge Albion had rubbed shoulders with the Newcastles and the Sunderlands in the Northern Victory League that followed in the aftermath of World War I. Still, a long, long time before that, a team with the divine-sounding name of Darlington St. Augustine's were the first to fly the flag for the town. They were formed around St. Augustine's Church in 1883. It seems in the year God created Charlie, He went ahead and created a future club for him too in one go, and then He rested.

Based at Chestnut Grove, Valley Street, St. Augustine's were the top team in Darlington at the time. So, them coming in for young Charlie showed how highly he was regarded in town. You see, while Rise Carr had merely dabbled with the Second Division of the Northern League recently, St. Augustine's were the inaugural champions of the First Division in 1889-90 and had just finished as runners-up in 1901. And, barring the three Northeastern giants of Football League fame, this competition was the area's next big thing.

Charlie made his debut on September 7th, 1901. Manchester United did not exist in the papers yet but, still answering to Newton Heath, they were embarking on their last campaign before the name change. They could have used someone like Charlie to steady the ship but they were too busy sinking towards bankruptcy. So Charlie focused instead on shoring up St. Augustine's defence. The Saints may have dropped to fifth in the table by the end of 1901-02 but there was no denying their stinginess at the back. Roberts' influence was starting to take effect. There are no Charlie quotes to back this up but, for proof, see the 'Goals Against' column. It was the lowest tally of all their Northern League campaigns – except for the title-winning first season of 1889-90.

Yet this was not enough for the teenage centre-half. He wasn't satisfied until he was accessorized with a necklace made up of a cup winners' medal. Not the big one – that won't come around for another seven years - though the Cleveland Cup was nearly as old as the FA Cup. This regional competition had been battled over for 20 years up to then. And it is still being contested today, only they call it the North Riding Senior Cup. It is a trophy that Middlesbrough have made a habit of keeping but, as far as Manchester United are concerned, the Saints' victory over 'Boro gave Charlie his first taste of success... and prepared him for more.

The Bishop

Charlie had been playing for Darlington St. Augustine's for only one year when mightily-impressed fellow Northern League outfit Bishop Auckland came asking for him. The teenage centre-half was in demand. The Bishops were only a year older than St. Augustine's but Charlie would be the wiser were he to join them. With all due respect to St. Augustine's, their plans for the future centred on them folding for good during World War I. On the contrary,

Bishop Auckland were destined to become the most famous and successful of all amateur clubs. And they should safely remain on their perch for as long as Sir Alex refrains from shifting his attentions to the non-League setup.

Also of ecclesiastical origins, Bishop Auckland were the Champions of the Northern League in 1902 for the second year running. Them coming in for Charlie showed how highly regarded he had become after one season in the league. Their old Kingsway Stadium has always possessed a magnetic attraction for the more prominent of the amateur stock. And, when Charlie joined them, a connection was forged between the Bishops and Manchester United that would surface again half a century later. Right after the Munich Disaster, the Bishops kindly sent three of their players to help man United's depleted reserve side. All three were English amateur internationals to boot, and one of them – Warren Bradley – turned out to be so good that, for a couple of seasons, he was able to replace Johnny Berry after the right winger's career ended with the crash.

So, for the first time in his life, Charlie was going to parade his skills away from home, albeit just up the street from Darlington. As his career evolved, a pattern emerged whereby with every new step he was moving further away from his hometown and closer to the footballing summit. Thus, this initial move with one foot out of the door constituted a right of passage in building his character. At least with his new club being so close to Darlington, Charlie could happily keep his day job at the works. And he apparently kept it no matter the occasion, even if it consisted of an FA Cup tie against the mighty Preston North End: "It was a red-letter day in the history of the club. I had been working in front of a furnace from six o'clock that morning till twelve o'clock, but I was on the field, ready to do my best, at 2:15 with the rest of them!" The Bishops obviously did not mind him making iron during the week as long as he kept their defence ironclad on the weekend. Defending, of course, was Charlie's speciality, with forward surges and leadership qualities as welcome add-ons. Consequently, he spent the entire season proving he was the best centre-half in the League. The evidence? Check the lineup for the inter-league match on April 14th, 1903. Twenty-year-old Charlie Roberts was selected to represent the Northern League against the Northern Alliance XI. As for Bishop Auckland, despite the rearguard reinforcements, they dropped to fourth place in the standings, meaning that again Charlie had unluckily missed out on a championship medal… for the time being. However, in his one year at Kingsway, he had done enough to show that he was on the destined track to become the greatest Bishop of all.

Charlie and the Mariners

Do you ever get the feeling someone is watching you? Your every move is being scrutinized. Eyes that blend into the crowd, you know they are there, and when you run along the grass they write down a comment. You leap into the air to head the ball and they jot down another remark. You send a long pass forward and they scribble an observation. And when it is all over, strange men in dark suits approach you. This is how Charlie felt when representing the Northern League in the inter-league encounter. Only the spying eyes belonged to Mr. H N Hickson, manager of Grimsby Town Football Club. *First Division* Grimsby Town. Yes, Charlie Roberts was being discovered. Incidentally, another pair of eyes in the crowd belonged to Newcastle United officials who also liked what they saw. So Mr. Hickson had to swoop in on Charlie at work, much like Richard Gere did to Debra Winger in 'An Officer and Gentleman' and whisk him away to the First Division with a professional contract.

It was only a matter of time. Since childhood, Charlie had excelled in the game. The talent; the temperament; the physique – he had it all. And, after honing his art for a couple of years in the minor leagues, he was ready for the big time. No more puddling: the furnace might as well be shut down from now on as far as he was concerned. Charlie was on his way to the professional world of the Football League. But perhaps he ought to have looked at the Division One table before agreeing to join Grimsby. When they watched him play on April 14th, sure enough, they were in the top tier. However, just four days later, their relegation was confirmed. Grimsby have always blamed their drop on the 'Lancashire Ring': a few Division One teams had apparently conspired to ensure the East Coast team would no longer be around forcing costly trips across the Pennines. Well, if anyone knows when something smells 'fishy' it is the Mariners, and the stench was so foul it took until 1929 for them to come back up!

It seemed Charlie would have to wait till then to make a top flight appearance for the club. Although he signed his first professional contract on April 24th, it was too late to sort the paperwork out in time for the ultimate league match of the season the next day. At least he was able to cross counties fast enough to blag a medal in the Lincolnshire Cup final to go with the one from last year's North Riding Cup. Grimsby put their demotion emotions aside on April 30th to beat Lincoln City. Charlie picks up the story:

"At first I objected as I thought I would be taking someone's place who had played in the previous rounds. But I was told this was not so. I played in the final and, after a drawn game, we beat them the next day by three goals to two. I received a lovely gold medal in my first week as a professional!"

There were around 10,000 spectators present to see Charlie make his league debut on September 1st, 1903. Even the sun was in attendance on an early Tuesday evening. The venue was Blundell Park, Grimsby, and Bradford City were kind enough to send a team over for the occasion. Despite Charlie being kitted in a jersey that was half blue and half chocolate, there was no point being nervous – the entire opposition as a team were playing their first ever Football League outing. At the risk of sounding inconsiderate, the Mariners went on and won 2-0 with goals from Dunn and Rouse. In defence, Charlie did a tidy job to guarantee a debut day clean sheet.

The sheets would get messier over the next few months but only in exchange for rave reviews. Charlie took the step up in his stride. Inexperience? What's that? It made no difference to a player who would go on to prove during his career that he was years ahead of his time. Accordingly, in no time he was made captain of the team! As much as it sounds like a Roy-of-the-Rovers type rise, the young man from Darlington was turning in classy displays on a weekly basis. And, bizarrely, it was to Grimsby's detriment: his form was so hot that soon word was out. He had spent a year each at St. Augustine's and Bishop Auckland, but his progress was so rapid he wouldn't even see this season out at Blundell Park.

Charlie Turns Red

They were lining up to sign Grimsby Town's prodigious centre-half. Nottingham Forest wanted him. So did Derby County. Cup finalists Manchester City sought to add him to their constellation of stars like Billy Meredith and Sandy Turnbull. But there was an additional figure lurking mysteriously on the darker side of the discussion table, ready to trump the unsuspecting First Division sharks at their own game. The accent was Mancunian but the colour was distinctively red. It was time for Manchester United to enter the Charlie Roberts Story.

The name was new although the club went back a long way to 1878. The team formerly known as Newton Heath was formed as a railway outfit. By 1902, however, they had nearly run out of tracks. But then club captain, Harry Stafford, collaborated with a wealthy Manchester businessman named J H Davies to stave off bankruptcy. The club was converted into a steamroller fuelled by Davies' money. Two years on, it had been re-branded with a new name, new colours, new players, and a new manager. Or secretary, as they referred to him back then, though his name remained Ernest Mangnall either way.

About the only thing that had not yet been revamped was that fiendish locale at Bank Street that they called home. Some Manchester United die-hards will loudly boast that they would go to hell to watch a game if United were playing there. In the first decade of the twentieth century, they were able to back their claims at every home encounter and it had nothing to do with the fact that the 'Red Devils' themselves were in action. Along one side of the ground, instead of being offered prawn sandwiches, you were treated to the view of the adjacent factories belching smoke and fumes from gigantic chimneys. But it was not your sense of sight you had to worry about. The smell of these fumes has been described as 'acrid', 'toxic', 'noxious', and 'putrid' though it was probably an accumulation of all. Hearsay has it that fans would make frequent trips to the toilets just to experience a more pleasant odour! Naturally, Bank Street did not fit in with Mr. Davies' vision of Manchester United, but the new stadium project was still a few short years away. Before then, Davies' aim – through means of varying transparencies – was to build a powerful team that would be fit to grace the new place. And Charlie Roberts, it was decided, should be the rock around which to build this team.

To that end, Manchester United formed a two-pronged attack on Grimsby Town on Friday, April 22nd, 1904. United chairman, J J Bentley cornered his Grimsby counterpart, Mr. Bellows at the Holburn Restaurant in London where club dignitaries were congregating for the following afternoon's FA Cup final. Concurrently, Harry Stafford, now United's Jack-of-all-shady-trades, headed to Grimsby to talk directly to Charlie. Understandably not willing to lose their prized asset, the Mariners were playing Hard to Sell. But then United dangled four big ones in front of their eyes. Some reports quote a higher figure of £600, which only speculates that United might have dangled four big ones and probably slipped another two under the table, as was one accounting technique used in the day. Soon Harry and Charlie were on the phone from Grimsby. Forget City, Forest, and County, Charlie was informing his chairman. It was only United for him. *Second Division* Manchester United. Lord knows what Stafford had dangled in front of him! With all this incentive, Grimsby were now happy to part with the player.

Now Charlie had learned the lesson from last year when he signed too late to turn out in the Mariners' remaining league matches. So, a runner was immediately ordered to rush the paperwork to the Football League offices as soon as possible with no diversions along the way. Charlie and Harry, meanwhile, hopped on the train and headed to Manchester in preparation for Saturday's match. Oh, to have been a passenger on that historic journey just to eavesdrop on the conversation – one man who was inarguably Newton Heath's greatest captain riding alongside another destined to be his United equivalent, exchanging views on previous feats and future missions, yet united in cause.

Interestingly, there were some critics who viewed the big fee for a player of less than one year's professional experience as a risky piece of business. But United knew what they were getting. Heck, they got the chance to face Charlie in three league matches in 1903-04! The away game on November 28th was stopped early because it got too dark to continue. It is safe to assume the United management based their judgment on the other two matches! In the original away fixture, Grimsby were winning 2-1. When it was replayed on April 12th, the Mariners triumphed 3-1. In hindsight, United should have accepted the result of the November encounter and moved on. Where the rearranged fixture fell, it intercepted an unbeaten away run that would otherwise have stretched to seventeen league matches – a United record that would have stood to this day. So, thanks for nothing, Charlie!

Of course that defeat might have been averted had United signed Charlie earlier. Just like Grimsby were too late in purchasing him a year earlier to stave off relegation, Manchester United's promotion hopes were almost over by the time they made their move. Even the chairman, Mr. Bentley, said so. And it is not hard to tell which particular away defeat he had in mind when he spoke.

For the record, Charlie and Harry made it back to Manchester in time for the Division Two match with Burton United on April 23rd, 1904. About 8,000 fans were present at Bank Street but it was not all about Charlie. Another player was making his debut that afternoon – George Lyons at inside-right.

The line-up in full was: Moger; Bonthron, Hayes; Downie, Roberts, S. Robertson; Schofield, Lyons, Grassam, Arkesden, and A. Robertson. United won 2-0 with goals from Billy Grassam and Alex Robertson, but I will leave it to the *Athletic News* reporter to select the man-of-the-match:

"Roberts was almost the best man on the field. His presence certainly strengthened the line, and he may safely be looked to as a player who will give a satisfactory account of himself in the future."

Gone Fishing

A highlight of Charlie's spell at Grimsby was the times he went fishing. Not the leisurely 'catch-and-release' strolls down the stream. Not at Grimsby! In fact, one of the first things Charlie did after signing for the Mariners was to hop aboard a trawler and head into the deep North Sea. There he would spend weeks catching the big ones. Most footballers preferred their summers to consist of nothing more taxing than a nap on the beach. But Charlie was not your average one-dimensional footballer. To the contrary, he was a man of depths who sought to enjoy life a day at a time.

He even talked a fellow pro into setting off with him one summer. The chap in question was Walter Whittaker, an ex-Grimsby and Derby County goalkeeper. Walter was actually a Mancunian who had represented Newton Heath in his early days. He was a tall, strapping keeper and, in a Derby County team photo, he stood out like a giraffe among rams. On the boat he stood out like a lighting rod in the stormy Icelandic waters. As the sea got choppier, his response was to experience dizziness and nausea of the type for which even his spell keeping goal for the struggling Heathens could not prepare him. So much so that the main purpose of his presence on the trawler became to provide the comic relief for Charlie, who never hesitated from that incident onwards to recount Walter's discomfort at any relevant opportunity.

So deep sea fishing was not for everyone. Charlie, however, thrived on it, and off he would go summer after summer benefiting from its dual purpose. Physically, of course, it was so demanding that it generally kept his muscles bulging during the pre-season to make sure he was loaded on stamina for the year ahead, as evidenced once by a writer who went by the name 'The Surgeon': "There are quite a number of footballers whose ability in the sport line you would never suspect in a chance meeting, but the minute you bumped up against Roberts – getting the worst of the bump, incidentally – you would say 'Here is an athlete!'"

Additionally, he sure could use a few weeks absorbing the sea breeze and warmth of the sun, if only to stock up on health for the rest of the year. For that was, remember, when his body absorbed as much gaseous stench as Bank Street's resident factories could belch out. Or, as was more eloquently put by a writer of the time, he obtained "a pallid appearance due to the insalubrious environ of Clayton".

Big Time Charlie

Unlike hundreds of players who came after him, when Charlie joined Manchester United, in no way did that mean he had made it to the big time. If anything, it was United themselves who felt they were destined for the big time when they signed Charlie, and they duly implored him to get them there. Or, at least if he could first see to the promotion issue, United having missed out by one point in 1903-04. Charlie did not waste a moment. This is what one newspaper was moved to say about him after only his fifth appearance of the season:

"One man on the home side stood out by himself both in attack and defence, this being Roberts. He was continually harassing the opposing defence and supplying openings for his forwards and bringing his confreres both at half and back out of difficulties".

Doing the job of three men, there, Charlie. This verdict was from an encounter with Lincoln City on October 15th, 1904. It was a historic match because the 2-0 victory led to another victory and another and so on. Well, to make a long story short, it was some time in January of the following year that Manchester United dropped a league point again. Consecutive wins: 14, a record that still stands to this day. And it was all built on the strength of a defence led by Charlie Roberts. The same match against Lincoln City kick-started a run of seven clean sheets helped in no small part by our hero. That was another record the Roberts team held for over a century. When Van der Sar, Vidic and Ferdinand created all that fuss recently about consecutive clean sheets, it was because at long last someone had been able to improve on Charlie's achievements.

Forget Charlie's defensive invincibility. It was not the only thing he was famous for. Striding forward to create and score goals was what made him special among centre-halves. This season he struck five times, starting with the winner at Glossop North End on September 24th. Charlie tended to score when United really needed a goal, to guarantee a victory, for instance, or force a draw. Having said that, he did indulge himself on January 2nd with a brace in a 7-0 trampling of Bradford City.

In the event, Charlie had been at Manchester United only a few months when he proved he was the best centre-half around. And I don't mean the Second Division, but rather the whole country. That is because when the British Championship came around in February 1905, the international selection committee wasted no time in picking Charlie to represent England. And this just did not happen at the time! Not only did Charlie lack First Division experience, but he also played for a club that in 27 years of existence had never provided a single player for the England national team. Soon the Football League followed suit, calling him up for their representative XI. All this was great if you were Charlie Roberts or England, but not so much if you were Manchester United. The reason being that internationals insisted on playing their matches at the same time as league fixtures. Consequently, United had to do without their defensive lynchpin in four matches during the promotion race run-in. Total points lost in Charlie's absence: 3. Total points United finished behind the promotion spots: 3! It was all the club needed to flip into a rage with a capital R. And A, G and E for that matter.

So Manchester United had again hit the snooze button on their promotion call. But, had Charlie led them up at the first attempt, nobody would have appreciated how difficult a task that was. Therefore, hopes were sky high for 1905-06, though a crucial tweak had to be put in place first: the appointment of Charlie Roberts as captain of Manchester United. It was a momentous decision that would soon herald the rise of the club to the summit of English football. From this moment on, Charlie would proceed to put his case forward as the greatest captain the club has ever known. A leader of men, he was; a trendsetter; a principled, opinionated individual with enough talent to lead by example should he wish to. To start with, though, he focused his energy on getting United to the top flight.

And what a start! Charlie simply showing up for coin tossing duties was inspiring enough for United to batter Bristol City 5-1 on the opening day of the season. The next five matches were also won. The clean sheets were piling up behind Charlie, reaching a club record total of 17 by the end, which lasted for almost 20 years. Again he showed his strength going forward by providing four important goals in United's promotion drive. No wonder he earned the nickname "The Ghost in Boots": not only was he as paled-faced a fellow as you were likely to see, but he would also ghost out of nowhere into the area and cause the net to ripple.

As the race heated up with United chasing Bristol City while trying to keep Chelsea at arm's length, England came by looking for the best centre-half around again. This was exactly like last season when it did not have a happy ending for the Reds. Leaving United to play for England at this stage of the season? It was the last thing Charlie wanted to do, though it was still on his list. So, not for the last time, Charlie put Manchester United's cause ahead of his own and concentrated on attaining that Holy Grail, which back then simply meant the First Division!

On April 21st, 1906 – just under two years from the day Charlie joined – it finally happened. United beat Leeds City 3-1 to gleefully secure promotion at the expense of those pesky upstarts at Chelsea. The Reds were back in the top flight after the longest ever absence of twelve years. Of equal importance, at least as far as our story is concerned, Charlie Roberts was now a First Division player. He had achieved the first task he was brought in to do and, now, he had reached the big time.

England... or Not

It was a historic day when Charlie Roberts earned his first international cap. Never before had a Manchester United player been picked to represent England. But on February 25th, 1905, as he trotted out against Ireland at Ayresome Park in front of around 25,000 spectators, Charlie was carving a path for numerous future Red Devils to star for the Three Lions. Edwards, Charlton, Robson, Beckham, Scholes –take your pick. Yet the Mancunian connection was not the sole nod to history on that particular day. Charlie, remember, was still a Division Two player. Sure, there had been Second Division call-ups before, and here is the whole list: Billy Bannister, once in 1901, and Chris Charsley, once back in 1893! Thus, Charlie's selection was a big deal, especially as – and this is historic bit number three – he was only 21 years old. To find a younger England centre-half you have to go back till the beginning of time, or to March 1885, whichever came first.

As for the match itself, Charlie could not have made a more assured start to international football. He dominated his territory in the first half to such an extent that "the Irishmen were rarely allowed to travel more than twenty yards across the centre line". In the second half, however, they were able to score from a corner-kick to force a 1-1 draw. This was, after all, an experimental England team. In addition to Charlie, five other players were making their bow though the line-up was supplemented by some of the biggest names of the era, such as Vivian Woodward and Steve Bloomer, who notched his country's goal.

The International Selection Committee was so happy with Charlie's performance that it retained him and only one other player from the half dozen debutants for the next match. This brought a historic first encounter with Wales' star winger, Billy Meredith. Charlie and Billy would soon form one of the most influential partnerships in football history, both on and off the field. This, however, would be the last occasion they faced each other for another eight years. Out of interest, on Charlie's side for this game was winger Harold Hardman who later played for Manchester United but would not be satisfied with his involvement until they made him chairman. Meanwhile, Charlie was again in commanding form in this showdown as England defeated the principality 3-1.

By the end of the week Charlie had added a third cap to his collection, and this was for the big one: against the Auld Enemy on April 1st. Charlie's job was to make the trip to Crystal Palace a miserable one for Scotland. Most miserable turned out to be their centre-forward Sandy Young. His performance in direct opposition to one Charlie Roberts was deemed not of international standard and he was overlooked for the next two years. The Englishmen edged a dire contest 1-0 to win the Home Championship for 1905.

Charlie was one of the heroes of this triumph having appeared in all three clashes. Just by doing so, he had added a couple more records to his name. Not only was he the first centre-half to play in all England's yearly matches since the previous century, but he was also the first Division Two footballer to gain three caps, when the entire division had only collected two altogether ever before. He would have earned more but England had run out of matches that year. Remember, this was when the whole of Europe witnessed a combined total of 11 internationals in 1905.

Charlie was still 21 years old by the time he won these three caps. And then? Zilch. Nothing. He was never capped again for the rest of his career despite being the heartbeat of a club that won trophies galore over the next half a dozen years. If that baffles you now, it certainly baffled journalists and players alike back then. Charlie's omission became a popular topic of discussion over the years and, with time, three main reasons were ascertained.

Originally, Charlie would have kept his place for the following year's Home Internationals. But then the selectors remembered Manchester United's funk after his absence cost them promotion, and they duly replaced him with someone who would later become a good friend, Colin Veitch. As Charlie concentrated on getting United up, the powers that be frowned upon his turning his back on his country.

To make matters worse, Charlie further incited the FA's ire with his choice of sportswear. And it had nothing to do with a snood, pink boots, or a cape that might have hung from his back. His actual crime, in its full horror, was that he liked to don short knickers! At the time, the FA insisted that shorts should cover the knees. However, our Charlie was so proud of his pale thighs he would hike his shorts high up and fold the waistline a few times. Reports of mass fainting among the female contingent in the stands have never been confirmed but the authorities had seen enough, if not more. You could argue that, in making the effort to facilitate his mobility, Charlie was ahead of his time. But such an accusation could rarely be levelled at the indignant FA, and they made sure his international career was shorter than his shorts.

Regardless, what finally pushed the FA beyond the kiss-and-make-up point was Charlie's involvement in the PFA's forerunner, the Players' Union. As we will see later, he was not merely a member but rather a ringleader himself, along with Welsh teammate Billy Meredith. Ironically, the Wales FA never hesitated in selecting Billy, although they drew the line once he reached 46 years of age. As far as their English counterparts were concerned, Charlie was a constant thorn in their side. The main problem was that he demanded a future where footballers had rights whereas they sought to maintain a feudal *status quo*. Consequently, they made Bristol City's Billy Wedlock their default centre-half for all England games for several years afterwards and justified Charlie's exclusion by spreading hilariously-unfounded rumours that he did not have the staying power to last whole matches.

However, everyone knew who really was the best defender around. Journalists who followed the game regularly championed his merits down the years, especially whenever he was overlooked for another international contest. Here is what one writer had to say:

"There are sins of omission as well as sins of commission, and the greatest under both categories is the deliberate exclusion of Charlie Roberts. He is undoubtedly one of the greatest centre-halves, and his untiring energy has a most stimulating effect upon the side".

Another day, another testimony: "They say certain footballers are like prophets; they are seldom honoured in their own country, and every time I think about Charlie Roberts I am inclined to agree. He was England's best pivot."

Though my favourite was the straight-talking *Post* reporter: "Why was Roberts passed over for the centre-half position? He is the most skilful player in the English League. The Selection Committee stand condemned by their crass stupidity. We want a fresh Selection Committee. They don't know much about a player when they leave out men like Roberts, the finest centre-half in the world".

At least someone was happy with Charlie's omission – the Newcastle United and Scotland halfback, Peter McWilliam: "No doubt the English Selection Committee know their own best, but perhaps I can tell them something which they do not know, and that is that the selectors of the Scottish side have told me frequently how pleased they always are when they see Roberts' name omitted from the English eleven. I may add that those of us players who were selected, and who know Roberts' ability so well, were just as pleased to hear of his non-inclusion".

Whether being frozen out affected Charlie, he never let it show in public. He certainly knew his own worth and was satisfied with his fellow pros' opinions of him. In fact, in a survey that was conducted in 1911, as many as 90% of footballers picked Charlie ahead of Billy Wedlock as their ideal centre-half. They simply did not like Wedlock, as evidenced by this excerpt from the *Sheffield Daily Telegraph*: "One doesn't know what to say about Wedlock, who gains caps year after year in spite of the fact that there are at least four men superior to him every week".

The final word, however, goes to the legendary England forward Charlie Buchan whose Sunderland and Arsenal career spanned from 1910 to 1927. Not only did he recognize a great forename when he saw one, but also a great footballer: "If you ask me who is the best centre-half I have yet run up against, I certainly give the honour to Charlie Roberts. As an all-round player, others fall into insignificance compared with the old Manchester player... I remember in one international against Ireland, Charlie absolutely carried the English side on his shoulders. His defensive work was great and his placing to his own forwards was the work of a pass master."

Champion Charlie

If you were given the chance to go back in time and relive any era in Manchester United's history from formation in 1878 to the end of World War II in 1945, you could not do better than picking the half dozen years from 1906 to 1911. It was United's first golden era – and the only one before the arrival of Sir Matt Busby on the scene. This also happened to coincide with Charlie Roberts' spell in Manchester. It could be argued that he was lucky in that he joined United just as the club was about to take off in a big way, having obtained a wealthy new owner and a nice collection of stars. Alternatively, it could equally be claimed that United themselves were the lucky ones for obtaining the services of such a brilliant player, right when they needed a leader to drive them forth.

It certainly seems a case of the latter. When Manchester United signed Denis Law in 1962 and Eric Cantona thirty years later, in both instances, the capture was seen as the last piece in the jigsaw puzzle to complete an all-conquering side. With Charlie, things unfolded the other way out. *He* was the original piece put in place around which the rest were added to build Manchester United's first great team. And what a team that was! Possibly two puzzle pieces were needed for goalkeeper Harry Moger, seeing what a giant he was. But England international fullback, Herbert Burgess, compensated for that with his 5'5" frame. His injuries cost him his place to the returning Vince Hayes, who had served the club when they still answered to 'Newton Heath'. Both men were partnered by George Stacey, the mandatory hard man in defence. On the right wing could always be found the incomparable Welsh Wizard Billy Meredith while the younger version, George Wall, ran down the opposite flank. Between them were the forwards – Sandy Turnbull, Jimmy Turnbull, and Harold Halse – who seemingly offered goals on tap. Yet they were later supplemented by the even more prolific 'Knocker' West.

However, the most formidable unit in that team was the half-back line that rolled off the tongue: Duckworth, Roberts, and Bell. The 'Roberts' in there was our Charlie, of course, and he was flanked on the right by Dick Duckworth, on the left by Alex Bell. All three were exceptional footballers. What Beckham, Scholes, Keane, and Giggs produced in the last decade of the twentieth century, Duckworth, Roberts, and Bell formerly created in its first. Their inaugural appearance together in midfield can be traced back to a Division Two fixture on October 22nd, 1904. Manchester United thrashed their hosts Leicester City 3-0. Over the next few years, they gradually matured into the most dominant half-back line in English football, collecting every trophy on offer, major or minor they didn't discriminate. For decades after, the names Duckworth, Roberts, and Bell were remembered reverently, at least in Manchester if not the land.

A century on, it may be mightily difficult for that trio to convince you how good they were, so perhaps they should dazzle you with stats instead. The first seven times the three of them formed the half-back line, United won on every occasion with a total goal aggregate of 22-3. It was not just beginners' luck – they stretched it on much longer. Out of their first 34 league matches together in midfield, United won a staggering 29 times; the goal aggregate, 91-35!

And the outcome of all that? Well, 1906-07 was a season of consolidation. It was, after all, the club's first season back in the top flight for 12 years. Back then they were known as Newton Heath. The first time the name 'Manchester United' appeared in Division One was on September 1st, 1906, skippered by Charlie Roberts. If that was not prestigious enough, he went ahead and claimed United's introductory goal too. That it led to victory over Bristol City and his international nemesis, Billy Wedlock, was the icing on the cake. He notched only one other goal that campaign though, as ever with Charlie, it was a crucial one: a header from a George Wall corner-kick to ensure United's first ever top flight home derby did not end in defeat.

1907-08, however, was something else. Manchester United swept aside anyone in their way as impressively as 48 goals in 14 matches indicate. The highlight has to be on October 12th when champions Newcastle United were demolished 6-1. Never before had they let in so many at St. James' Park. Charlie grabbed one goal and most of the accolades: "exceeding all expectations... in the most redoubtable half-back line in years." Unsurprisingly, United marched to the title with such inevitability that they were able to ease off in the last couple of months. You have to admit though that they did ease off a bit too much one afternoon in March to allow Liverpool a surreal 7-4 win. Most of the blame, however, could conveniently be placed on fullback Ted Dalton. In his one and only appearance for the club, he was so confused he possibly spent the first quarter hour marking the ref!

On April 11th, 1908, United finally guaranteed the title with five matches to spare, should they wish to use them. Captain Charlie Roberts was the man who brought the first championship to the city of Manchester. He had appeared in 32 league matches, one more than he ought to have. On January 25th, Charlie was one of several missing injured United players, and he turned up at Bank Street immaculately dressed in his civil attire. Manager Ernest Mangnall took one look at him and deduced that, if he could walk, he could play! Charlie had no option but to put on his jersey and short shorts and hobble his way through a 1-0 victory over Chelsea. It was performances like this one that helped bring United success.

A lot of the players starred in this historic season, but local reporter 'Wanderer' knew exactly who had shone the brightest: "To Charlie Roberts more than any man Manchester United owed their promotion and their success in heading the league. In match after match, his energy has been remarkable – a sixth forward and a third back."

Sticks and Stones

Manchester United's reward for winning the League championship in 1908 was to qualify for Europe. Well, for a tour of the continent, to be exact. The European Cup in all its future guises was still half a century away, of course, so, in the meantime, Mr. Davies wanted to thank Charlie and his men for their achievement. And this was a big deal at a time when even the England national team had yet to step outside the British Isles. United themselves had not travelled anywhere since Newton Heath hopped on the train to Glasgow late in 1893. This foreign excursion certainly was the best thing up until sliced bread.

The first stop was in Paris on May 2nd, 1908. It was the city of culture, of romance. Yet the main topic of conversation among the players was the use of this particular green herb they had come upon in their St. Petersburg Hotel in the Opera District. Some, much to health freak Billy Meredith's liking, postulated it might be a kind of poultice, perhaps, to be applied on aching joints. Yes, for Charlie and the boys, it was the first time they had seen spinach! Indeed, most of the trip was an eye opener for the travelling party, and that only highlighted the prevalent unawareness of a country by another at the time. Even Hungary was deemed too hot for a pale Englishman's liking, as affirmed by one amused reporter: "In Budapest, the sun had left its bronze impress even upon the face of Charlie Roberts!"

Charlie must have wished he was only struck by the sun. As ever with Brits on footy duty abroad, trouble was lurking ahead – only it was the Hungarians who provided the hooligan factor. United had blazed a glorious trail through Eastern Europe, winning all eight friendlies and scoring 35 goals in the process. Seven of these strikes were reserved for Ferencvaros Si Torna on May 24th. Apparently, the home crowd were not too happy with that last one, nor with the ease with which the English Champions obtained some of their goals, and nor with a mid-game breakdown in communication between the referee and some of the United players. When the final whistle sounded, the Magyar faithful took it as a signal to attack the visitors. The Reds ran into the dressing tent but not quickly enough. The outcome was that Charlie was thumped with a stick on the way in, as were several of his teammates. Inside was hardly safer as stones tore through the tent. The final phase of the battle continued as more stones were pelted at the players as their carriage wheeled away back to the safety of their homeland. It was there that Mr Mangnall declared that he would never set foot in Budapest again.

Incidentally, this was not the first time Charlie had been stranded in the eye of a mob storm, though on that occasion Mr. Mangnall did not swear to never visit Yorkshire again. This happened in February 1906 when Manchester United facilitated their promotion cause by tonking Bradford City 5-1. Simultaneously, United full-back Bob Bonthron facilitated his own defensive tasks by clobbering City's Jimmy Conlin whenever an opportunity presented itself. It is worth adding that Conlin was a wee fellow whereas Bonthron could be described as 'in shape', though that particular shape was round. Hence, after the match ended, a seething horde consisting of Yorkshire's meanest made a beeline for Bob with the aim to maim. A mighty scuffle ensued as players and officials from both teams rushed to minimize Bob's batterings. Charlie, as ever, was quick to show his captain credentials by riding to the rescue of his player, even as this meant putting himself in real danger. As he picks up the story: "I have never experienced anything like it. I pushed several men away who were going for Bonthron. I was glad to get out of it". Luckily, the punch-up only hurt Charlie's feelings and not his fillings.

Whistling in the Snow

After Manchester United landed their first championship in 1908, in no way were they obsessed with going for a historic 18th or 19th title. For the record, they would have required a further five titles back then to eclipse Aston Villa's tally. And, although United began 1908-09 looking like they would retain their trophy, focus soon shifted away as soon as another competition came into view. The FA Cup, you see, was the most prestigious gong around at the time. Even back then, The English Cup – as it was generally known – had been around longer than any of United's players, including the old geezer on the right wing. And in all that time, United had always found a way of exiting the competition as quickly as possible, except for a couple of occasions when they were made to wait around until the quarter-finals. Charlie himself had hardly experienced much joy in this competition, even going back to his non-league days. His highlight up to now had been skippering Division Two Manchester United to a shock 5-1 defeat of holders Aston Villa in 1906. Thus, it was imperative that the club do something about their miserable cup track.

A plan was devised for the first two rounds of the competition: Charlie and the lads at the back would guarantee a clean sheet, and forward Harold Halse would score the solitary goal. It worked a treat whether facing non-league Brighton or second-in-the-table Everton. For the next round against Blackburn Rovers, United decided to liven things up a bit. Well, a lot, actually – Rovers were trounced 6-1 with six Turnbull goals! However, that achievement was only half as decent as it appears because, in reality, Sandy Turnbull grabbed a hat-trick and so did his namesake Jimmy.

United were now in the last eight where their best runs had always ended. And planning to do the same to them were hosts Burnley, in addition to the elements – a blizzard descended from the Pennines of the kind that had even Charlie questioning the wisdom of his insistence on wearing short knickers. As he described it, "it was like playing on a sheet of ice in a blinding snowstorm". Accordingly, United froze in the conditions and were trailing 0-1, their cup journey seemingly coming to an inevitable end. With only eighteen minutes left, however, a ray of hope came piercing through the snow – the referee deemed the worsening conditions unplayable. In fact, he was shivering so much he could not blow his whistle to stop the match. Instead he asked Charlie for help! So Charlie dug his hand deep into the ref's pocket, searched all around, and all he could find was the aforementioned whistle. He stood up and, to the horror of the home fans, blew for time. On the other hand, the away supporters laughed so hard you could not tell whether they were shivering any longer. Incidentally, lest he be accused of bias, let it be clearly stated that the referee, one Herbert Bamlett, did not become manager of Manchester United until some 18 years later!

The replayed tie was held a few days later. Charlie remembered it very well: "We were greeted with such a round of booing and hissing as I have never heard before or after". Of course, United won the match, by three goals to two, and for years afterwards Charlie could still hear the taunts every time he played at Turf Moor: "Stop the game, it's snowing!"

Charlie's Reds had reached uncharted territory. The city was buzzing, especially considering the semi-final opponents: Newcastle United. Position:

Six points clear at the top of the table. Objective: Claiming the first Double of the 20th century. Over 40,000 spectators converged on Bramhall Lane to watch the top two sides of the era. The game lived up to expectations with one particular centre-half leading the way: "Charlie Roberts was the king of the play… bobbing up here, there, and everywhere". With the score still 0-0 deep into the second half, United had to revert to the formula that served them so well in the earlier rounds. It worked to perfection, Harold Halse grabbing a goal with 15 minutes left to play. From then on, Charlie called the forwards to drop back and help in defence. Even the likes of Meredith obeyed orders, kicking the ball into Row Z, if necessary, though towards the end they were so exhausted they could barely get the ball as far as Row K or L. Nonetheless, United held on to edge an epic contest. Despite their disappointment, the Newcastle players waited for a quarter of an hour in the rain to applaud Charlie and his men. He headed to the final, match ball in hand, a present from Newcastle's captain, Colin Veitch, who had snatched it off one of his own players.

A Glorious Day

April 24th, 1909 was one of the biggest days in Manchester football history, except for Manchester City fans. Their best players had already hoofed it to Bank Street where all the country's focus was now on Manchester United, the cup finalists. This was a momentous occasion, their first appearance in the final. In preparation, the players spent the last week in Royal Forest Hotel in Chingford, resting, relaxing, even playing golf if they had to. Unfortunately, Charlie had to take a break from taking a break and rush back home when he was informed that his daughter had come down with bronchitis. He rejoined his club, however, in time for a crucial intervention. Sandy Turnbull's idea of preparation involved aggravating a leg injury, and the discussion was ongoing whether he should participate in the final. That is when Charlie chipped in with some prophetic words: "Let him play. He might get a goal and, if he does, we can afford to carry a passenger". Sometimes you got the feeling Charlie ran the club.

Whoever penned Charlie's bio entry in the Cup final programme seemed to agree: "Roberts is the sort of player who can 'make' his side. For the greater part of this Cup final he will be seen directing Manchester forces by the very strength of his individuality. When he gets the ball, his true, almost immaculate footballing mind immediately thinks out a plan of attack. He sees in a flash that an opposing back is badly placed and, with a speed that suggests instinct, he sends the ball quickly and accurately to his colleague".

It was an awesome sight when Charlie 'directed' his men onto the field at the Crystal Palace in London. Donning a new white kit with a red 'V' in the front and the Red Rose of Lancashire on the chest, he entered the fray 'at a merry trot' that mesmerized the awaiting media. The picture still exists today showing him in all his glory. The full line-up consisted of Moger in goal, Stacey and Hayes at the back, the famous halfback line of Duckworth, Roberts, and Bell, and the dangerous Meredith, Halse, J. Turnbull, S. Turnbull, and Wall up front. Their opponents for the game, appropriately enough for Charlie, were Bristol City. Appropriate because City were the opposition the day he first captained United; they were the other team that accompanied him from Division Two in 1906; and they were the victims of his goal on his Division One debut. And, if that was not enough, their centre-half was none other than Billy Wedlock, his rival for the England spot. This game, it was hyperbolically presumed by the press, would decide once and for all who the king of the centre-halves was.

Accordingly, both men began well, treating the 80,000 fans to solo performances. Soon, however, Charlie grabbed the upper hand. Twenty-two minutes had elapsed when he collected the ball, strode forward in his majestic style, and sent a superb pass that put Halse clean through. Halse fired goalwards but the ball smacked the underside of the bar and bounced out... only for Sandy Turnbull, Charlie's own pick, to volley venomously into the net. United were ahead and the Duckworth-Roberts-Bell triumvirate began to dominate. Charlie was everywhere, cleverly snuffing out a dangerous Bristol City attack one minute, driving his team ahead the next. That said, he did provide a moment of comic relief when he met a Meredith cross with an acrobatic effort. As the *Umpire* reporter explained it, "the goalposts are only eight feet high, and to have received Roberts' shot they would need to be 80 feet"!

Things got more serious in the second half, thanks to Vince Hayes pulling up injured. He left the field for over ten minutes before returning to hobble up front as Halse fell back to midfield after Duckworth had in turn dropped to fullback. United were now carrying two passengers – at no extra cost, as it proved. Bristol City got one splendid chance in the last minute but Hilton, displaying the accuracy of a water sprinkler, shot wide from four yards. Shortly after, the referee blew for time to signal Manchester United as winners of the FA Cup for the first time. Just seven years earlier the club had been on the verge of bankruptcy. Suddenly they had appeared as if out of nowhere to initially lift the championship and now the cup. The captain on both occasions was Charlie Roberts and, when he stepped up to lift the cup, he was starting a tradition that in time would be achieved by Manchester United more than any other club. For now, though, this was a unique moment that would not be repeated until after World War II.

It was imperative then to have a fitting celebration, and an action-packed romp of London would see to that. First stop was the Alhambra Music Hall as special guests of the management, where Charlie locked the Cup away for safe keeping while he watched the show. A while later he took off with three

Billy Goat. United's mascot

teammates to meet his Mancunian mates at the Trocadero Restaurant where the heavy duty celebrations began. This went on for hours until about a quarter to nine when Sandy Turnbull stepped up to drop a word in his ear. Charlie had forgotten his promise to famous comedian and hardcore United fan, George Robey, that he would have the players and the Cup at his show… at nine o'clock! So Charlie and Sandy darted back to Alhambra to grab the Cup only for chairman J J Bentley to stop them. Once they explained the situation he said: "I think I had better come along or I can see the Cup being lost in London". Which was fine by them, especially as they made him pay for the cab fare.

They made it in time to the Pavilion Music Hall where Robey was performing, but most of the team were still missing. Charlie had no alternative but to hastily summon his mates from across the street. He tells the story better from here:

"I brought about a dozen of my friends from Manchester, including two or three of aldermanic proportions. One had a bald head, and another had a silver plate in his side. I stood on one end of the stage and Sandy at the other while George Livingstone, Jimmy Turnbull, Mr. Bentley, and Harry Stafford stood at the back. And with my friends mixed in it, it was the greatest Cup team you ever saw!

"The screen went up and I thought I should have fainted as the crowd began to cheer and clamoured for a speech. I was winking at Robey to get the screen down and then the laugh that I had been bursting to let out came forth in its full strength. The team I had collected to represent the Cup winners included a poultry dealer, a bookmaker, a builder, and a greengrocer among them!"

The first of many: United celebrate their first major trophy on the steps of Manchester town hall.

That, apparently, is how they celebrated in 1909, though not everyone enjoyed a happy ending that night. If you take a trip to the Manchester United Museum today, you will be welcomed by the head of a goat on display. Named 'Billy', it actually belonged to Charlie back in the day. It was given to him by Frank Benson of the Bensons touring theatrical company on stage at the Manchester Empire theatre. Charlie kept Billy – the goat, not Meredith – in his backyard, though both went to matches, one to run down the wing, the other to act as the club mascot. In the post-final celebrations, the United players, in an advanced state of merriment, decided to share their alcohol with 'Billy'. This, I hasten to add, is not a practice that is carried on with today's match mascots.

Evidently, 'Billy' took a liking for the taste of the drink, much to his own detriment. The goat consumed so much ale that it died from alcohol poisoning. As much as Charlie should be held responsible, he *did* at one stage ask 'Billy' whether it had had enough, to which the goat presumably replied 'naaaah'!

In years gone by, as Billy's head hung off his living room wall, Charlie had a mischievous tale to tell anyone who inquired about it: "Shall I tell you how Billy died? Well, it was this way. Elated over a certain victory, Billy strayed from the straight path of teetotalism, and was never the same goat afterwards!"

Charlie Forms the PFA

Tommy Docherty famously led Manchester United to their first major trophy in nine years when they won the FA Cup in 1977. Infamously he was sacked before the next game. His successor, Dave Sexton, had won seven matches in a row at the climax of 1980-81 when he was asked not to bother returning for the next season. Swedish winger Jesper Blomqvist started in the 1999 Champions League final as a glorious 'Treble' was completed. He never kicked a ball for United again. The history of football is filled with falls from grace and Manchester United are not immune, as the previous examples illustrate. But the most shocking fall from grace the club has endured took place in the summer of 1909.

It had only been in late April when the Reds arrived back in Manchester clutching the Cup, to be welcomed by thousands of fans as they made their way on carriages. Thousands more waited to serenade them at Town Hall as old black and white photos still show. There's Charlie Roberts standing at the top of the stairs, for once immaculately dressed instead of flashing his knees; Cup in hand; officials and teammates at his side; the toast of the town. Just a few weeks later, he opened the newspaper one morning to find out that all of Manchester United's players had been suspended from playing football!

It all began during a reserve United fixture back in April 1907. Fullback Tommy Blackstock went up to head a ball and came down dead. Charlie was one of the pallbearers at the funeral and, like the rest of his teammates, was appalled to discover that no concession was existent in the rules to provide compensation for Tommy's widow. They decided to do something about such injustices. So, a few months later, on December 2nd, footballers from numerous clubs met at the Imperial Hotel in Manchester to form the Association of Football Players Union – PU for short, PFA for anyone under 70. To give all the credit to Charlie alone would be unfair, especially to a couple of his teammates. Herbert Broomfield, United's reserve goalkeeper, was made PU secretary, which made sense – he had every Saturday afternoon off to complete the administrative matters. And then, of course, there was Billy Meredith, the man who woke up every morning wondering what to rebel against that day.

Nonetheless, as this is the 'Charlie Roberts Story', it is understandable to focus more on his role in all this. After all, despite not holding any official position, it was he who in time would become the organization's loudest voice. In the years ahead, his leadership qualities would come to the fore. Sure he was famous before – for on-field excellence and success – but soon his name would be propagated to a national level, bringing him acclaim and rebuke in equal measure.

The beginning was low key. The Players Union called for things like changing the maximum wage (which stood at a whopping £4 a week for the sixth year running), compensation, freedom of contract, and the right to use the law of the land if necessary. These demands are commonplace today but they were revolutionary back then, so thought the FA who labelled the players selfish. Living up to the old-fashioned status of aloofness and arrogance they displayed at the time, the FA then took steps to quash the union by granting club officials forgiveness of any sin if they denounce this new body. Suddenly the players were alone without the backing of their clubs. In reality, they really had no power... unless they hooked up with the GFTU, which was a sensible way of saying 'The General Federation of Trades Union'. This here was organised labour at a nationwide scale. Should they join, the PU would gain a new power – the ability to strike. And that was what Charlie and his fellow rebels advocated once they had finished celebrating the Cup triumph.

Now it was the FA's turn to fret, and they responded by taking some sinister measures: all players must sign new contracts rejecting the PU or they will be suspended! Sinister indeed, though not surprising to Charlie who remarked: "In six years in the game I have never heard one player say a good thing about the FA". Without exaggeration, at the time, this organization was so evil you need not have told them to go to hell – a simple 'go back home' would have sufficed. The players were given three weeks to respond, but Charlie immediately faced up to the challenge:

"I wrote to my fellow players and called a meeting. We agreed unanimously to stick to the Union and risk whatever penalties might be inflicted by the FA. Scores of letters arrived at the Union offices from players on holiday saying they would resign until September, therefore get their summer pay, and then they would rejoin. I thought about doing the same, but I ultimately decided to have no underhand work. I openly told the FA that I refused to resign from the Union".

Brave words from a brave, principled man. It was at times like these that Charlie demonstrated his leadership characteristics. His teammates were lucky to have him and Billy Meredith at their club. While players at other teams folded en masse, the Manchester United men trusted Charlie enough to follow him no matter the risks. And there were risks indeed, either of suspension or wage loss, even testimonial cancellation, as would likely happen to Charlie just when he thought he would be financially set for years ahead.

Sure enough, on July 1st, 1909, came the announcement that shook the football world: "The Whole of the English Cup Winners Suspended Sine Die! Manchester United Without a Team!" It was a unique moment in the club's history. Try to remember the time Cantona was banned for letting it all out, or when Rio opted to hold it in. Now multiply that by eleven. That was the misfortune that befell United in the summer of 1909. But fear not, for matters got worse when the players turned up at Bank Street to pick up their four quid. Charlie remembers it well:

"We waited for our manager but he did not appear. All we could get out of the office boy was 'There are no wages for you, as the FA have suspended you all'. 'Well, something will have to be done' said Sandy Turnbull as he took a picture off the wall and walked out with it under his arm. The rest of the players followed suit and, a few minutes later, hair brushes, glasses and several other things were for sale at a little hostelry outside the ground".

That must have been some surreal sight – United's stars pawning club items for cash! Of course the office boy reacted by verging onto a nervous breakdown until Charlie calmed him down: "Come along with me and I will get them back for you. It's only one of their little jokes". As ever Charlie was the mature face of the common footballer, a leader in the truest form. And the FA knew that as they approached him with a bribe one day that summer: "If you resign the rest of the players will follow you, and your club will guarantee you £1000 instead of £500 for your benefit match".

They say money talks. Well, this time money screamed... but Charlie was not listening: "When I thought of the scorn of my fellow players had I deserted them, and of the Union being disbanded, I banished all idea of accepting the offer". It is worth remembering that a sum of £500 at the time would have comfortably afforded you a house or two!

Charlie's stance bought him more support, as evidenced when the Manchester United board gathered the players for a status update with the new season only one week away. Now the reserves joined forces with the first team in rebellion. All 27 players on the club's books were thus suspended, leaving the management with no option but to inform Bradford City that the opening fixture would have to be postponed! Champions the year before, current holders of the Cup, but now without a single qualified footballer to kick a ball! Lest he be accused of turning his back on Manchester United, Charlie gave his justification to the *Manchester Evening News*: "Roberts said they had no grievance with the club, but they were fighting for what they believed was a just principle".

It was a good job they kept fighting for as long as they did, for soon someone else joined in. Tim Coleman was an international inside-forward with Everton. He was also a friend of Charlie's, having played alongside him in Football League representative contests. After returning from his summer holidays all refreshed, he decided to deliver on his promise of rejoining the Union. Other players took a look at Coleman's action and followed suit. In no time clubs were missing hordes of players with the 1909-10 season only days away. With the threat of fixture cancellations looming, the FA were finally forced to act. They called a meeting on August 23rd in the neutral venue of Birmingham. It began in a civil manner with Charlie one of eight Union players around the discussion table. He also brought along GFTU representatives in a 'big brother' capacity. It was a body the PU was eager to become affiliated to and the FA was trying to block – for fear of striking. Things were rosy for four hours until the FA decided they were not going to sanction the back pay of £28 for each of the suspended Manchester United players. What business do professional footballers have getting paid, huh? This brought an abrupt end to that particular meeting.

Another get-together was held three days later, the main focus of which was a one-hour ramble by the FA chairman. By August 28th, relations had deteriorated to such extent that Charlie was banned from entering the Grand Hotel for the meeting – the only one of around 300 players to be barred - a telling statistic that proves who the main thorn in the authorities' side was. So he occupied himself outside instead by trying to recruit non-unionists while still finding the time to discuss the matter with any misguidedly opinionated players.

This proved to be the decisive meeting. Acting on Charlie's behalf inside was his friend Colin Veitch, the Newcastle United captain. He had actually resigned from the PU only so he could represent them undercover. Veitch tried his best, but he was no Charlie Roberts. So, while he *did* talk the FA into finally recognizing the PU and removing the suspensions so football could resume, there was a major condition to all that: there shall be no affiliation with the GFTU! For Charlie and his inner circle, this tasted more like a defeat. Without joining the land's union, professional footballers remained powerless to hurt the FA where it really hurts. Charlie was left to ponder:

"I know of no class of workers who are less able to look after themselves than footballers. They are a lot like sheep. A representative from the Union could speak to them and they would immediately decide to join. Two minutes after, a manager could go and say a few words, and then they decide not to join". It was Charlie's way of saying that, if you walked up to a random professional footballer and offered a penny for his thoughts, you would be overpaying.

The Union dragged the battle out until October when all the members gathered to vote on whether to join the GFTU. Charlie's fears were confirmed:

they voted 470/172 not to join! The United players could finally receive the money owed to them, but the regret remained that a great opportunity had been wasted. The captain had a famous quote for the occasion:

"I would have seen the FA in Jericho before I would have resigned membership of that body, because it was our strength and right arm. But I was only one member of the PU and, to the shame of the majority of the players, they voted to resign from the GFTU. The only power they had they took away from themselves, and the FA knew it".

The FA knew what they were doing too when Charlie applied for the league game with Newcastle United on October 2nd to be his benefit match. At a rough estimate, his take would have been around £800. But the nice men from the FA took their sweet time approving until it was too late. Royally miffed, Charlie again threatened to strike but Colin Veitch, in town with Newcastle, convinced him not to. Even the papers were sympathetic, the *Athletic News* particularly moved to tweak Kipling:

> *Oh, there'll surely come a day*
> *When they'll grant you all your pay*
> *And treat you like a Christian ought to do;*
> *So, until that day comes round,*
> *Heaven keep you safe and sound,*
> *And, Roberts, here's our best respects to you.*

It would not be until Christmas Day when Sheffield Wednesday and Santa jointly dropped by that he enjoyed a testimonial. The FA's pettiness, however, proved one thing: Charlie Roberts was now officially the authorities' enemy Number One. No caps or claps should come his way, and only because he dared to fight for footballers' rights.

The funny thing was that little had changed regarding those rights. As the saying goes in the nether world, it is the second mouse that gets the cheese. So, while Charlie and his men put their neck on the line, all he got was the nickname 'Jack Johnson', for he had fought bravely like the world heavyweight boxing champion at the time. Instead, it would be the second wave of rebels, fifty or so years later, that would reap the benefits. And, of course, the biggest piece of cheese is the one on the menu at today's version of the PFA. That it remains the oldest player association in sports history, and that its members are so lavishly rewarded, is down to a group of Manchester United players who decided to take a stance a century ago and abide by it long enough for it to make a difference. And their leader and loudest voice was one Charlie Roberts.

The Outcasts

No talk of the summer of 1909 is complete without mention of a team that sprouted from a park in Manchester one day in late August. They were called, believe it or not, the Outcasts FC. Ah, yes, the Outcasts – a name that belonged more fittingly somewhere in the Wild West, or Siberia perhaps, but that captivated both the local and national press. They even had a team photo taken, a spur of the moment thing, apparently: a matching kit was optional, their star player donned a flat cap and you should see the knees on their captain. However, whatever you do, do not challenge them to a match. "Boys, we could play a hard league game on Saturday and win too", that captain was quoted saying, and he was most probably correct. The team photo may have given the impression that these were a ragged assortment of pub players, but they were, in fact, some of the top footballers in the land. They were the FA Cup winners, to be precise, and the captain in question was none other than our boy Charlie.

As inconceivable as it sounds, this *was* Manchester United training in the park. It would not have been a great surprise in the earlier, deprived days of Newton Heath, but, since then, the club had stocked up on silver both in the bank and the trophy cabinet. Champions, Cup winners, international stars, they all were. But what else could they do? The players, remember, were still under suspension. Thus, entry into Bank Street was a major no no, and Old Trafford was still a few months away from completion. Always the good guy, Charlie did not want Manchester United's players unfit should the ban be lifted for the start of the season. So he summoned the players to train at a park in Fallowfield that belonged to Manchester Athletic club! The eager Sandy Turnbull got there first and his reward was to mow the grass. Soon the Manchester United stars, in the news all summer, arrived to practice in the park. Word was out in no time as Charlie recalls:

"After we had been training a day or two, a photographer came along to take a photo. Whilst the boys were being arranged, I obtained a piece of wood and wrote on it 'The Outcasts FC', and sat down with it to be photographed. The next day the photograph had the front page of the newspaper, much to our enjoyment and to the disgust of our opponents. It gave offence to several critics and the powers that be, but it is one of my cherished relics today".

It was a picture that came to symbolize Manchester United's rebels in the midst of battle. How much extra support it brought them, or how significant it was in ending the ban, can never be known. What is clear, however, is that the whole episode proved that Charlie was bigger than the club. Just think about it. What other United skipper would prize the players away from the club and train them on his own? In comparison, even when the King of Mean, Roy Keane, dared to utter a few words out of the party line, he was banished to a land beyond the border. It could be argued, of course, that United of a century past were nowhere near as huge as they are today. Then again, it was Charlie, and his actions that specific summer, that helped build a mere football club into an empire.

The Golden Era

Ever wonder why it hurts so much when Manchester United lose? How did we become so spoiled for success that, unlike other clubs' fans, it is harder for us to deal with disappointment, no matter how rarely they may occur? Between you and me, it is Charlie's fault! It was Charlie and his men who first gave Reds a taste of success then set the standards that we have become addicted to. Not content with winning the championship in 1908, they went on to add the FA Cup while consistently challenging for any trophy around for years afterwards. This was the time in which the famous Duckworth-Roberts-Bell trinity inscribed its name into history. The team was bristling with stars, but they were all connected to the man in the middle of the constellation, who held them all together. They were driven by him and they eagerly followed his orders to form the ideal team ethic. The two seasons after the 1908 title triumph show that Manchester United finished 13th and fifth in the standings, except these positions are misleading. United should have been much closer to the top but they were busy compiling a list of excuses not to: injuries, mud heaps at Bank Street, or a variety of other ailments.

1908-09 is a prime example. Champions United initially took off using the previous year's swashbuckling formula to win the first five matches. Little did they know, however, that it had an expiration date. They were still top in mid-October, but a series of misfortunes kept befalling them. Finally, when their coach passed by a funeral on the way to a match with Aston Villa, Charlie was moved to exclaim: "That's done it!" The Reds lost 1-3. Superstitious Charlie! A weakness detected in his makeup? Well, I never said he was flawless. United were still in third place on March 20th but all their efforts were now being focused on the FA Cup run. Eventually, they ended in 13th place, yet they could have jumped as much as seven spots up had they simply beaten Bradford City in the ultimate fixture. Charlie certainly tried his best… for ulterior motives. Were Bradford City to lose or draw, they would go down, Manchester City would be saved, and Charlie would be guaranteed a bumper crowd for his testimonial in the following campaign. Unfortunately, his teammates did not share a similar regard for City's wellbeing. This was also the club's eighth outing in three weeks, and they succumbed to a 0-1 defeat. Still, the Sky Blues could have avoided the drop with a draw against Bristol City. However, and you may have heard this before, with City being City, they contrived to score a last-minute own goal to go down! It was just like the infamous Denis Law

*Saturday, 19th February 1910: Charlie leading
United on Old Trafford's opening day.*

backheel, only self-inflicted.

The summer of 1909 was the time of the Outcasts, of course, and, after they prepared for the new season by training in the park, the first three matches were like a walk in that park – all three were won. United were leaders again, staying joint top until mid-November. Then the after-effects of their summer spat with the authorities started to bite: refereeing decisions kept going against them as the FA sought revenge! Even their own ground did not provide much solace. Old Trafford was nearing its opening date, but apparently Bank Street did not want Charlie and the lads to leave. It changed into a quagmire that seemed bent on swallowing them up! So bad was the state of the home pitch that it affected United's stylish passing game. No one was happier than Charlie when the Reds bid farewell to Bank Street on January 22nd, 1910, as evidenced by the couple of goals he bagged in a 5-nil pummelling of Tottenham. The last link to Newton Heath was severed.

An incredible match took place shortly after. The Reds were trailing Champions Newcastle 0-3 at halftime. Charlie did not like it one bit. He rallied the boys, notched a goal, and ensured a momentous 4-3 comeback victory. But the exertions were taking their toll. At the end of February, United visited Villa Park where Charlie proceeded to dislocate his fingers. Just as bad, goalkeeper Harry Moger was absent with an injury. His replacement, one Elijah Round, provided as much cover as a bra-less strap. The outcome was a 7-1 win for Aston Villa! Luckily, that did not create a new record defeat for United, though it did equal the old one. From then on, Villa ran away with the title although, to their credit, the Reds kept the fight up until April 9th. Their final position? Fifth, or, as I prefer to sugarcoat it, 'joint third'.

1910-11 did not get off to the best of starts, unless you consider the coach crashing into a lamp post on the way to the game at Arsenal as a good omen. Charlie cut his shin open and learned a valuable lesson: it is never too early before a match to put on your shin pads! He soon added pleasure to pain, though, as United won 2-1, and they actually proceeded to win seven of the opening eight league outings. This season they meant business, hovering around the top until January 2nd when they took hold of first spot and would not let go. As ever, Charlie was in exceptional form, dictating the play and driving his men on. Then bad news struck on April 15th. United were still top – one point ahead of Aston Villa with three matches to go – but Charlie had been injured against Sheffield United. The prognosis was not good: he would be out for the remainder of the campaign. In the previous two seasons, injuries had cost him 21 league matches during which the Reds were only able to muster eight victories. Did they now have the bottle for the title, or were they going to bottle it?

First off, they dropped a point at Sheffield Wednesday then headed to Villa Park to face their closest rivals. Earlier in the season, United had beaten the Villains at Old Trafford and also bundled them out of the FA Cup. But with no Charlie Roberts around this time, Aston Villa survived a hard, feisty tussle to win 4-2. *They* were joint top... with a game in hand. Surely now Villa had the title in the bag. Only the bag had a hole in it! Their match at Blackburn ended in a draw. Still, Villa were one point ahead as they travelled to Liverpool on the last day of the season. Meanwhile, Manchester United were entertaining third-placed Sunderland with Charlie watching from the stands like the helpless crowd. The prospects looked bleak when the Villains took the lead at Anfield but United concentrated on the immediate task at hand. Goals flowed in both games and, by the end, a vibrant United had thrashed Sunderland 5-1. But all that could be to no avail depending on the result from Anfield. Charlie remembers the tension very well:

"At the end of the game, our supporters rushed across the ground in front of the stand to wait for the final news from Liverpool. Suddenly, a tremendous cheer rent the air and was renewed again and again, and we knew we were champions again".

Indeed, the Scousers had done the Mancs a great favour by battling back to defeat Villa 3-1. And, thus, Charlie lifted the trophy for the second time, but for the first time at Old Trafford. Coincidentally, United showed Liverpool their gratitude when '11 came along again, winning their 19th title in 2010-11 to eclipse the Scousers' previous tally. Only on one previous occasion had a team repeated a championship success exactly one century later, and that was also Manchester United, in 1908 and 2008.

Which brings us to a mysterious double photo of which Charlie was the main figure: After the title success, Manchester United arranged for a team photo with the trophy, the picture still exists to this day. However, a near-identical photo is also about, but the League trophy having been replaced with the FA Cup trophy, which United had last won two years earlier! The only other noticeable difference is that one photo shows Charlie holding a ball in his hands while the other shows him folding them while the ball rests in the forefront. The two pictures have baffled historians down the years, the best explanation provided is that Charlie possibly borrowed the Cup from the owner at the time. To further muddy the waters, a new trophy had been designed by Fattorini's of Bradford and won by Bradford City for the only time in their history that season at Old Trafford. Answer on a postcard…

Harry Halse's Hat-trick a Half

Question: Who was the first player ever to lift the Charity Shield? Surely it cannot be Charlie Roberts. After all, he is already credited with being the first Manchester United footballer to hold both the championship and the FA Cup aloft, to earn a full England cap, and to captain the club in the First Division under the new name. Inevitably, however, in what appears to be a personal quest to be the answer to as many pub trivia questions as possible, Charlie is indeed the first man to get his hands on the Charity Shield as well. Not just for the Red Devils, but the first ever. Out of habit? Perhaps, though what helped was that the first time the Shield was contested – in 1908 – United happened to be the champions.

There were a few differences for that inaugural Shield. For a start, they did not call it the Community Shield. Also, it did not originally pit the Football League champions against the FA Cup winners. Instead, the champions of the next best league, the Southern League, were invited to challenge. And thirdly, the Charity Shield was not yet deemed the traditional 'curtain raiser' but rather the 'curtain drawer', for the simple fact that it was scheduled at the end of the 1907-08 campaign. So, on April 27th, Charlie led his men onto the field at Stamford Bridge to take on Queens Park Rangers. United were favourites but, jaded after a long season and ruing a missed spotkick from George Stacey, they were held to a 1-1 draw. Nowadays that qualifies you to a penalty shoot-out. In earlier times you got to share the trophy with the other team. But, on the occasion of the very first match and only this once, the authorities decreed that there should be a replay.

The problem with said decree was that United already had other plans: previously arranged obligations including the notorious trip to 'sunny' Budapest as part of the club's first continental tour. The only option was to push the match back until the beginning of the 1908-09 campaign, thus creating the curtain-raising tradition. The fixture had another historic significance. It was United's only competitive August outing in the first forty years of their existence up to 1919. This time Charlie finally received the Shield from Alderman Sir William Treldar after the refreshed Reds trounced QPR 4-0. Charlie played his part in the famous halfback line which "endowed Manchester United with huge prosperity from start to end". He probably also expressed a little gratitude to Jimmy Turnbull, who rattled in three goals. Jimmy would go on to complete hat-tricks in three different competitions that season – a feat that only Denis Law has ever replicated for the club.

So Charlie lifted the shield high in the sky as the photographers snapped away to satisfy the excitement shown in that glorious first ever tie. Charlie, of course, was unaware at that moment what a habit-forming act he was initiating. Nearly every future great United skipper for a century on would be repeating his act as the Reds racked up a record number of Charity Shield successes. Interestingly, later that evening, part of the celebrations was a stop for Charlie and his lads at the Alhambra Theatre where they watched the match on film. As a result, it is possible that, somewhere in the midst of time, there is footage of Manchester United's first champions waiting to be unearthed.

Three years later Charlie was able to get his fingerprints on the shield a second time, obviously becoming the first man to do so. Manchester United were the Football League champions of 1911, Swindon Town their Southern

League counterparts. Again the Mancunians were hot favourites but sneaky Swindon waited for Charlie to step off the field for treatment and took the lead. Regardless, the captain soon returned to drive his men forward. At least one man responded: Harry Halse. He took over and scored a hat-trick… in each half! It was the most prolific performance in Manchester United's history and no future Red would ever be able to match it unless your name happened to be George Best. According to Billy Meredith, who admittedly had an inclination for hyperbole, every time Halse scored that afternoon, he cheekily told the exasperated Swindon goalie 'I'll be back in a minute!' He was one sparkly character, that Harry. The only time he was capped by England, he scored twice! And, when he delivered those half dozen goals in the Charity Shield, he helped produce a unique scoreline in Manchester United's history of 8-4. Of less uniqueness was the sight of Charlie raising yet another piece of silverware.

Still, there are other medals in his collection, specifically the ones he started garnering in 1908. Not satisfied with proving they were the best team in the land, Manchester United flexed their muscles in their own backyard as well, winning the Manchester Senior Cup on the last day of April. In recent times, teams have let their reserve outfits contest this trophy. However, in Charlie's era, all the big boys were out in force to face Bury, especially as they were chasing their first success since the days of Newton Heath. A 1-0 victory duly provided Charlie with his third medal of the year. He was back for more in 1910 when he 'made the opposition forwards ineffective'. But he should not go around bragging too much considering the opposition in question belonged to lowly Stockport County. And United must have enjoyed the Manchester Cup so much for they won it twice in 1912-13! The one in September was a replay left over from the previous season after they ran out of dates when the final ended in a draw with Rochdale. Then in April, United marched on to the final again and defeated Bolton Wanderers to retain the trophy.

Charlie, however, did not win it all. About the only medal missing from his collection was one from the Lancashire Senior Cup. It was another regional competition that commanded more value back in the day, only Manchester United always seemed to struggle in it. Only once before had the club taken the trouble to win it and that was thanks to Newton Heath's efforts in 1898. When United finally repeated the success in December 1912, Charlie was unfortunately out injured. The Lancashire Cup thus remains the only trophy he failed to lift from what was available to him at Manchester United. But that should not be such a bad thing. Try asking Roy Keane which medal he would have preferred to miss out on!

Of Football League Fame

There will always be some who doubt the greatness of Charlie Roberts. If he was so brilliant, there is no way England would have ignored him, regardless of the occasional spot of bother he had put them in. Well, if the FA were big-headed enough to turn down the chance of winning the first three World Cup finals, then they were small-minded enough to freeze out the best centre-half available to them. For proof of his exalted status at the time, check out the parallel career he carved out representing the Football League. You could argue that inter-league matches were not as glamorous as full internationals but, in reality, they were more harder to get selected for. Not only did you have to be the best Englishman around, you also needed to outshine all the other Brits in the League, at a time when the best footballer in the world was a Welshman.

The Football League, much like England, played three representative fixtures each season – against their Scottish, Irish, and Southern equivalents. Unlike England, however, the selectors were smart enough to station Charlie Roberts in the heart of their chosen eleven at every possible opportunity. He was only twenty-one and still plying his trade in the Second Division when he was first deemed to be superior to all the centre-halves in the top flight. The date was March 11th, 1905, and the Scottish League were afforded a 2-0 halftime lead for hosting the game at Hampden Park. On the hour Steve Bloomer pulled a goal back then watched in amazement a couple of minutes later when the unknown youngster at centre-half strode forward and walloped home an equalizer from long range. Charlie's debut strike proved crucial as the Football League marched on to record a 3-2 triumph.

He was next called up in October 1906. The opponents came from the Irish League but it did not matter to Charlie – again he scored. With defenders like these, who needs strikers? Well, obviously the forwards were still required to heap a 6-0 mauling on the Irish. He was next selected to face a Scottish League XI in a March 1907 tussle which finished goalless, but there is an explanation for the stalemate. Scotland's centre-forward Logan was comprehensively tamed by Charlie, whose luck on the attack finally ran out: two shots were saved by goalie Muir and a mighty header bounced back off the post.

Something unique happened in February 1909: Charlie lost his first representative match, the English League succumbing to their Scottish rivals 1-3. But they improved to earn a 1-1 draw in March 1911, thanks to the man from Darlington. "Roberts was the best of the English League's halves", said one report before redundantly adding that "his tackling was good and he always placed the ball with judgment".

A special match took place on October 9th, 1911. Manchester United were the reigning champions again, a fact reflected by the presence of four Reds in the Football League XI to face the Southern League. Charlie was there, of course, now captain of this selection. Behind him was right-back Leslie Hofton, on his right was Dick Duckworth, and in front ran Harry Halse. Even the halfback on his left, George Hunter, would later turn out for United. You had to feel sorry for the Southern League's Peart who was totally overshadowed by our Charlie. Shortly into the second half, however, Charlie was penalized for bringing Freeman down and Bradley converted the spot-kick. Within two minutes, Charlie headed home from a corner and called it even. A late goal then gave the Football League a 2-1 victory.

As the years went by, Charlie continued to be the Football League's first-choice centre-half. England's loss was their gain. In 1912-13, he was 'splendid' in a goalless draw with the Irish League. As late as March 1915 he was still getting called up, earning a ninth cap at the age of 31. Extra hype was afforded to the meeting of the English and Scottish Leagues because the Home Internationals had been cancelled due to a little incident called World War I. Accordingly, 45,000 bravehearts turned up at Parkhead to see their forward, wee Willie Reid, utterly dominated by Charlie 'by reason of his weight and height'! The home eleven were blitzed 4-1.

This turned out to be Charlie's last representative outing. His international career, with either England or the Football League, had spanned 11 years and 12 matches. Only once did he finish on the losing side. With a track record like this, he ought to have been an automatic choice for England for years. And he surely would have… were he not a principled, forward-thinking fellow who tended to put Manchester United above country.

A little-known fact, mind, is that Charlie *did* get to don the England jersey one more time in an obscure game. In January 1913 he was chosen to captain an England North selection that would serve as trial opponents for the full national team. The fixture was scheduled for Monday, January 13th at Manchester City's then ground of Hyde Road. As soon as Charlie travelled the short distance there, he was informed that Billy Wedlock had withdrawn at the last moment and that *he* would be lining up in England's colours instead! For eight years the FA had banished him as an outcast but, now that it suited them, he was supposed to serve their purposes at the drop of a cap.

In the event, the North XI destroyed England 5-0. It was a poor performance all around by the full selection. One of the fullbacks gave away a penalty while the other one skipped such formalities and scored an own goal. As for Charlie, a surprised match report described him as 'dead off colour'. For explanation of his display, we need to go back in time a couple of days to Saturday. In a hard league fixture against Everton, Charlie had exerted himself beyond normal as injuries reduced Manchester United to nine men. So, in effect, he was neither mentally nor physically prepared to show his best in England's shirt. It is doubtful whether even a splendid performance would have mattered. The petty selectors, though shameless enough to grovel for his help, were in a win-win situation. A good Roberts shift would have given England victory until they were no longer out of Wedlock, a bad one and they would not blink an eye in duly dropping him. You wonder though whether at least one member of the authorities put his pettiness to the side one day in the future and thought to himself: "We got it wrong all along regarding Charlie..."

Once Upon a Football Game

Manchester United fans have had to put up with a lot of jibes over the years. They have been called 'gloryhunters'. They have been accused of being prawn sandwich munchers. And not coming from Manchester is seen as another stick to beat them with. Yet all that really matters is that, for every single home match, over 75,000 – that is seventy-five thousand – souls cram into Old Trafford to watch that rectangular piece of land where so many legends have worked their magic down the decades. It is the same greensward that, a very long time ago, Charlie Roberts became the first man to run onto, leading his team to herald the opening of this Arena of Glory.

Charlie again? As if he needed any more accolades! This was yet another honour for this fellow who seems to have experienced a Forrest Gump-like existence: been involved in everything and done it all. The date was February 19th, which has a dual significance in Manchester United's history. In 1958 it witnessed the rebirth of the club after Munich, the phoenix rising to play the first match. And way back in 1910, it announced the start of United's life at their new, lush home of Old Trafford. As luck would have it, the fixture list dictated that Liverpool would be the inaugural visitors. Inevitably, being as Scouse back then as they are now, they proceeded to steal the glow of the occasion with a 4-3 victory. But a consolation exists: on that day the new stadium offered as much home advantage to United as it did to Liverpool. It was right after that day that Charlie and his men racked up eleven straight home wins.

This was just one of many memorable games that Charlie was involved in during his career with Manchester United. Another interesting one had taken place on January 1st, 1907, before United had become Champions of England. United manager, Ernest Mangnall, came to the realization that to move ahead, sometimes you have to veer left or right. So he snuck into neighbours Manchester City's 'Everyone Must Go' player sale and convinced four of their best players – Billy Meredith and Sandy Turnbull included – to switch Manchesters. Just over two years earlier, City had tried to enlist Charlie and failed, and now nearly half their team came over to join him instead. Duly, their debut against Aston Villa on New Year's Day was one of the most eagerly anticipated matches in United's history... and Charlie was there. The *Manchester Guardian* picks up the story: "When Roberts led the United team with its famous recruits on to the field there was a scene of wonderful enthusiasm. A greater roar of cheering has probably never sounded over a football ground". The Reds won this match 1-0 then set about to bring home their first League title.

Then there was the time Charlie woke up and found himself on a football field. It was a familiar place, Bank Street, in fact. Strangely, there were no other players around although the stands were packed with spectators. A dream it was not for this actually occurred on December 16th, 1905. Yet the record books do not back this up – Manchester United did not play on that date! In truth, they did, but they never completed the match. United were leading Leeds City 1-0 with just over a quarter of an hour left. Then a thick fog unlike any you have seen – or seen through – descended on the field. That created a visibility problem for Charlie who clashed heads with another player and collapsed to the ground unconscious. The referee had seen enough. He stopped the game and ushered everyone off before Charlie had regained consciousness. Luckily he did not suffer any concussions though there were repercussions. When the fixture was replayed, United's lead turned into their only home league defeat of the season. However, it would be futile to fault Charlie for that unless you classify a tendency to drop unconscious from a knock to the head as a flaw.

A trait that he *did* possess was wit, as evidenced by this anecdote by Thomas Taw from his book 'The Life and Times of Dick Duckworth'. In February 1911, Manchester United were on their way to an FA Cup tie in London when they ran into the Darlington team at the train station. Darlington, of course, was Charlie's hometown, and its players were excited to meet him. When one of them stated that it would be fantastic were the two teams to meet in the cup final, Charlie was quick to quip: "Yes, wouldn't that be a good thing for us!"

There is another fascinating anecdote, altogether true, which illustrates many things about the atmosphere at United at the time, not least the respect the players had for their captain. It was said that one of Charlie's teammates – unidentified but possibly the impish Sandy Turnbull - enjoyed the odd beer... during the game! However, he always felt it imperative to ask the skipper for permission. Surprisingly, Charlie was usually cool with the request, because he knew that the Reds were generally so good they could cope with the temporary one-man disadvantage, and he would tell the thirsty soul: "Alright, I'll give you five minutes". Off he would rush for a good chug then return fully refreshed and doubly eager to repay his captain and serve the team!

However, if there is one quality to remember Charlie by then it is his leadership. A memorable match from January 1913 provides a succinct demonstration. The Reds went in at halftime trailing second-placed West Brom by one goal and one man. The cause seemed lost... but not for Charlie: "We might as well lose by three as by one...attack should be the only object!". He bravely drove the ten men forward until six minutes from the end when Charlie himself headed home the equalizer. A legend in his own lifetime!

Internal Wars

A word of caution: never trust your noisy neighbours whenever they get their hands on some greasy money! It is well-documented how, when Manchester City recently developed a 'sunny' disposition, they started boasting about splashing £125 million for a Ronaldo or pre-printing kits with a Rooney on the back. Much less known, however, is that City first used their evil ways over a hundred years ago. Newton Heath fans still gripe about losing their greatest striker, Joe Cassidy, in 1900, but, of more pertinence to our story, is the time the City sharks came after Manchester United's greatest defender, Charlie Roberts. It was the summer of 1912 when they came waving £1,500 about. The United management was surprisingly tempted, which left Charlie flabbergasted: "This information greatly upset me as I was deeply attached to my club and my fellow players". United finally saw some sense and said 'no'. City would not be satisfied, however, and, turning their attentions to Ernest Mangnall, they prised United's original master-manager away instead. It was a move that precipitated the end of the Reds' first era of dominance.

If that was shocking news, it was not as shocking as the fact that Manchester United actually contemplated selling their captain and heartbeat. The reason was found in the finances. In fact, it was virtually the only thing in there for the club's money was mostly going to service the cost of building Old Trafford. Hence, in a situation that eerily parallels the club's recent financial predicament, United were tempted to cash in. And it was a temptation that would rise to the surface again one year later.

At the end of 1912-13, Charlie's contract ended, so he went to see the new manager, Mr. JJ Bentley, about a fresh one. His demand for a two-year deal was fine, but the club would not provide a legal guarantee for a second benefit. Testimonials back then came around every five years and they were a player's best source of financial security. Charlie had been with United for nine years already so it was in his right to have a benefit in 1914. A cash-strapped board, however, branded him greedy and came up with a fresh excuse: it would deprive the younger players of having one! Astonishingly, Mr. Bentley informed Charlie to find a club that would pay £1,500 for his transfer. Charlie was duly astonished: "Fancy, United almost ten years before had paid Grimsby Town £600 for me, and now they wanted a profit of £900, and yet we sing 'Britons Never Will Be Slaves'!"

In all honesty, Charlie did not want to leave Manchester where he already had a thriving tobacco business. He was willing to back down but only with a promise of a three-year deal instead. The board again refused. That was bad enough, but then they went ahead and sanctioned a similar offer for another player who had only been with United for two years. Charlie finally flipped. Charlie Roberts, Manchester United's captain and formidable warrior of nine years, had seen enough: "I was angry with my club. It appeared to me as if I was not wanted, and I was determined then to sever my connection with United!" Charlie sure was sentimental: "It was almost taken for granted that I would finish my career with United as I had seemed to be part and parcel of the club". But he was also realistic, "I have always looked at football as my business, and through it my wife and children have to be kept, and sentiment about sport won't feed them when they are hungry". Most United fans claim they would play for the Reds for free and I would too... but only if I had another source of income.

For four weeks in May, an out-of-contract Charlie missed out on £18 in lost wages. Something had to be done. He reluctantly signed the diluted contract – a piece of paper that exists to this day – then turned around and informed Mr. Bentley that he was determined to renew negotiations in September! Around this time, Charlie also sent in his resignation as captain although he did not find out whether the club accepted it until he opened the paper one morning to see a photo of Manchester United's new skipper, his teammate George Stacey. Nonetheless, Charlie was intent on doing his best as long as he was a United player. So much so that, as the new season approached, he was 'happy as a lark' when he got back in the mix of things with all his teammates in a practice match at Old Trafford. That same night there was a final twist:

"I was having a game of cards in my club at Clayton about 11:30pm when I saw David Ashworth, manager of Oldham Athletic, pop his head round the cardroom door. He said that two of his directors were at my house since nine o'clock! I went along with Mr. Ashworth and found the two gentlemen making themselves quite at home and enjoying a cup of coffee in my house".

Apparently the United board had made the decision to end their association with Charlie, no doubt helped by the nifty £1,500 Oldham were prepared to hand over for the 30-year-old. Incredibly, they were bringing to a conclusion a glorious career after nine years that felt like nine minutes... under water. Well, it did if you focus solely on the suffocating Players' Union feuds, the England rejections, contract squabbling and such. The other times, however, brought pure joy for both club and star. Charlie had amassed 302 appearances for the Reds, just a few short of taking the club record off Heathen Fred Erentz. The scoring record for a defender was all his though, his 23 goals keeping him ahead for seventy years until Gordon McQueen took over. But the numbers of course only tell part of the story. When it comes to achievements, Charlie was the first Red to do almost everything. Under his leadership, Manchester United won two First Division titles, the FA Cup, two Charity Shields, and four Manchester Senior Cups. And we should not forget the 1906 promotion that started the whole thing. No wonder there was uproar among Reds fans when they heard United had sold their mighty defender and captain: "The news spread like

Charlie Roberts captain of Oldham.

wildfire, and I was simply besieged the whole day in my shop by supporters of United wanting to know whether the rumour was true".

The United management knew they would have to face a backlash but their options were limited. When they originally came into some funds, the first thing they did was sign Charlie. Now that money was tight, they used him to ease the burden. Basically, it was either Charlie Roberts or Old Trafford! So it made sense to stick with the stadium in the long run. In the very long run, it should be stressed, for United were now entering the grimmest period in their history with the next trophy not scheduled for another thirty-five years. And so they bid farewell to their legendary captain with this handwritten letter from Mr. JJ Bentley:

"Dear Charlie, enclosed please find cheque value £250 – percentage of transfer fee. In passing it tonight, the directors again asked me to impress their appreciation for your services to the club, and to wish you a successful future. Kind regards. Faithfully yours, John J. Bentley".

Meanwhile, Charlie was happy to sign for this plucky little club – his words, not mine – especially as the three officials at his house stood there star-struck, hardly believing what a coup they had pulled off in obtaining a player of such stature. They catered to his every demand in the contract and, with Oldham being a reasonable distance from his business in Manchester, everyone was satisfied. Within a year and a half, as Manchester United slid towards the abyss, Charlie guided Oldham to the heights.

A Famous Latic

They had never seen anything like him when Charlie walked in to Boundary Park. Sure, Oldham Athletic had the odd international player here or there, and they had heard of Charlie's heroics over the years or his face-offs with the authorities. But now this larger-than-life character was standing here among them. This was the man who had joined Manchester United when they were still a Second Division club and led them until they became the superpower in the land. And, now, here he was in the flesh at Oldham.

Oldham? It was the definition of 'unfashionable' in the dictionary and its synonym in the thesaurus. The club had been around only since 1895 though you would not find a mention in the papers, considering they originally answered to the name 'Pine Villa'. It had nothing to do with luscious landscapes, for, in keeping with Oldham's image, the club was born and bred in a pub. A few months before the turn of the century, they switched to their current moniker when they shacked up at Boundary Park. Fashionable that was not, and normally Charlie would never have ended up there were it not but a short distance from his shop.

Charlie's presence also owed much to the club's ambitious manager. David Ashworth had guided the Latics into the Second Division of the Football League in 1907 at the same time that Manchester United embarked on their first title-winning campaign. Promotion was secured in 1910 by the skin of their teeth, and the same skin was used again to evade relegation shortly after. By 1913, however, Mr. Ashworth had led Oldham to mid-table safety, in addition to a historic run to the semi-finals of the FA Cup. The club was on the up and some of the players were even getting capped by the likes of England and Scotland. It was with this steady improvement in mind that the Latics decided to hand Manchester United £1,500 for Charlie's services on August 23rd, 1913. £1,500, incidentally, was a record fee for Oldham at the time. Heck, it was a record fee for anyone anywhere at the time. Indeed, for about three months that autumn, Charlie was the costliest footballer in the world!

Murmurs were heard back in 1904 when United splashed £600 on acquiring the inexperienced Charlie, and similarly now eyebrows were raised at this exorbitant fee for a 30-year-old. He may have been past his peak by now, but Charlie did not need to be at his peak to be "still the best centre-half in England". In fact, a match report from his last season at Old Trafford shows he had maintained his impeccable standards. United were facing leaders Everton who were buoyed by their new signing Tommy Browell. He was a sensational striker who was later snapped up by Ernest Mangnall for Manchester City. But this is what the 'Observer' had to say of his tussle with United: "Browell was so very much overshadowed by Roberts that the crowd never got even a glimpse of those shooting powers which have made the boy centre-forward famous".

Regardless, Oldham did not seem to care about the size of the fee as they placed their prized new signing in the heart of their line-up, between right-half Hugh Moffatt and left-half David Wilson. Moffatt-Roberts-Wilson! It does not have the same resonance as Duckworth-Roberts-Bell but it would do for the Latics, what with all three players having been internationally capped. Charlie made his debut on September 6th, 1913, but why dwell on a 2-6 defeat to Bolton? Thereafter, the team excelled to amass six victories in eight matches, including one at Preston when Charlie got the only goal of the game. This run saw just one defeat – to Manchester United. It was Charlie's first return to Old Trafford, and 55,000 fans turned up to welcome their idol back. This easily constituted United's biggest crowd for a league match at Old Trafford, at Bank Street, or at the very first home of North Road, for that matter. The emotion of the occasion visibly got to Charlie causing the visitors to crash to a 1-4 defeat.

This Oldham team that Mr. Ashworth put together though was top notch. If Paul Scholes loved the 1990 version, he would have absolutely worshipped that pre-World War I side. Apart from the half-back line, Howard Matthews stood in goal assisted by the fullback pairing of Hodson and Cook. Scottish international Joe Donnachie operated down the left flank, Tummon the right. In between them marauded the balding England international George Woodger, Gee, Kemp, or a couple of ex-Reds – Broad and Walters. Throw in the legendary Charlie Roberts as captain and you got the finest assortment of footballers in Oldham's history.

In the following season the Latics would provide the conclusive evidence. This season, meanwhile, they settled on submitting their claim. They extended their good start through winter, some of their better performances included holding leaders Blackburn to a 1-1 draw and earning revenge against Bolton when Charlie got on the scoresheet again. By New Year's Day, Oldham were fourth in the table, four points behind Blackburn but with a game in hand. Incidentally, in third place were Manchester United who were doing well seemingly oblivious to the fact that Charlie had left. Strange as it may seem, it was at this very moment in time that the news finally hit them, so they did the logical thing and plummeted down the table to 18th!

United did improve slightly to end the campaign in 14th spot, whereas Oldham maintained their form to finish fourth, a mere one point behind the First Division runners-up. This was easily their highest ever placing and it proved one thing without any doubt: If you want to be the top team in Greater Manchester, sign Charlie Roberts! Further confirmation of their new status came on April 21st, 1913, when a David Wilson goal against Hurst FC gave Oldham their first ever Manchester Senior Cup success. It would be their only one until after World War II but, for Charlie, it was his third in a row. As a matter of fact, it was his third Manchester Cup medal in 17 months. If that was getting repetitive, he did experience something this season he had not done before in his career: he was ever present in all of Oldham's matches.

Charlie's Championship Chase

At no other time in the entire history of the Football League did an unfancied team come as close to winning the championship as Oldham Athletic did in 1914-15. Watford stumbled upon the runners-up spot in 1983 but you would not describe an eleven-point gap to Liverpool as a title challenge. Queens Park Rangers finished only one point behind in 1976 though they had already gained some prestige when they won the League Cup. But for a team that has only ever spent a dozen years in the top flight, Oldham's deeds remain unparalleled. For that, you have to take into account the Charlie Roberts factor.

We will look at the Latics' heroics a short while later. What made them more impressive was that they were achieved after the departure of David Ashworth who had managed the club since 1906. Instead, for the new season, Charlie had another manager. After serving under Ernest Mangnall in each of his first nine seasons with Manchester United, he was now on his fourth gaffer in four years. Mangnall left in 1912, Mr. Bentley took over for 1912-13, Mr. Ashworth coached him in his first year at Oldham, and now Mr. Herbert Bamlett was put in charge. A new manager though not a new acquaintance – Charlie had been into Bamlett's pockets before!

You may remember that he was the referee who was too cold to abandon that infamous FA Cup quarter-final tie between United and Burnley in 1909 and had asked Charlie for a strange favour. A few years on, when Bamlett blew the whistle on his refereeing career, he decided to dabble in management. Oldham offered him a job within a few weeks after his retirement! Bamlett's path would one day lead him to Manchester United. Some would say he was the worst manager in their history, but that is only if you base it on actual results. Though he led United to relegation in 1931, he had performed the same trick twice previously with Middlesbrough! Regardless, his first attempt as a gaffer produced the greatest campaign Oldham Athletic has ever known.

Which brings us back to Charlie. While Oldham had demonstrated their capabilities in 1913-14, in Charlie they had a decorated captain who could sit them down at the start of the new season and inspire them by simply listing the trophies he had collected. More could still be added, he urged them, and so the first thing they did was to get a 3-1 victory over United out of the way, with Charlie assisting one of the goals after dribbling past several ex-teammates: "I was anxious to turn the defeat we sustained there the previous season into a victory – so beloved by a player against his old club". A further four wins in five matches sent them into second spot in the standings. Add a few draws and some more wins and that brings us to November 14th, 1914 – the day a 4-1 thrashing of Tottenham Hotspur lifted Oldham to the top of the table for the first time ever. They entered December on just the one defeat, and Charlie was as majestic as always. Just read this review:

"Roberts was a host in himself in the centre of the Oldham line. Quick on the ball, wonderfully clever with both feet and head, he played a masterly game, and was ever in the right place at the right time". Or this one: "Charlie Roberts was on top of his form… He simply dominated the game, and the Everton inside-forwards could hardly get a kick of the ball". Or yet this other one from the victory over champions Blackburn and their own lynchpin Percy Smith: "Roberts was in his best vein on Saturday. He and Smith tested their artillery powers against each other, but after Roberts had delivered one particularly telling aim, Smith realized that they better steer clear of each other so far as was possible". He may have walked around sporting a frail look, but Charlie knew how to administer a good, old-fashioned 'reducer' when he needed to.

So the Latics headed into spring as the top team in England, destined for their first championship success. It was a surreal sight but this was the most surreal of seasons. Back in June, Archduke Ferdinand had been fatally shot by a Serb – which brings Rio and Vidic to mind – only that particular confrontation led to World War I. Throughout the campaign, as soldiers died, footballers played on, though Oldham's quandaries, as evidenced by Charlie's Christmas Day trip to Bradford Park Avenue, were initially limited to the 'Benny Hill' variety:

"As usual at holiday times, the train we travelled by took it into its head to go as it pleased, with the result that we arrived at Bradford twenty minutes before kickoff. So we commenced to dress in our taxi, and you can take it from me that it isn't a very pleasant job taking off your ordinary attire to put on football clothes in a taxicab as you fly through the streets on a cold winter's day!"

Later on in the season, however, Oldham's problems took a serious turn, mainly because - Charlie apart - the players were not familiar with the much-maligned run-in nerves. Two consecutive matches were lost in March. Charlie used his experience to try and hold the team together but, on April 3rd, they finally cracked. The leaders were away at Middlesbrough where their best efforts consisted of trailing 1-4 after 55 minutes. The Latics were visibly frustrated and none more so than left-back Billy Cook. If you could not stop them drop them, seemed to be his motto. Once the referee had seen enough he ordered Cook off when Boro's Carr went tumbling to the ground. Ironically, this was the one time when Cook had not sinned and, astonishingly, he refused to leave! That would be shocking today and it was equally shocking back then. Captain Charlie was there: "It was an incident that I had never seen before, and I don't want to see repeated. I asked Cook to obey the referee, but still he was adamant. The referee then gave him one minute to make up his mind and, as he still refused, the official left the field and the game came to a premature termination". The football world was stunned by Cook's actions, the FA not so much – they banned him for one year and decreed the result should stand.

Oldham dropped to fourth but Charlie gathered his men – minus Cook – and spurred them on. Two victories later, the Latics were back on top. That April 10th, 1915, League table was one of the strangest ever. With just three matches left, Oldham were on 44 points and the destiny of the title was in their hands. However, in keeping with the uniqueness of the season, a hugely competitive division meant that a host of other teams were still in with a chance of snatching the title. In fact, it was still mathematically possible for Burnley – on 36 points but with a game in hand – to catch the Latics, and they were all the way down in twelfth place! About the only club that was out of the running was the mighty Manchester United, resting glumly at the very bottom of the table. But fear not, for soon United would forge an unlikely alliance with Liverpool to even out the other century of hatred – the two rivals would fix a match to guarantee United's safety.

In hindsight, perhaps Oldham ought to have engineered a similarly evil pact. As they sat on the summit with United on the bottom, it seemed that all the money they spent to sign Charlie was worth it. He was now on the cusp of his third championship medal, what with the last two games scheduled at Boundary Park where Oldham had lost just once all season. The problem was that, for the rest of the players, this would be their first title... as well as probably their last – the authorities having decided to halt competitive football as they deemed it too tacky for the gravity of the ongoing war. Call it nerves, jitters, or 'squeaky bum-time' if you are Sir Alex, but it got to the Latics, who proceeded to lose at home for only the second time this season, going down 1-2 to Burnley. Still, Oldham just needed to win the ultimate fixture to be crowned champions. But on April 24th, Liverpool arrived at Boundary Park having suddenly recovered their scruples, and, in the name of the League's integrity, played as if the outcome of the whole war depended on it. The Scousers gleefully won 2-0 before realizing they had just handed the title to Everton by one point.

One Last Stand

So close! The Latics had seemed certainties for the title – "it looked all Lombard Street to an orange on Oldham being champions", as Charlie put it, using an expression so classic it deserves frequent airing. But they inexplicably blew it and deeply hurt Charlie in the process. Even years later the wound had not fully healed: "I won't say anything further on the subject, because it makes me absolutely sick to think about it. I never in all my football career felt so much upset about anything. I dearly wanted to see Oldham win the league, and secure my third championship medal". He did indeed boast two medals already, but captaining unfashionable Oldham to the title would have arguably been his mightiest feat.

Instead, the Latics had to settle on the consolation of second place, which still constituted their greatest ever campaign. For Charlie, it was also his last campaign of competitive football for, with the Great War in full flow, teams were now divided into regional leagues. It would be four years before peacetime footy returned and an aging Charlie was not prepared to wait around that long. Heck, he would not even see the first wartime season through.

In 1915-16 the Latics were placed in the Lancashire Section Principal tournament with 13 other clubs. Their chance for championship glory had passed by forever, but they participated in this competition simply for the love of the game. Wages? There were none, thanks to the FA's wartime decree of only allowing a payment of one whole pound a week purely for expenses! It was a state of affairs that did not sit well with one Charlie Roberts, co-founder of the PFA. Nonetheless, he played on for free, even re-discovering his scoring touch to net three goals in six matches around the New Year. But this proved to be the captain's last stand. Around this time, possibly during a match with Stoke City on January 22nd, 1916, he contracted pneumonia. On top of that, he simultaneously aggravated a knee injury. For months and months he struggled and hoped that his knee would get better, all along his face was sporting a defined look of misery. But the damage was so bad that, for the rest of his life, the previously supremely fit athlete now had to use a cane to help him walk. A leather ball may be allowed on a football field but not a wooden stick. Consequently, Charlie was forced to call it a day.

And so a glorious career came to an abrupt end. Charlie had played 414 league and cup matches scoring 29 goals. He had captained Grimsby Town, Manchester United, Oldham Athletic and the Football League with distinction. When the Great War finished, he was still in the public's mind, but there were new stars to adore. A couple of decades later, an even longer war engulfed the world and, when it was all over, very few still carried the memory of Charlie vividly. As the years rolled by, football entered a new age where Charlie's name became unrecognizable, like many pillars of his bygone era. However, a century on, his legend still exists. It has been preserved in time by cuttings and microfilms, like fossils in an ancient rock: the aura; the glory; the larger-than-life character; the caps; the accolades. Those accolades alone would have been enough to justify his grandeur, but Charlie backed that up with numerous league and cup medals, as well as an extensive list of 'firsts' that would have threatened Neil Armstrong's claim to fame had Ford invented rockets instead of cars. Charlie Roberts, the player, will always be an all-time great.

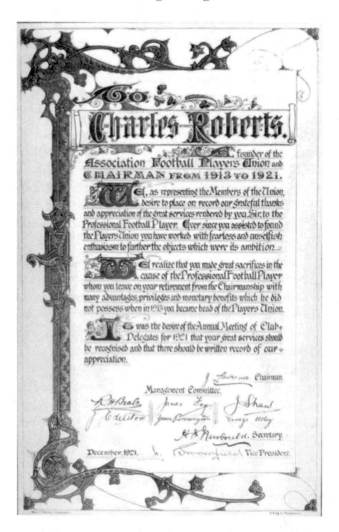

The Chairman

The call came to head to Manchester. The Great War had ended, won by the Allies and whoever survived it. Footballers who could still run sought to resume their daily lives. A group of professionals from London clubs decided to form a new players' association. No one had heard from the old Players' Union since 1915, but something had to be done about wages so low the only way to get paid less was to not get paid at all. Thus, footballers from all over the land were summoned to meet in Manchester on January 13th, 1919.

When they arrived at the meeting, however, they were welcomed by a famous face. The charisma, the aura – it could only be one man. Charlie Roberts, who had sat alongside Billy Meredith and Herbert Broomfield in the original union's first meeting eleven years earlier, had gotten wind of this fresh movement and was quick to lend a hand. The old union was still in existence, rallied Charlie, and the new London representatives were eager to merge into it. The Players' Union would now be stronger than ever before. What's more, now that he was no longer active on the field of play, Charlie was willing to fight the administrative battle himself. You could argue that he was the PU's leading crusader all along, but now he was officially unveiled as the organization's chairman, just as he was in 1913 before the war pushed such matters to the margins. He loved the game too much to simply leave it behind. And the FA need not worry, he reassured them, for this time there would be no strikes. Talking softly there, Charlie, and carrying a wooden stick.

A stick would have come in handy throughout the past decade in Charlie's ongoing conflict with the authorities. You see, Charlie did not form the Players' Union and just forgot about it. On the contrary, he was always there, nurturing it, ensuring it grew. And always in the background there was the FA trying to smother his creation. The Union asked permission for a match between its English and Scottish members, for instance, in September 1912. The FA did not sanction it until April 1914! Luckily it was worth the wait as the game raised £120. For the record, the Englishmen won 2-0 with Charlie's help. He was always involved. The Union used to hold an annual Sports Festival, with the 1912 edition at St. James' Park a particularly memorable one for Charlie. The main event was the dribbling competition, and the final boiled down to four players: two from Sunderland plus Billy Meredith and Charlie himself. Now, they don't call him the 'Welsh Wizard' for nothing, but this only made Meredith's fall from grace harder, because the winner turned out to be Charlie Roberts, King of the Dribble.

During the war, Charlie fought a separate battle with the authorities, especially when they decided one day that footballers should play for free. His whole idea of a union was for circumstances such as these, and apparently it rankled that he never received unanimous support: "Now I know that all those players holding agreements are in wonderland as to what is to happen when the game is resumed professionally after the war. If players never saw their helplessness before, surely they can now. Haven't they had their chance? Did they take it?"

Still, his main ire was directed one way: "A player should not be debarred from picking up a few shillings extra because one or two members of the FA (who are very comfortable, thank you) think that professionalism in war time is 'all wrong'. I know of managers today who are getting as much as £10 per week. Referees are being paid; in fact, everybody appears to be getting paid except the player".

Accordingly, Charlie was now the most qualified man in the world to be

Union chairman, if only to take care of some unfinished business. His first task was to double the wages to £2 a week. A few months later the maximum increased to £4.50. And better yet, it jumped to a whopping £9 in time for 1920-21. You have to remember that post-war attendances were booming yet clubs withheld the 'takes' from the players, whether they were deploying them or transferring them, as Charlie pointed out: "The player being transferred is in a blind alley – everything is subject to the consent of the Football League, and they, as representatives of the clubs, keep the amount the player receives down as far as possible".

Under Charlie's command, the Union grew stronger then ever. He took his role very seriously, feeling he could finally walk the walk. He recruited the biggest names for the committee to raise the Union's profile, and he worked continuously on bringing in funds. The Union's bank account started off with £50. A year later it had £2,000! Another year on and they could afford to invest £2,500 in the stock market. What helped, of course, was that over one thousand players had now joined Charlie's Union.

In September 1921, Charlie had to resign as chairman, only because he was stepping to the dark side – he had accepted a position as manager of Oldham Athletic. For nearly 14 years he had risked his international career, his name, and his finances for the Union's sake. The Union would not forget. As he stepped down the committee presented him with a tidy sum of £53 in appreciation, a gold watch, and an illuminated address. Charlie was chuffed: "You don't know how I feel here today!" His final words as chairman were: "I like to think to myself that in the future I can say, 'Charlie, you have done your duty to your fellow players'." Any random six-figure-a-week Premier League footballer can testify to that.

A Stressful Spell

There is no denying the class of Charlie Roberts, the centre-half. Charlie Roberts, the captain, was a legend in his own lifetime too. The achievements of Charlie Roberts, the co-founder of the PFA, are also a source of pride. And, in view of his success in later life, you can also champion the merits of Charlie Roberts, the businessman. Just do not mention Charlie Roberts, the manager! Martin Buchan famously took a mere 109 days to decide that management was not the job for him. If only Charlie had followed suit he would have spared himself half the headache. Instead it took him a good 18 months to come to the same conclusion.

At first it all seemed appealing. His old boss, Herbert Bamlett, parted company with Oldham Athletic in the summer of 1921, destination Manchester United via Wigan Borough and Middlesbrough, where he practiced relegation until he perfected it in time for Old Trafford. Having captained the Latics in their glory years, Charlie made a sentimental return as gaffer in July 1921. Those 'glory years', unfortunately, had been left behind on the wrong side of World War I. Of that team's players, only three or four had waited around for Charlie. A quick glance at the Division One table would have given him a clue before he took over: Oldham had dropped into the lower half in the first post-war campaign then, with better aim, zoned in on the lower quarter in the second. The hope was, however, that Charlie – through his glamorous profile and experience if not his pale look – could turn their fortunes around. And at first the 'Roberts effect' *did* work as, eight matches into the season, the Latics were only two points behind leaders Burnley. But then another problem surfaced. It had nothing to do with the fading force at Boundary Park, but rather with Charlie himself – he just could not stand the strain of watching his team! If it was acceptable behaviour to cover his eyes with his hands and peak through his fingers he would have done so. As flimsy an excuse as it might sound, he just could not handle the stress. Some would call that a weakness and Charlie, after all, is not perfect. But there is something you have to remember about his personality. He was a leader, an achiever, a hands-on operator who could get the job done. If he were on the field he would have inspired his men with his drive and ability. When that is ingrained in his makeup, he simply could not rely on someone else to accomplish the job, especially players as average as were available to him at Boundary Park. Even in his personal notes he expressed just how average they were, this after one particularly heavy defeat: "A. Marshall, by carelessness lost the match ten minutes from time".

By December 1922, Charlie had seen enough. This managing lark was not the pastime for him. His solitary claim to fame is that he remains the only man to represent the club in the top flight both on the field and in the dugout. It is hard to imagine he could have done better in the hot seat for the Latics seemed already doomed. Another of Charlie's old bosses, David Ashworth, returned to manage Oldham next, and he promptly got them relegated in 1923. They got so used to dwelling in the lower reaches they did not revisit the top flight for 68 years. As for Charlie, he was relieved this stressful episode was brief. In fact, if his story was ever written, his entire spell in management would constitute the shortest chapter in the book.

The Further Adventures of Charlie Roberts

Charlie' stint as manager started at the age of 38 and finished at 39. In truth, he did not need it – he was already midway through building a small business empire on the side. Yet his love of the game meant he was always looking for ways to stay involved. He had sampled football as a player, as an administrator with the Union, and as a gaffer. About the only job he had not taken was as coach. It is hard to imagine how much coaching he could have done walking on his wooden cane, though he probably put it to good use on any underperforming players! Regardless, he was offered the opportunity to coach in 1928 when a new team popped up in East Manchester. A consortium of local businessmen figured they could take advantage of booming attendances, so they formed Manchester Central FC to play at Belle Vue. Charlie would not come anywhere near the hot seat, naturally, but he was part of a dream coaching duo with his old teammate Billy Meredith. He did get the name 'Charlie Roberts' onto the players' roster, through with a 'Jr.' attached at the end – his son was part of the team. Charlie Jr. participated in Manchester Central's first season in the Lancashire Combination and his prowess as a player can be gauged by the fact that his dad soon advised him to focus on the family business instead!

Central did well in the Lancashire Combination and, at the end of every season, they would apply to get into the Football League… only to be turned down. It transpired neither Manchester United nor City wanted them in, and the two giants lobbied against them for fear of revenue loss! This was especially true of United, who were passing through a lean era. Any less support and the Reds might have gone out of business. In the event, it was Central who disbanded in 1932 instead.

Although it seems as if Charlie's role was anti-United in this episode, it was in fact the club's directors who were the bad guys. He had actually locked horns with them in a separate matter around the same time. The Reds were struggling dearly in the autumn of 1930, at least if collecting a total of zero points from the first twelve matches is the criterion to go by. If the board and the players did not care, at least the fans did, forming a protest group and calling for game boycotts. The first – and only – respected figure to back the supporters' movement was Charlie, of course. Led by super-fan George Greenhough, they approached the ex-captain specifically because of his legendary status and inclination for the moral right. Charlie was only too happy to come to the rescue, proving he still had United's best interests at heart.

The plan was to get Charlie onto the Manchester United Board. However, the directors were so terrified of him they rejected the application on account of him not owning any shares. Fair enough. Yet when Mr. Greenhough sought to pass him some of his own shares, the petty Board again pounced to block the transfer. So Charlie was moved to attacking them through the press. United's predicament was all their fault, he thundered, for it was their ineptitude that led to the steady decline. As ever, the players themselves had his sympathy, though he did recommend the club buy nine new ones! On October 18th, he addressed around 3,000 fans at a supporters' rally, again attacking the Board while advising against the planned boycott of an upcoming match versus Arsenal as it would not garner public opinion. Undeterred, the fans went ahead with the boycott, only it backfired – all the publicity attracted Old Trafford's biggest gate of the season barring the Mancunian derby. Nonetheless, the fans' stance, coupled with Charlie's involvement, exposed the Board's weakness and ineptitude. In due time, the directors would yield to a new owner, name of James Gibson, who would instigate the saving of Manchester United. Charlie had again played his part, even if that came to his detriment – the directors were so miffed at him for singling them out that they banned him from coming anywhere near Old Trafford, which, if you remember, is the stadium he had personally opened.

What is also worth noting is that Charlie certainly enjoyed the odd moment in the spotlight. And addressing the masses could have become a frequent occurrence in 1928. For the previous two decades, he had been an active member of the Conservative Party, specifically the Clayton Conservative Club. Politics had become another facet of Charlie's multi-dimensional persona, and it gave further credence to his desire to live life to the fullest. When he finally ran for City council, his timing for once was off - the prevalent feeling at the time was in favour of the untried Socialists. Charlie quickly learned his lesson: "I contested the Moston Ward in the Manchester City Council elections. I was beaten by the Labour candidate, and I must admit I lost pretty well all my enthusiasm for politics from that date". It was a venture that can be safely filed alongside his spell in management as topics not to delve deeply into.

Charlie Wins the World Cup

Did you know that Charlie Roberts was the first Englishman to win the World Cup? It is true. It happened in the 1930s! He did not win it as a player, nor as a coach, but as the creator of a tactical concept. At least as far as Vittorio Pozzo was concerned. Pozzo was the master-manager who led Italy to two World Cup successes in 1934 and 1938. They also bagged the gold medal at the 1936 Olympics, because it fell in between. The connection to our Charlie began during Pozzo's younger years when his well-off family sent him to school in England to become an engineer. However, once he watched the glorious Manchester United team in action, he concluded that education was over-hyped. Instead of reading his books, he took to studying Charlie's approach to playing centre-half, even getting a private lesson or two from the star himself on the intricacies of the role. Pozzo idolized Roberts so much he refused to return to his homeland at first. Eventually his family lured him back by providing him with a return ticket.

Years later, having settled back in Italy, Pozzo became coach of the national team. Still influenced by his early days watching United, he decided that the *Azzuri*'s own centre-half should be the fulcrum of the side rather than simply a pedestrian stopper. So he went looking for the fittest and smartest player to be his 'Roberts' and found the perfect specimen in Luis Monti. Only Monti blemished Charlie's role by incorporating the elements of thuggery and ruthlessness that are required of the typical Italian defender. Considering he was born in Argentina, it is safe to assume said characteristics were demanded on the naturalization application. Obviously Italy did not mind one bit as they strode to two consecutive World Cup triumphs, thanks in no small part to one Charlie Roberts.

The Legacy

Work is the way of the world. There is almost no escaping it. But there are exceptions. Playing until you cannot run anymore is the way of a footballer's world. Unless your name is Ryan Giggs then you can play through the millenniums. Other professionals in this day and age may not even need a job after their career is over, thanks to either their astronomical wages or their extracurricular deals. Back in Charlie Roberts' time, before the full benefit of the PFA effect, that was not the case. Knowing Charlie's propensity to wear short shorts, I suppose he could have modelled underwear on the side. As it is, he chose to build a business empire instead. And the product used to amass his fortune? Tobacco. Now, some would say this is not the best recipe for healthy living, but you have to remember that a century ago there was absolutely no awareness of the product's dangers. Who knows, perhaps future generations would one day look back on us and judge us for chewing gum!

So, it is true – cigarettes will slowly kill you, but Charlie was not in a hurry, and he set about gradually growing his business. He bought his first tobacconist in Clayton in 1907 from an ex-Newton Heath director and, just like Manchester United outgrew their previous incarnation, so would the retail shop. When injury ended his career, it was the cue for Charlie to sell more cigarettes! Soon that one tobacconist grew into a chain of shops before in time becoming a wholesale firm. By the 1930s, Charlie was easily the most successful

Charlie's grandson Ted at Old Trafford.

of his old teammates post-retirement, not that he was necessarily into bragging. Speaking of teammates, one of the cigarettes he launched was DUCROBEL. The name may be dodgy, but it was actually an amalgamation of the famous halfback line of Duckworth, Roberts, and Bell. It is a blessing then that Charlie did not spend much time as a member of the five-man forward line common at the time. The DUCROBEL cigarette can still be found to this day on display at the Manchester United Museum, presumably in the smoking section.

It was a good job Charlie built a big, prosperous business, for he simultaneously raised a big family to match. It was thus shrewd on his part to provide them with a flourishing environment in which to grow. The seeds of the Roberts clan were first sowed during his short spell with Grimsby Town, so at least one good thing came out of his time there. That is where he first met Mary Cammiss, a young lady of the same age who hailed from nearby Knottingley in Yorkshire. You could tell their love was true because when he was signed by United, she followed him to Manchester even though that was not part of the contract. But Charlie was a man who had his priorities in a certain order, for he promised Mary they could be married... once he had first delivered on his resolution to get United promoted. He even made that public during a dinner held by the manager, Ernest Mangnall, for all the players. When the boss made a speech declaring that he had promised his own fiancée they would wed once promotion was attained, Charlie stood up to announce that he was under a similar obligation... though not to the same woman! You could imagine Mary's horror then when the Reds missed out on promotion by three points in 1905!

Fortunately, relief was just a year away, both for United (on April 21st) and for Mary (on May 7th). Charlie and Mary tied the knot in Selby near her parents' home then set about filling the world with Robertses. Their first-born, Charles Jr., sadly died soon but, undeterred, they proceeded to give birth to nearly a whole team of children, their names rolling off the tongue like Charlie's lineup from his Manchester United heyday: William, Charles (another one), Madge, Jack, Mamie, Hilda, Richard, and Chris. However, after the eighth child, God did not bless them with anymore!

With time, the memory of Charlie faded from the public's conscience, but his descendants carried it with them all along. Even today, years into a new millennium, they are always eager to proudly proclaim his greatness. And foremost among them is Ted Roberts, William's son, who has taken it upon himself to preserve every significant tidbit in the 'Charlie Roberts Scrapbook', a historic shrine to his famous grandfather. Ted is always keen to share Charlie's deeds and accolades with anyone who is interested, whether that be an inconspicuous historian or a prominent figure, as he explains:

"The PFA held a centenary Gala Evening in 2007 and Gordon Taylor, chairman of the PFA, invited me and the other grandchildren of Charlie to this splendid event. Much was made of the early years of struggle to gain recognition. Then, in 2010, Manchester United celebrated one hundred years at Old Trafford and once again I was invited to attend the celebrations during which I met the great and good of the football club. At half-time in the match against Fulham, I was taken down onto the pitch, introduced to the full-house crowd, and asked to place the final bolts in a time capsule vault which is situated just off the playing surface in front of the Directors Box. What an honour – there was a tear of pride when I thought of Charlie, trotting out at that exact spot one hundred years before. I put my hand on the vault to say 'thank you' to all those players and managers of the last century of years who have given us such wonderful football".

Rubbing shoulders with the elite is a more recent occupation. In younger years, it was Ted who handled the bulk of the work required to run Charlie's tobacco business, maintaining it and expanding it as deemed fit. Nowadays he spends his time between England and sunny Spain enjoying a much-earned retirement. But his endeavours only mirror the hard work that Charlie put in when it was originally his turn, as Ted recounts:

"Charlie bought a News and Tobacco shop in 1907 at 591 Ashton New Road, Clayton, Manchester. The football ground at Bank Street was just a short distance away, as was his home in North Road, Clayton. The home would have been typical of this working class area of Manchester: three bedrooms – one for the boys, one for the girls, and one for Charlie and his wife. My dad had his own bed but his other brothers had to share top to tail, as had the girls. It had an outside toilet and was jolly cold in the winter!

"Charlie would serve the fans arriving for the game prior to kick-off and, if United had won, he would be back in the shop to serve the home-going fans and accept the congratulations. If United lost then he would stay at the ground until the coast was clear! The business was mainly retail, but gradually during the thirties wholesaling increased. The boys would deliver the tobacco products around the city on their bicycles. In 1936 the business was incorporated into a Limited Liability concern as Charlie Roberts Tobacconists Limited, with Charlie and my father being the two directors. Growth was limited in the war years as tobacco products were rationed. There was no time for talk of football and Charlie's fame was rarely mentioned.

"Growth in the sixties was rapid, and a new warehouse complex was built in the late seventies on the ground behind the site of one of Charlie's early shops at 365 Ashton New Road. In the early eighties, taking a leaf from Charlie's book, I organized a cigarette called UNITED, in a red and white pack to boot, to be made for our company and distributed by my friends throughout the UK. I was appointed Chairman. At one point we were making and selling some 28 million UNITED cigarettes per month. The warehouse was destroyed in two arson attacks in 1992. Following the attacks, the City Council acquired the site late in 1992 under a Compulsory Purchase Order. A splendid stadium, built for the Commonwealth Games of 2002, was erected on the site and this stadium is now the Etihad Stadium, home of Manchester City. The remains of the building lie beneath the field, and Charlie's spirit roams around the stadium for evermore, or until we find out who authorized the attacks!

"Charlie loved football and would watch both United and City whenever a good match was on. He became a shareholder in Manchester City sometime in the thirties, and we held those shares and their sub-divisions up until the late nineties when the company was taken over and we were obliged to sell. Manchester United fell out with Charlie sometime in the thirties and I believe he has the singular honour of being the only past player to be banned from using the Directors Box at Old Trafford. I understand there was a groundswell of fans that wanted Charlie to be the manager, and he made many outspoken criticisms of the Board and Management. Mrs. J H Davies, who gave £5,000 to the club to stave off bankruptcy, said she would have given them £20,000 if they had made Charlie Roberts the manager, and advocated that he be given a salary of £1,000 a year. Charlie's international career was over whilst only 21 years old and yet his name lives on in football circles over a century later. He was a very great footballer and a great man to boot, and it surely cannot be long before his role and sacrifice is recognized, and he is admitted into the National Football Hall of Fame".

A Legend

They lined the streets in their hundreds. All eyes were on the six footballers in the middle: Billy Meredith, Dick Duckworth, Jimmy Turnbull, Herbert Burgess, Vincent Hayes (all of Manchester United fame), and Jimmy Henderson (of Oldham Athletic). But they were not here to play a football game. Instead, they were the pallbearers at Charlie Roberts' funeral. The great footballer was being laid to rest at St. Cross Church, just a short distance from the old ground of Bank Street where they had first witnessed him in all his awe. At the entrance to the church, a dozen members of the Clayton Conservative Club, ranging from the prestigious to the ordinary, formed a guard of honour. Inside wept his widow, Mary, and all his children. Mr. James Fay, secretary of the Players' Union, was there, as were Messrs Whittaker and Crickmer of Manchester United, accompanied by a wreath of red and white carnations, similarly tied with red and white ribbons. Mr. J H Davies' widow also sent a floral tribute, as did Grimsby Town, who had not forgotten Charlie after 35 years.

Football was Charlie's life, and it was football that brought about his death. For the previous two years he had been suffering from increasing spells of dizziness, the result − it was concluded − of a brain tumor caused by years of heading that heavy ball. The doctors at Manchester Royal Infirmary advised him to have an immediate operation on his skull. Sadly, it was not successful. Charlie passed away on August 7th, 1939. He was only 56 years of age. At least he was spared the horrors of World War II, which began just over three weeks later.

If you happen to walk along the redeveloped shop fronts in Ashton New Road, Clayton, look for a commemorative plaque showing a footballer in full flight. It is a tribute to Charlie Roberts, the captain of Manchester United's first great team and a player who could have embellished any of the subsequent ones; the footballer who redefined the art of the centre-half; the man who formed the PFA, which in itself is a far greater tribute than any engraved stone; the man who threw himself into management, politics, and deep sea fishing simply for the love of life; the father who raised a loving family; and the businessman who built a tobacco empire. He may have spent only 56 years on this earth, but he lived life to the fullest. And, if it is permissible to slightly alter one of his famous quotes, it is safe to say: Charlie, you have done your duty to all.

Charlie Roberts

Born: 6.4.83 in Darlington
MU debut: 23.4.04
England: 3/–

Season	Club	LEAGUE Apps	Goals	FA CUP Apps	Goals
1903–04	GRIMSBY T	31	4	2	–
1903–04	MANCHESTER UNITED	2	–	–	–
1904–05	MANCHESTER UNITED	28	5	–	–
1905–06	MANCHESTER UNITED	34	4	4	–
1906–07	MANCHESTER UNITED	31	2	1	–
1907–08	MANCHESTER UNITED	32	2	4	–
1908–09	MANCHESTER UNITED	27	1	7	–
1909–10	MANCHESTER UNITED	28	4	1	–
1910–11	MANCHESTER UNITED	33	1	4	–
1911–12	MANCHESTER UNITED	32	2	5	–
1912–13	MANCHESTER UNITED	24	1	5	1
1913–14	OLDHAM ATHLETIC	38	3	2	–
1914–15	OLDHAM ATHLETIC	34	–	5	–
	TOTAL	374	29	40	1

LEGEND

PROMINENT FOOTBALLERS.

A. TURNBULL,

MANCHESTER UNITED.

"Controversial and heroic in equal measure"

SANDY TURNBULL BY IAIN McCARTNEY

The noise was deafening, incessant, vibrating through his whole body, making the hairs on the back of his neck stand on end, creating a nervous tension, a feeling surpassing all others. But this wasn't a familiar arena such as Hyde Road or Ewood Park, nor was it the more familiar, much loved environs of the depleted Clayton or the ultra-modern Old Trafford. No, this was far from home. It was Arras, France, around seventy miles south-east of Calais and to some, hell on earth.

Those alongside Lance Sergeant Alexander (Sandy) Turnbull, service no. 28427, of the 8th Battalion of the East Surrey Regiment, shared his nerves and anxiety and, like their colleague at arms, they were never to depart this grim, unfamiliar and totally unfriendly place.

For once, Sandy Turnbull could not claim victory through his undoubted skill as a goal scorer and creator, and, as he climbed the roughly built wooden ladder out of the mudded trench at approximately 3:45 on the morning of May 3rd 1917, he was not simply venturing into the unknown, he was taking the first steps in his final journey, a journey that led to his ultimate death, but a demise that even today has a huge question mark over it.

Alexander Turnbull was born on July 30th 1884 at 1 Gibson Street, Hurlford, a small Ayrshire village a handful of miles southwest of Kilmarnock. It was a mining community, like so many others in the area, with the coal face providing the main source of income for villagers, with Turnbull's father Jimmy one of those who spent his working life in such a dark, dismal and claustrophobic environment. Hurlford, and indeed Ayrshire itself, was also a footballing hot-bed, providing the necessary 'get away from it all' distraction that held one's sanity together away from life underground.

Football, for those not young enough to take on adult responsibilities, was also a pleasant distraction from the three R's and the classroom desk and, as was common at the time, the day to day drudgery of school work was abandoned around the age of fourteen, with young master Turnbull forsaking his short trousers and learning to become the bread winner of the family following his father's early untimely death. Naturally he became a miner, while his mother Jessie remained at home raising her other six children, all but one younger than Sandy.

But Sandy Turnbull was more fortunate than his late father and many others within the community, as he had a talent, an undoubted ability, something that would enable him to escape the dark, unhealthy confines of the coal face. He was a highly rated footballer.

If Hurlford had been without a football team, then there was no shortage of others close by, with a host of excellent junior sides within easy travelling distance. But there was little need for the promising young footballer to venture outside the village boundaries, as Hurlford Thistle, a team he most probably watched win the Ayrshire Junior Challenge Cup in 1895-96, offered him a place within their ranks.

So, Saturday afternoons were now spent plying his trade at Struthers Park, and other spartan grounds scattered across the Ayrshire countryside. But it was a countryside that contained more than green fields and coal mines, as many promising footballers were nurtured amongst the kick-and-rush merchants who, more often than not, played to simply make up the numbers, forcing others to develop their skills lest they suffered some horrific injury from the rock-hard toe caps of either football or working boot, depending on the individual's financial predicament as to whether or not they could afford a pair of the former.

As the English Football League began to develop, with the promise of employment often used as an incentive to attract players from other areas, clubs also began to travel further afield in search for new additions to their playing staff. A prime area for recruiting new players was Scotland, as many of the players from north of Hadrian's Wall were considered of a superior talent to those from nearer home. They possessed a finer degree of ball skills and their often diminutive stature, which gave them a lower centre of gravity, enabled them to do things with a ball that seemed beyond the scope of others.

The first club to find themselves captivated by the imposing 5'7", 12-stone figure of Sandy Turnbull, as they cast their nets far and wide in their attempt to become one of the top sides in the land, were Bolton Wanderers and so impressed were they by his imposing stature, and his ability to look after himself in the physical hustle and bustle of the penalty area, that they quickly agreed to sign him in the summer of 1902.

Whilst he was looking forward to a completely new lease of life in Lancashire with Bolton, Manchester City, under the guidance of Tom Maley, (brother of Glasgow Celtic manager Willie), had also cast their eyes over the player and were impressed by his goal scoring prowess. So much so, that they moved in before the contractual papers from the Wanderers had arrived at the Turnbull home and offered the player better terms to move a few miles further down the road.

Signed on a contract that would pay something in the region of £3 per week, a figure that many today would perceive as a paltry sum though it was actually exceptionally good money compared with that of a miner (who would earn around a third of that), the young Ayrshireman, who would certainly have informed his mother that she had no need to worry about his weekly wage no longer coming directly into the house, as he would send some of his new found wealth back to Scotland, headed south. He joined a football club that had been relegated from the First Division at the end of the 1901–02 season, but City would immediately spring right back to the top flight the following season, while Bolton, ironically enough, dropped down to Division Two. So it was as a Second Division footballer that Sandy Turnbull began his fledgling Football League career.

Leaving his family may have been a wrench, but giving up the long hard toil of working in the mines would not have cost him any sleep, and he would have snatched the professional contract offered by City and instantly scribbled his signature on it before any of the City officials could have had a change of heart.

Exchanging the rural countryside of Ayrshire, with its vast acres of farm land, for the industrial sprawl of Manchester must, however, have been something of a rude awakening for the budding footballer and felt more like a journey into the unknown rather than the road to fame and fortune.

There were certainly no fanfare of trumpets to herald Sandy Turnbull's arrival in Manchester and undoubtedly, he would not have expected one as it was not as if he had been signed from one of the top sides in the Scottish game, but even he must have been uncertain as to what lay ahead, as the *Manchester Evening Chronicle* reported in their July 22nd edition that "Manchester City had signed Turnbull from Hereford (sic)". At least they had spelt his name correctly!

The Manchester City supporters were given their first real sight of the new arrival in the 'Blues' versus the 'Stripes' pre-season practise match on August 16th, 1902, and his early appearances in the City second team were certainly more than promising. Two goals against Bury Reserves on October 4th were followed by another against Preston North End's second string seven days later, with a second

Sandy in City's colours

double strike on October 18th against Liverpool Reserves. Even Manchester United's first-team understudies could not contain the new arrival when their respective second elevens met on November 8th, as the name of Turnbull once again appeared amongst the scorers, notching City's third in a 3-3 draw.

For those who watched the Manchester City reserve side, they would be slightly aggrieved if they did not witness a Sandy Turnbull goal and, as each game passed by, great things were soon expected of the player, who had taken up a role that would be classed as that of a midfielder in the modern game, tucked in behind the deeper lying centre-forward. It has, however, also been written that the new signing failed to make an immediate impact at his new home and that some even held the opinion that the club should cut their losses and either send him back to Ayrshire or try and sell him. His early record in the City Reserves suggests otherwise and it was on the back of those goals and his all-round performances that he was given his first team debut as the right-sided partner to a certain Billy Meredith, against Bristol City at St John's Gate on November 15th, 1902.

In a confident debut, Turnbull scored one of City's goals in the 2-3 defeat, claiming another seven days later on his Hyde Road debut against Glossop in a 5-2 victory. The opportunity presented to him had certainly been snatched with both hands, or perhaps more emphatically, both feet. City were to lead the Second Division for most of the season, but it was the Christmas holiday period that was to see them edge their way in front of challengers Small Heath. On December 20th, they could be found a mere one point in front of their Midlands rivals, but a 1-1 draw against United on Christmas Day, a 2-0 win at Preston on Boxing Day and a 2-1 win at Doncaster twenty-four hours later saw them three points in front with a game in hand.

Everyone needs that little piece of luck if they are to achieve anything and City had theirs, as they sought the Second Division championship and a return to the top flight of the English game, on January 10th, when their table-topping fixture against Small Heath at Hyde Road was abandoned after forty minutes. Had the visitors managed to clinch a victory, then the records books may well have told a much different story. As it was, City more or less wrapped the title up between January 31st and March 7th, when they showed devastating form, scoring thirty-one goals in five successive games, all of which, it must be added, were played at Hyde Road. The run included a 9-0 victory over Gainsborough Trinity and 7-1 against Burslem Port Vale.

Sandy Turnbull's name, however, wasn't exactly prominent in the list of scorers, managing only three in those five fixtures, outshone by the likes of Gillespie with nine, Bannister with eight and Meredith with seven. United almost threw a spanner in the works on April 10th, winning 2-0 at Hyde Road, but three days later Birmingham lost 0-3 at Barnsley, a game they needed to win and a defeat that left them three points behind with only one game remaining. City were Champions.

Twelve goals in twenty-two appearances was a healthy return and certainly contributed to Manchester City's return to the top flight. But alongside players such as the above mentioned trio it would have been difficult not to shine. However, as the weeks and months moved on, the boy from Ayrshire would soon be up there alongside his, for now, more illustrious teammates. He was becoming a firm favourite of the Hyde Road crowd due to his 'devil may care' approach, his all-round contribution to the team and, without any doubt whatsoever, his goals.

Back in the First Division, Turnbull, described in the *Athletic News* as "a clever, virile player", continued to score goals, improving on his first season's tally, with sixteen from his thirty-two outings, along with a further five in the FA Cup and it was in the latter that he really hit the headlines.

He kick-started City's assault on the famous old trophy with a First Round double in the 3-2 victory over Sunderland at Hyde Road. This was followed by another in the 2-0 Second Round victory at Woolwich Arsenal's Manor Ground. Middlesbrough's Third Round visit to Hyde Road was to end goalless, but four days later at Ayresome Park, he scored City's third in their 3-1 win, a victory that clinched a place in the last four. The semi-final paired City with Sheffield Wednesday at Goodison Park and a Turnbull double (or single depending on what sources you read) secured a 3-2 victory.

According to teammate Billy Meredith, Turnbull's sixty-seventh minute goal, City's third, in the semi-final against Sheffield Wednesday, was the "best I've ever seen". The Welsh wizard said: "I never saw anything like it. I had centred square, and 'Sandy' took the ball first time when it was well off the ground and drove it into the net with marvellous force. The amazing thing was that the ball kept low all the way. You will understand the pace of the shot when I say the ball hit the net at Goodison Park and came out while the goalkeeper was still tumbling."

At Crystal Palace in the Final, however, it was the irresistible Meredith and not Sandy Turnbull who claimed the plaudits in the 1-0 victory over Bolton Wanderers, a win that presented City with their first major trophy. In the First Division, however, there were some indifferent displays, and conceding eight goals in four games while only scoring once, could be looked back upon in anguish, as could the final five games of the campaign, when they won two, lost two and drew one. Had the results been better, then they certainly would not have finished second, three points behind the Wednesday.

Turnbull was soon scoring goals for fun and, in season 1904-05, he put away ten in seven games. This tally included a hat-trick against Sunderland in a 5-2 win on December 3rd and four in the 6-0 hammering of Derby County a fortnight later. These were goals that saw him not simply finish top of the City goal scoring chart, but also that of the Football League. It was also a season that saw City push for the ultimate crown of First Division champions and, as the season moved towards its finale, there were only two points separating the

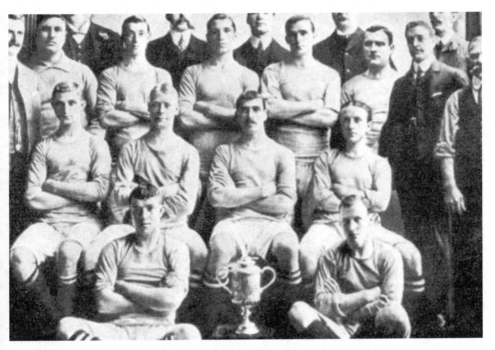

Turnbull (seated on ground, left) with
Manchester City's 1904 FA Cup winning team.

Hyde Road side and title rivals Everton and Newcastle United.

A 1-1 draw against Sheffield Wednesday at Hyde Road, knocked City back somewhat, although a 2-0 win against Everton at Goodison Park kept the dream alive. Strangely, the Turnbull goal machine had not simply stuttered along in those final few games of the season, but had virtually dried up. His goals against Notts County at Hyde Road and Sheffield United at Bramall Lane on January 14th and 21st were his last in the League until March 11th against Blackburn Rovers at Hyde Road, but this was not about to signal something of a return to scoring form, as the final seven games of the campaign were to produce only one further goal.

That was to come on the final day of the season at Villa Park, Birmingham, on April 29th, a game that City had to win in order to take the title, whilst hoping that Newcastle United would slip up against Middlesbrough. Victory for Villa and the Gallowgate club would see Newcastle clinch the championship on goal average.

Villa had won the FA Cup the previous Saturday and so were on something of a high, looking towards clinching the ever elusive 'double', while City knew what they had to achieve, setting up a pulsating encounter, with the volatile and partisan crowd adding to the atmosphere around the packed ground. At the final whistle there was much unrest as the players made their way off the pitch, with some of the crowd determined to rent some physical abuse upon the City players, making it necessary for the police to use considerable force in order to restrain them.

As the second half progressed, with things clearly not going City's way as they were 1-3 down, (they were to eventually lose 2-3), tempers became frayed and some rather over-physical challenges brought retaliation in the form of mud-throwing between players, which soon progressed to punches, with Sandy well into the thick of things.

As the *Bolton Football Field* reported: "Turnbull was in his dourest dribbling mood, dashing about with the ball with his whole heart set on victory. Leake (the Aston Villa captain) found him a real hard opponent and, becoming annoyed at the rough impact, gathered up a handful of dirt and hurled it at the City man. Turnbull was not hurt and responded with an acknowledgement favoured by the bourgeoisie – thrusting two fingers in a figurative manner at the Villa man. He then says that Leake appeared to look towards the referee as though appealing, and not catching his eye, 'gave Turnbull a backhander'. The latter immediately responded with his fists and Leake was restrained by his fellow players from retaliating further."

Closer to home, the *Manchester Evening News*, under the heading of 'Disgraceful Scenes at the Villa Ground. City Lost Championship', included the following in their report of the afternoon's events – "Had Turnbull taken advantage of a very easy chance, the visitors might at least have made a draw of it".

"An Unpleasant Incident - There was little doubt that Turnbull's failure was due to the excitement caused by the unpleasant incident which had just previously taken place. There is a difference of opinion as to what actually happened. On the one hand it is alleged that Leake, the Villa centre-half first attempted to strike Turnbull and that the latter retaliated by striking the Villa player on the mouth with the back of his hand. Others aver that Turnbull was the aggressor, though no-one suggests that the blow was such a one as Turnbull would have struck had he seriously intended to strike Leake. That the latter had been provoked in some way was plainly shown by his desperate rush to get at Turnbull; indeed it was only with difficulty that he was restrained. What the referee thought about the incident was plainly shown by the fact that, after consulting both linesmen, he threw the ball up and allowed play to process".

"Mr Johns' was apparently in an excellent position to see what happened and unless he was guilty of unpardonable weakness, nothing had happened to justify his sending either or both players off the field. There is something to be said in extenuation of a resort to fisticuffs in the heat of the moment, though it would be for the better for the game if all such offences were seriously dealt with, but nothing can excuse the conduct of several Villa players at the close of the game."

With football as divided regionally then as it is today, it was only to be expected that the Birmingham-based *Sports Argus* saw matters in a completely different light, their correspondent writing – "To think that Leake, the mildest-mannered man and the most jovial who ever stepped on to a football field should be the victim of so unprovoked an assault as that committed by Turnbull is entirely to make one's blood boil. It is a mistake to say Alec (Leake) tried to retaliate after being struck once, as my correspondent seems to think. He had good-naturedly asked Turnbull – 'what he was doing' on the first offence, thinking that it might have been one of the mishaps of the game, when the City sharpshooter struck home a second time. This was too much even for Leake's complacency and though George clung to his neck like the 'Old Man of the Sea' and four to five other Villa players assisted the pacificatory efforts of the goalkeeper, Leake was with difficulty held in a leash. This was not the last of the affair but I am not going to raise the veil that ought to enshroud the proceedings in the dressing room."

It is little wonder that the *Sports Argus* were rather reluctant to mention anything relating to "the proceedings in the dressing room", as this would have cast a completely different light on the whole affair, bringing to question the actions of the Aston Villa players that afternoon. The *Bolton Football Field*, however, had little to lose or gain by publishing the events as they saw, or were related them by an eyewitness, portraying Turnbull as not so much as a sinner, but more the sinned upon. The same eye-witness was to relate what he saw to the *Manchester Evening News*.

The man on the spot recalled the events off the pitch as follows: "What I saw was this – Turnbull was coming off the ground (I think he was almost the first of the City players) and was going down the covered passage to the visitors dressing rooms when someone, not a player, sprang out from the urinal and grabbed Turnbull, pulled him inside the Villa dressing room and the door was shut behind him. I thought the whole thing was in fun until, within a few seconds, the door was opened and Turnbull was pitched out heavily, by whom I could not see. He was yelling with pain and fright, and he had obviously been badly handled for his right cheek was grazed with a black mark or dirt (something like a cyclist describes as a cinder rash) and he had a mark on his ribs where he had been kicked (so he said)."

"Naturally, this caused a great uproar and for a few seconds it looked as though there would be a free fight, but the officials kept their heads and so did the players. Turnbull was in such pain that a doctor was called for, but there was not one to be got on the ground and after being attended to by the trainer, the injured player was able to leave the ground with his fellow players."

Having been unable to get within striking distance of the City players, the local Brummies decided to hang around outside the ground and, as the City coach attempted to leave, stones were thrown and police reinforcements called in an effort to disperse the unruly mob. Unable to hide behind a veil of ignorance and indeed without the proverbial leg to stand on, the Birmingham newspapers were later to admit that, yes, something had occurred, although they were not as forward as their Bolton or Manchester counterparts in pointing any fingers at the Villa players.

A commission was set up to look into the events at Villa Park, but it soon transpired that there was much more to the picture than the incidents involving Sandy Turnbull and Alec Leake, and it came to the fore that Billy Meredith had reportedly offered a sum of money to a Villa player in order to allow City to win the match. It must be added that this commission was clearly out to get City for anything that they possibly could and they added the Villa match into the boiling pot well and good.

Meredith, in his defence, protested that he had done nothing more than offer his congratulations to Leake upon his team winning the FA Cup and, although no evidence was produced to portray the Welshman as being guilty, he was banned from football from August 4th, 1905 until April 1906.

What was even stranger was the fact that the FA Commission also banned Sandy Turnbull for a month for his involvement in the incidents on and off the pitch, while the referee, RT Johns, was also suspended for failing to control the match properly. No-one who had worn claret and blue faced any charges or received any suspension or warning. Having won the FA Cup and challenged for the First Division championship up until the final day of the season, City should have built on such success, but failed to do so and, before long, everything suddenly crumbled around them with an almighty crash.

Billy Meredith was somewhat aggrieved that due to his suspension, as he continued to plead his innocence, Manchester City were unable to offer any financial support, due to already being under the watchful eye of the FA Commission. The Welshman took it upon himself to publicly criticise the club and open a huge can of worms when he claimed that he had indeed offered Leake the bribe and had been authorised to do so by his manager, Tom Maley. There was now no turning back. The Football Association had already, perhaps due to some southern bias and jealousy, carried out an investigation into the financial side of City, which had brought about their sudden surge to the top of the English game, but, with only one or two minor irregularities found, they took no action. This time, however, when one of the club's employees was making the accusations, they decided to look a little more closely into their affairs.

On Thursday May 31st, 1906, the FA reported its findings, having discovered that, despite the maximum wage of £4 per week, City had been constantly overpaying over a number of years, with Meredith earning £6 and Livingstone £6. 10s. A total of seventeen players, some having already left the club, were suspended until January 1st, 1907, while manager Maley and Chairman Forrest were suspended sine-die, with two directors banned for seven months. City were also fined £250 and the suspended players ordered to pay a total of £900 in fines. Amongst those seventeen players left kicking their heels was Sandy Turnbull, as the whole episode became rather unsavoury, with one party blaming the other for the mess in which Manchester City found itself.

As the day that their suspension was due to be lifted drew nearer, numerous clubs began to show more than just a passing interest in a number of the banned City players, including Sandy Turnbull. Following the Manchester 'derby' on December 1st, 1906 – the first meeting between the two clubs in the top flight of the Football League and a game won 3-0 by City – United officials made their move for the contracts of a number of those suspended Hyde Road players. The FA had agreed that deals could be done in December, but no-one was to know if any of the players had been approached well before then, with signing-on fees already agreed.

Glasgow Celtic were rumoured to have made a £1,000 bid for fullback Herbert Burgess, while it was also suggested that he was going to Everton as part of a player exchange. He eventually signed for United for £750. Four days after the Hyde Road 'derby', it was reported that United had not just signed Burgess, but also Jimmy Bannister, Sandy Turnbull and the man at the centre of it all, Billy Meredith. The latter cost United nothing, as the Welshman had an outstanding agreement with City saying that he was entitled to a benefit match and at least £600, something that the FA said that they could force City into honouring. In the end, they agreed to a free transfer and upon signing for United, Meredith was handed £500 by an 'unknown gentleman', who also paid his outstanding £100 fine. A mere £350 secured the signature of Sandy Turnbull.

So, A. Turnbull was now on the Manchester United payroll, making his debut in red along with his former blue teammates on New Years Day 1907 against, ironically enough, Aston Villa and he ran out behind captain Charlie Roberts to a rapturous welcome from around forty thousand supporters. The pitch, however, wasn't as welcoming as the fans, as it was in very poor condition with large patches of mud and even larger pools of water scattered across it.

Both sides plodded manfully throughout the opening forty-five minutes but without either goalkeeper being put under too much pressure. But within fifteen minutes of the re-start, the crowd erupted in a joyous wave of euphoria, as United took the lead with what was to prove to be the only goal of the afternoon. Meredith worked his way down the right, taking the ball almost to the corner flag, before crossing with uncanny accuracy to the feet of Sandy

Turnbull, who had no trouble placing the ball out of the Villa keeper's reach.

The new-look United stuttered against Notts County four days later, losing 0-3, but got back on a winning track in the next two fixtures, thanks mainly to Turnbull, whose solitary goal was enough to beat Bolton Wanderers 1-0 on January 26th, having also scored one and George Wall the other the previous Saturday against Sheffield United, the latter from another pinpoint Meredith cross.

Despite the excellent start, the goals dried up and it was not until March 25th, against Sunderland at Clayton, that he scored again, and he was only to score a further two in the remaining six fixtures as United ended the season in 8th place, which in itself was an excellent finish, as they had only just returned to the top flight having spent twelve years in the Second Division.

Season 1907-08 exploded into action with a 4-1 win over Aston Villa at Villa Park and, if Sandy Turnbull felt aggrieved at not beginning the new season with a goal, he well and truly made up for it in the weeks ahead. Five days after the opening fixture, Liverpool arrived at Clayton and were defeated 4-0, with Turnbull snatching a hat-trick: a right-footed drive for his first and two second half headers for his second and third. This was followed by a double against Middlesbrough, which had the local press extolling his praises and pressing for his inclusion in the Scotland international side. He strengthened his international cause with a further five goals in the following five fixtures as United stormed to the top of the table, before notching his second hat-trick of the season against Blackburn Rovers at Ewood Park on October 19th.

The previous Saturday, champions Newcastle United had been hammered 6-1, strengthening United's credentials as the country's top side. Then against Lancashire rivals Blackburn, United made it eleven goals for and only two against in consecutive games with an equally emphatic 5-1 victory. Here, Sandy was in his element; a diving header opened the scoring, with a fine drive for his second, before the customary cross from Meredith presented him with his third.

Another goal in the 2-1 home win against Bolton Wanderers the following Saturday took his tally for the season to thirteen, before injury forced him out against Birmingham City. Although it was only one game on the sidelines, it took him another ninety minutes before he got back into the goalscoring routine, notching both United's goals in the 2-1 win at Sunderland. Seven days later, the 4-2 victory at Clayton against Woolwich Arsenal didn't simply secure United's place at the top of the table, but also saw them register their first-ever ten-match unbeaten run. It also saw Sandy Turnbull taking his goals tally for the season to twenty in fourteen games as he notched all four!

It took Turnbull a mere three minutes to open his account with a low drive, adding his second half an hour later. Although the Londoners admirably managed to pull it back to 2-2 just short of the hour mark, there was no stopping the United inside-left who headed home a Duckworth cross for his hat-trick, edging United in front, before guaranteeing victory with his fourth.

United's unbeaten run and Turnbull's assault on the goal charts came to an abrupt end at Sheffield Wednesday on the last day in November, when the team in second place in the table recorded a 2-0 victory. But life at the top of the First Division was not always a bed of roses for the Manchester United inside-left, as the fixture against his former club at Clayton four days before Christmas was to prove.

In front of some 40,000 supporters, United took a tenth-minute lead through George Wall and, with halftime approaching, Turnbull increased that lead when he headed home a Billy Meredith free kick. After the break, United continued to control the game with Sandy adding a third. Then the game took on a more physical outlook, so much so that United lost Burgess through injury and were soon to be reduced to nine men when the referee sent Sandy off for what was adjudged to have been 'rough play', thus becoming the first player ordered off in a Manchester 'derby'.

The correspondent for the *Manchester Guardian* in attendance at the match wrote: "Sandy Turnbull and Eadie made themselves ridiculous early in the game by repeatedly making grimaces at each other and, in the second half, Turnbull lost self-control so far as to strike Dorsett to the ground. He was promptly ordered off the field by the referee". Suspension ensued, causing him to miss two games in mid-January, but he was soon back to the fore on February 1st when Chelsea visited Clayton on FA Cup business. However, it was a drab and what many perceive to be a typical Mancunian day that saw Sandy return to the side and an afternoon that clearly showed what the conditions at Clayton were really like.

"Manchester United beat Chelsea 1-0 in the second round at Clayton, a place where thirteen belching chimneys confront the spectator in the grandstand; where steam in great volumes threatens to envelope the whole place at any moment if the wind but swings round to the west; where the playing pitch is but a bed of grit, though it rolls out as flat and as taking as a running track. Manchester United may be a great team, but they will always have the advantage over opposing teams that appear at Clayton" wrote one correspondent present.

The groundsman had marked out the pitch on the morning of the game but had to do so again fifteen minutes prior to kick-off as the early morning frost began to disappear in the sun and the pitch softened. It was later to resemble "a ploughed field" down the middle, but the visitors could not overcome either the conditions or the spirited and "lucky" United team in the "witches' cauldron". It is thankful, however, that Sandy Turnbull scored before those playing conditions worsened, taking only two minutes and thirty seconds to find the back of the Chelsea net, firing the ball home from twenty yards following a free kick. However, the reporter from the *Sporting Chronicle* appeared to give as much credit to the "evil power that presided over this witches' cauldron" than Sandy Turnbull's football skill, with the shot being "willed to strike the upright and go off into the net."

The name of 'Sandy Turnbull' appeared on the score sheet in the following round in what was a rather uneventful return to Villa Park, United winning 2-0, but any hopes of a Cup Final appearance were put to rest in Round Four with a 1-2 defeat at Fulham. His solitary strike against Birmingham (the addition of City to the club name was still a long way off) at Clayton on February 29th, however, maintained United's place at the top of the First Division with an eight-point gap between them and second-placed Newcastle United. There was even the further advantage of having a game in hand.

A 0-1 defeat at Woolwich Arsenal on March 21st was followed four days later by a 4-7 defeat at Liverpool, closing the gap to five points, but there was now a cushion of two games in hand to fall back on. It was, however, rather ironic that both those fixtures had seen the name of A. Turnbull missing from the United lineup. But he was back on the team sheet on March 28th as United returned to their winning ways with a 4-1 home win over Sheffield Wednesday, striding towards that initial First Division title.

On April 4th Bristol City held United to a 1-1 draw in front of some 20,000 spectators, while nearest rivals Newcastle United lost 0-2 at Everton, and Sheffield Wednesday – who had recently appeared in the picture - defeated Blackburn Rovers 2-0. This saw the Yorkshire side climb into second spot, eight points adrift of United, but having played a game more.

Newcastle had four games left, Wednesday five and United six, so the ball was very much in United's court. However, on Wednesday, April 8th, no 'if's and but's' remained as the destination of the Championship trophy was well and truly decided, with United only having the minimum of input into that final outcome. The North-East, rather than Lancashire, produced the results that determined the 1908 First Division champions. Sheffield Wednesday travelled to Middlesbrough while, a few miles up the road, Newcastle entertained Aston Villa. United had only to make the short journey across Lancashire to face Everton. Whether it was nerves or whatever, both Sheffield Wednesday and Newcastle United didn't simply lose their 'must win' fixtures, they were both soundly beaten, the former 1-6 and the latter 2-5. United, courtesy of goals from Harold Halse, George Wall and Sandy Turnbull, defeated Everton 3-1.

Yes, Sheffield Wednesday could win their remaining fixtures and draw level with United, and even Manchester City could sneak up on the blind side to also draw level on points, but to do so, the team in pole position would have to lose their remaining six games, an event that was very unlikely to happen.

Or was it?

On April 11th Notts County left the obnoxious surroundings of Clayton with both points from a 1-0 win but, strangely, it was defeat that also brought the title to those Spartan surroundings, as Manchester City lost 1-3 at Nottingham Forest and Sheffield Wednesday lost 1-2 at Bolton Wanderers - results that well and truly confirmed that United had become Football League champions for the first time. It was an ideal ninety minutes to be crowned champions and the home supporters, despite their delight in the achievement, were critical of their team's performance. However, it was a result that also raised more than one or two eyebrows with the events on the field causing much debate in Manchester and beyond.

The visitors were to be found in 19th place in the First Division, sandwiched between Bolton Wanderers and Birmingham, with all three on twenty-eight points, although the Midlands side had played a game more. So, claiming anything from the visit to Clayton was totally unexpected but, as the afternoon progressed, became much more than simply a pipe dream.

With news of a proposed move to the banks of the Ship Canal filtering around the ground and indeed all of Manchester prior to kick-off, the United supporters were more than content to debate the pros and cons of the move, dismissing the visitors as mere cannon fodder, with two points little more than a foregone conclusion. The opening forty-five minutes did little to create any excitement from the spectators scattered around the ground and indeed some of the performances from the home players were noted to be well below their usual standards. Shortly after the second half got underway, those performances were momentarily forgotten when the referee pointed to the penalty spot following a foul by a County defender, but within seconds there were looks of astonishment as it appeared that none of the United players wanted to take the spot kick. Sandy Turnbull, as likely a character as any to take the kick, declined as he said he had a damaged ankle and was also suffering from a sore head following a couple of knocks. Always in the thick of things, few would doubt the robust inside-forward. So, it fell to George Wall to place the ball on the spot.

As reliable as any with the ball at his feet, Wall surprisingly hit the spot kick well and truly wide of the goal and was even more surprisingly congratulated by the Notts County players for his efforts, as the United supporters expressed their own personal thoughts with loud boos! The minutes slowly ticked away and, the longer the game went on, the less effort was contributed by the United players, so much so that, with full-time beckoning, the visitors charged up field and snatched both points with practically the last kick of the game.

If the crowd had been cold in their reception of Wall's penalty, then it was nothing to compare with the abuse hurled towards the United players at full-time despite the news reaching the ground that both Sheffield Wednesday and Manchester City had lost and there were now no doubts whatsoever that Manchester United were champions. Many felt that an enquiry should have been carried out as regards the outcome of the game, but none were forthcoming.

United surprisingly failed to score in their following two games and, even more surprisingly, won only one of their remaining five fixtures, a 2-1 victory over Preston North End on the final day of the campaign. At full-time, the events of the Notts County fixture were forgotten as the supporters invaded the pitch and congregated in front of the main stand shouting for their heroes to take a victory bow from the window of the president's area.

Sandy Turnbull contributed as much as anyone to that first League Championship, notching a more than creditable twenty five goals during the campaign. However, as the defence of the title kicked off on September 5th, 1908, his name was missing from the Manchester United line-up, and it was not until the visit of Liverpool to Clayton that he had the chance to resume where he had left off some five months previously. In the thick of the action from the outset, a header across goal, from a Meredith free kick in the fifteenth minute, left Wall with the easiest of opportunities to open the scoring and help maintain an opening five-match unbeaten run.

Despite the goals of the previous season, it was not until October 24th, the ninth League fixture of the season, that Sandy's name appeared on the score sheet, netting twice against Nottingham Forest in the 2-2 draw. It was also something of a surprise that he was indeed able to actually feature in that, and many other United fixtures, due to his total involvement in the game, his robust nature and the knocks that materialised from his physical play. Indeed, he had to leave the field of play in two of the previous three fixtures to receive treatment for injuries, but on both occasions returned to the fray, and against Bury on October 3rd, he even managed to force the ball home, only to be given offside.

October 31st saw United, who had slipped to 4th in the table four points behind Everton having begun the month in top spot, making the journey to the north-east to face Sunderland at Roker Park. Again the United trainer found himself earning his money, with injuries to Burgess and Downie forcing United to play much of the game with only nine men. Sunderland stormed into a 2-0 lead early in the game, but by half-time Sandy had pulled a goal back. It was, however, to no avail, as the depleted United side were no match for their hosts, who eventually ran out 6-1 winners.

Injury struck again on the first Saturday in November, when Chelsea visited Clayton and once more the unfortunate individual was Sandy Turnbull, who was carried off the pitch during the second forty-five minutes, with a twisted knee. It was an injury that would keep him on the sidelines until the Christmas Day fixture against Newcastle United at St James Park.

Turnbull was back among the goals in the 4-3, January 1st victory over Notts County, but the new year failed to bring much in the way of success to Manchester United, as they were to win only one other game between the first day of 1909 and April 12th, with one four-game run even failing to produce a goal.

By early April, they had dropped to eleventh place with thirty-three points from their thirty-two games and were now some sixteen points behind leaders Newcastle United. It was a picture that was to show little in the way of change, as they finished the campaign in thirteenth, a mere four points better off.

With players of the calibre of not just Sandy Turnbull, but his namesake Jimmy, the irrepressible Billy Meredith, Livingstone, Wall and Bannister, why there was such a shortage of goals from the United front line and indeed the team as a whole, is a mystery, as following the four against Notts County, a meagre nine were added to the 'goals for' column over the course of the following twelve games.

Of those nine, Sandy Turnbull could be credited with one, scored against Liverpool in the 1-3 defeat on Merseyside on January 30th, but he was also to miss half a dozen of those First Division fixtures. One of them, the 0-3 defeat at home to Blackburn Rovers, was due to his presence being required in Glasgow to take part in the Scotland international trial match between the Anglo Scots and the Home Scots, for the forthcoming fixture against England at the Crystal Palace. Sadly, he failed to make the final eleven. However, although there was a distinct lack of goals and points from the League fixtures in the latter half of the 1908-09 season, with the final placing a disappointment having failed to build on their title success, the FA Cup took on a completely different outlook.

The draw for the Third Round of the competition paired United with Brighton and Hove Albion of the Southern League and, despite their somewhat lower status, the visitors gave an excellent account of themselves on a very heavy pitch and considered themselves unfortunate to lose by the only goal of the game, scored by George Wall, in the thirtieth minute.

What Brighton lacked in experience - they had only been formed eight years previously - they made up for in effort. The 8,074 crowd witnessed a bruising ninety minutes that saw Billy Meredith sent off for 'kneeing' an opponent and at different periods during the game, Jimmy Turnbull, Hayes and Bell of United and Martin of Brighton were off the field receiving treatment for injuries. Sandy also came in for some close attention from the opposition, but for once managed to avoid injury and also the wrath of the match official, but, unfortunately, the referee could not do likewise with the crowd, as a number of his decisions were not to their approval and they waited outside the dressing rooms for him at full time. He was, however, able to get away from the ground safely and without any confrontation.

On the training ground at the Blue Cap, Sandiway, the United players attempted to erase the memories of the 1-3 defeat against Liverpool and prepared for their Second Round FA Cup tie against the other half of the Merseyside duo at Clayton seven days later. They were, however, without the services of Billy Meredith, suspended due to his sending off in the previous round. Rather surprisingly, United had no reserve player capable of stepping into the Welshman's shoes, so something of a re-shuffle was carried out, with Livingstone coming in at inside-right and Halse moving out to the right.

With Everton already having beaten United a couple of months previously, their confidence was high, but they themselves were not without selection problems, so the packed crowd were indeed anticipating something of an enthralling encounter. The visitors opened briskly, but for all their endeavour, they went in at the interval a goal behind – Halse firing an unstoppable shot past Scott shortly before the break. United maintained their advantage as the second half got underway, but could not increase their lead, although both Wall and Sandy Turnbull came close. Everton often put the United defence under pressure, but like their Manchester counterparts, failed to get the better of the defensive line that stood in front of them, and the game was played out with that one solitary goal deciding the outcome.

It was a home draw again in Round Three and yet another Lancashire derby, with Blackburn Rovers making the short distance south to Clayton. Much to the enjoyment of the home support, it was certainly nothing similar to the nail-biting ninety minutes of the previous round. United threw off their shackles and the misery of the 0-0 draw against Sheffield United the previous Saturday to hit Blackburn for six in a game that the *Athletic News* reporter referred to as "sensational" and a result that "will rank as one of the most surprising results in the history of the Cup contest".

He continued: "That the Rovers would be beaten was not altogether unexpected, but few of those who witnessed the great game in the Bank Street enclosure could have been prepared for the surprising events secured after the interval, when the United were leading by a goal scored by Sandy Turnbull nine minutes after the start."

Blackburn brought around 6,000 supporters to Manchester for the cup tie, monopolising the tram cars to Clayton and creating plenty of noise as they packed themselves in behind one of the goals as soon as the gates opened at one o'clock. However, Sandy stunned them into silence as the small army of ambulance men were kept busy with fainting casualties as the ground swelled to capacity.

Twice in as many minutes Jimmy Turnbull came close to scoring, while

Blackburn scorned an excellent opportunity at the opposite end. But with less than ten minutes played, Wall and Sandy Turnbull worked the ball out to the United right. The cross from Harold Halse found Wall close to goal and he in turn passed the ball to Sandy who was left with the easiest of opportunities to give United the lead. A minute later, Sandy was in the thick of the action again, but on this occasion, he was in collision with an opponent and had to leave the field with a "damaged forehead". He was soon to return to the fray and played a major part in United's devastating second half display.

Two minutes after the restart, Wall beat Crompton in the Rovers goal but could only watch as his shot went agonisingly wide. It was, however, only a brief reprieve for the visitors as goals from Jimmy Turnbull and Livingstone soon gave United a 3-0 lead. Davies pulled one back for Blackburn but, with ten minutes remaining, Sandy Turnbull took the game by the scruff of the neck and re-established United's three-goal advantage with a shot from close in. Five minutes later, Jimmy Turnbull made it 5-1, running straight through the Rovers defence and, with the now silent Blackburn support making their way to the exit gates, Sandy Turnbull added a sixth to complete the rout.

Did the Football Association have something against Lancashire clubs, a London bias perhaps, coupled with jealousy of their success? It certainly appeared as if they wanted as few clubs from the red rose county in the competition as possible, as once again United were paired with one of their local rivals, coming out of the velvet bag after Burnley, sending them to Turf Moor on Saturday March 6th.

The day was far from ideal football weather, as when the gates opened at 12:25, snow had already began to fall and before long had turned into a cold, mind and body numbing sleet. It didn't, however, put off the locals and travelling supporters alike, as the ground quickly began to fill and the atmosphere was certainly not spoiled by the weather.

The pitch was covered in frozen snow, but slowly began to soften as the game commenced. United, although playing down the slight slope on the Turf Moor ground, had to face the wind and sleet which blew towards them. Burnley attacked from the outset and within ten minutes were in front, Smethams sending the ball into the United area where Ogden managed to steer it into the corner of Moger's net. Sandy Turnbull and Halse were denied by Dawson, while Ogden almost notched his second but was denied by the post. Sandy should have put the scores level, but he took the ball too wide and saw the opportunity go amiss. The weather failed to improve, but the players stuck admirably to their task despite sliding and slipping across the quickly deteriorating surface, while Dawson in the Burnley goal continued to deny the United forwards.

With eighteen minutes remaining the outcome of the game was finally decided when a shrill blast of referee Bamlett's whistle brought the game to a premature end. The official, like his linesmen and the players of both sides, had endured the appalling conditions admirably, but he finally decided that enough was enough and called a halt to the proceedings. He was certainly not influenced by any of the visiting players or officials, although the former had wanted the game to be abandoned long before the referee made his decision – one that was certainly not well received by the home crowd. Rather ironically, Bamlett would become manager of United in April 1927, enjoying a four-year spell in the hot seat, an appointment that was in no way influenced by his brave decision in the face of hostility at Turf Moor!

So, it was back to Burnley the following Wednesday, with the home side still confident that they would secure a semi-final place. But it was not to be as United, with the conditions greatly improved, won 3-2, with goals from Jimmy Turnbull (2) and Halse. Now ninety minutes from a Cup Final appearance, only Newcastle United stood in United's way, and it was perhaps that this momentous occasion was a contributing factor in the 0–3 home defeat at the hands of Blackburn Rovers the previous Saturday.

Cup fever well and truly gripped Manchester, or at least those within the city of a red persuasion, as there was something of a mass exodus from early morning until around 2pm, heading for Bramall Lane, Sheffield from the London Road, Central and Victoria Stations. Countless saloons and special carriages had been booked, but demand was greater than supply and it proved impossible to cater for everyone. It is interesting to note that, despite the vast support that crossed the Pennines, there was still a crowd of 4,000 at Clayton to watch the United reserve side take on Blackpool.

Bramall Lane was a mass of humanity, with 40,118 paying £8,590 to watch what turned into an intensely fought encounter although many locals had complained about having to pay one shilling for the privilege of doing so, caring nothing for the travelling and meals outlay of the visiting supporters. If the outcome of the match were to be decided on form alone, then it would be Newcastle who would progress towards the final, as they led the First Division by six points from Everton, whilst having also played a game less. United floundered in fourth, some thirteen points behind.

It was indeed Newcastle United who enjoyed the best of the opening exchanges but, slowly, United managed to gain a foothold on the game and caused their opponents some nervous moments around their goalmouth. Nonetheless, amid the excitement of the first forty-five minutes, neither goalkeeper was beaten. With the wind now behind them, United had something of an advantage and this was increased somewhat following an injury to Newcastle's centre-forward Shepherd, who was forced into a rather inactive role out on the right wing. Things were soon to even out though as Sandy Turnbull limped

Sandy scores the goal that earned Manchester United their first ever FA Cup triumph

off to receive treatment, and play developed into stalemate with both sets of defenders happy to play something of an offside game.

Charlie Roberts almost broke the deadlock, but his header crashed against the Newcastle crossbar. Wall and Jimmy Turnbull also came close as rain began to fall heavily, then with 28 minutes of the second half gone and Sandy Turnbull having limped back into the fray, taking up a position on the left wing, the opening goal - and indeed what turned out to be the only one - was scored. Wall centred from the left and, amid something of a scramble for possession between a couple of players, Halse quickly sized up the situation and pounced on the ball to drive past a helpless Lawrence. Newcastle pressed forward for the equaliser, but to no avail, and it was United who could now make plans for a trip to London and their first FA Cup Final appearance.

According to the report in the *Umpire*, Sandy's performance, even before his injury, was regarded as "very moderate", with the knock not allowing the opportunity to redeem himself, as it kept him on the sidelines for the next seven fixtures. His injury was indeed a worry to manager Ernest Mangnall. There had been little hope of retaining the League Championship for some time, so his absence in those remaining First Division fixtures was not exactly the end of the world, but, with the Cup Final edging nearer by the day, Mangnall hoped that he would be able to field what he regarded as his strongest line up.

There was much debate in the week leading up to the match at Crystal Palace whether or not Sandy would be fit to face Bristol City and, although he travelled south with his team mates, it was not until half an hour before kickoff that the United manager decided to gamble on a player who had spent so long without kicking a ball in earnest.

Despite the advantage of a brisk wind, United were soon put on the defensive by the Bristol forwards, with both Roberts and Stacey clearing their lines. A foul on Charlie Roberts saw the resulting free kick headed wide by Sandy Turnbull in United's first serious attack, but they were soon to settle and began to cause their opponents' defence some anxious moments. A foul on Sandy by Annan saw the offended player once again head wide as United continued to press forward. Roberts dictated play from the back and, in the twenty-first minute, sent Halse through but, although in the clear, his effort slammed against the underside of the Bristol City crossbar and rebounded into play. It went, however, only to the feet of Sandy Turnbull, who drove the ball firmly home from close range.

Ernest Mangnall's decision had indeed paid off.

Play began to even itself out, but as halftime approached, United once again looked to be in control. Wall was unlucky not to add a second, while Sandy tested Clay in the City goal with a low drive which the 'keeper managed to turn round the post. An excellent one-handed save by Moger early in the second half maintained United's advantage, although they were soon hampered in their defensive department by an injury to Hayes. Following a few minutes on the sideline receiving treatment, the fullback returned to limp around in something of an inside-right position. Duckworth and Halse moved back, while Stacey switched wings, as United fought to defend their solitary goal advantage.

The injury clearly had an effect on United's play and it became completely disjointed, but the game should have been put beyond Bristol City's reach when a double Turnbull threat opened up their defence. However, Jimmy, a few yards from goal, blasted over. Minutes later, Sandy almost wormed his way through the City defence, but was rather unceremoniously brought down from behind by Annan. Despite being hampered by the injury to Hayes, United kept their opponent's defence on their toes and, with Roberts marshalling the reshuffled defence superbly, they hung on to secure a memorable victory, thanks to that solitary Sandy Turnbull goal.

With Manchester United's first FA Cup secured, the new season was eagerly looked forward to, but there were problems on the horizon, perhaps more so for United than any of their opponents. Had the game been nothing more than an ordinary Football League fixture, then it is more than likely that the name of Sandy Turnbull would not have appeared on the Manchester United team sheet, but such was his importance to the team, Ernest Mangnall, perhaps due to the prompting of his captain, Charlie Roberts, who had said to the manager that he should let him play, "as he might get a goal and if he does, we can afford to carry a passenger", took a calculated risk and included the player and was certainly more than relieved that his gamble paid off.

Turnbull's efforts were also appreciated by the United support, who warmed to his whole hearted approach to the game, with his physical involvement warming many hearts on those cold afternoons in the dull and dreary surroundings of Clayton. So much so that, following the final, the *Athletic News* carried a supporters' song:

> *"Why we thought you were 'crocked' Dashing Sandy,*
> *That to fame your road was blocked, Hard Lines Sandy,*
> *But you came up to the scratch,*
> *Made an effort for THE match ...*
> *When Halse hit the shiv-ring [sic] bar, Lucky Sandy.*
> *There were groans heard near and far, Deep ones, Sandy,*
> *But the ball was on the bound,*
> *And your boot was safe and sound,*
> *When the net your great shot found, Champion Sandy.*
> *For the score was but one up – not much Sandy?*
> *But the Bristol boys worked hard*
> *Though their efforts were ill-starred*
> *Give a cheer then with the band, For them Sandy."*

After a night of celebrations, which saw Sandy and his side-kick Billy Meredith, accompanied with the Cup itself (much to the pains of United secretary JJ Bentley), join staunch United supporter George Robey - one of the top entertainers of the day and the man who had actually supplied United's Cup Final shirts - at the Alhambra Theatre where the latter was appearing, it was discovered that the United secretary's fears were turning into a nightmare, as the lid of the famous trophy had disappeared. Had it been left at the theatre amid the jovial scenes of the night before, or had it got lost somewhere between there and the United hotel?   Such fears were soon put to rest as the lid duly turned up – in the pocket of Sandy Turnbull's jacket! The why's and where's of its disappearance and subsequent re-discovery were never recorded, with the incident simply passed off as nothing more than a prank, a piece of harmless fun, involving the United goalscorer.

On December 2nd 1907, a meeting at the Imperial Hotel, which five years earlier had become Manchester United's headquarters, saw the formation of the Association of Football Players' and Trainers' Union (now the PFA), with Billy Meredith and Charlie Roberts well to the fore at this inaugural meeting. Two years down the line, the PFA contacted the Football Association, making clear its intentions to challenge the maximum wage of £4, while also seeking to alter the 'retain and transfer' system. It also sought to join the 'Federation of Trade Unions'. Eager to see off any threat the fledging Association might poise, the Football Association withdrew its recognition of the PFA, a move which not only angered the players, but also brought the threat of strike action. This in turn forced the Football Association into banning all players affiliated to the Union prior to the start of the 1909-10 campaign, which in turn saw a steep decline in its membership.

There was, however, little, if any, drop in interest or indeed involvement from the players of Manchester United and, with the new season about to break over the horizon, there was a very distinct possibility that the opening fixture against Bradford City would not take place. So strong was the feeling of those United players, and some of their fellow professionals at other clubs, they were pictured posing behind a hand painted sign which proclaimed "The Outcasts FC", Sandy Turnbull sitting proudly in the front row. But they were not to remain 'outcasts' for long as, when it was seen that there was support from outside with Manchester United (Tim Coleman of Everton was one of those pictured in that infamous team group), others came forward to ignore the FA, which eventually agreed to allowing the PFA official recognition, in exchange for the dropping of the plans to abolish the maximum wage and substituting it with bonus payments.

So, it was a full-strength cup holders who got season 1909-10 underway with three straight victories followed by two draws, results that saw them level on points with Newcastle United, but with the advantage of a game in hand over their semi-final rivals from a few months previous. Sandy kicked off the campaign in his usual inside-left position, but it wasn't until the sixth game of the new campaign that he found the back of the net, scoring twice in the 2-3 defeat at Notts County.

As in the past, the physical side of the game seemed to follow him around like a shadow as, in the second game of the new season, against Bury at Clayton, he was once again forced onto the sidelines to receive prolonged treatment, leaving his teammates to plod away with a man short. He was also in the thick of the goalmouth action despite his inability to find the back of the net, coming close on numerous occasions and finding creditable mentions in those early season match reports.

Against Bury, he "made a fine wing alongside Wall", while the following week he was regarded as "useful" against Tottenham Hotspur in London. A "magnificent shot in international style" (whatever that might mean) almost opened his scoring account against Preston North End at Clayton in a game during which he also "did some clever things". But it was at Trent Bridge that he claimed his opening strikes of the season, although his goals only achieved personal success. Notts County had taken a second minute lead, but with only three minutes of the first half remaining, Sandy equalised with a magnificent shot from a Meredith free kick. His second of the afternoon came with County 3-1 in front and was scored from the penalty spot after Jimmy Turnbull had been brought down by Morley. But there was to be no fight back and a share of the spoils, as County held on to their one goal advantage.

October 2nd brought Newcastle United to Clayton and the battle between the League Champions and the FA Cup holders promised to be an entertaining affair, so much so that United captain Charlie Roberts had requested the game as his benefit match, most probably in anticipation of a bumper crowd. However, a dispute between the Players' Union and the FA as regards to the proposed benefit, which in reality should have been settled well before the game, saw the FA meet the day before and then fail to come to an agreement, putting the plans of the United captain on hold for the time being at least. Roberts was obviously disappointed when informed of the Football Association's decision - or indeed its lack of - and when he informed his team mates on the morning of the Newcastle match, several of his teammates declared that they would not turn out that afternoon as a form of protest.

It was most likely that Sandy Turnbull was one of those who felt so strongly about the outcome, but in a hastily arranged conference at the Players' Union offices managed to persuade the dissidents that they should turn out that afternoon. While United enjoyed the better of the first half, it could be said that the visitors won the second half on points, although many would argue that this was mainly due to the fact that United were without either of the Turnbulls for the last ten minutes and they faced Newcastle with only nine men. Despite the two injuries, the game, although physical, was in no way a dirty one, with only four fouls awarded throughout the entire ninety minutes.

The home side took the lead in the twentieth minute when a Sandy Turnbull shot beat Lawrence in the Newcastle goal, but could only watch as his shot cannoned back off the post. Fortunately for United, Wall was alert to the opportunity and ran in to prod the ball past the stranded 'keeper. United could have found themselves three goals in front before the referee brought the first half to a close, both chances falling to the feet of Sandy Turnbull, but his first effort flew over the bar, while the second was saved by Lawrence. Newcastle snatched a share of the points when Duckworth, in an attempt to clear, only succeeded in putting the ball past Moger, the ball skidding off the side of his boot as he attempted to block the shot from a Newcastle forward.

Seven days later United travelled to Liverpool and in a repeat of their last away day at Notts County, they were beaten 2-3, with Sandy Turnbull again the scorer of both the visitor's goals. By halftime United found themselves 0-2 down, the home side having scored in the seventeenth and fortieth minute, with debutant goalkeeper Rounds having little chance with either Liverpool effort. After the interval, however, it was a completely different picture, with the visitors scoring twice in the opening sixteen minutes. With the second half only a few minutes old, Halse was tripped inside the area, leaving referee Howcroft little option but to point to the penalty spot. Hardy was given no chance with Sandy's spot kick. Minutes later, following another assault on the Liverpool goal, United won a corner and, from the flag kick, Meredith's inviting cross fell invitingly to Sandy Turnbull who once again beat Hardy. The tempo was now raised as both teams pushed for the equaliser with Rounds keeping the home side at bay with a magnificent performance, but midway through the half he could do little to prevent Stewart from heading the winner.

Aston Villa's visit to Clayton saw United record their first victory in six games and once again the Turnbull duo were in the thick of the action. One United attack saw Sandy charging into the Villa penalty area only to be brought down, but, taking the kick himself, drove the ball into the arms of Cartlidge. He made amends for this miss thirty minutes into the second half when he headed home a Meredith corner and, soon afterwards the Welshman was again the supplier, with Halse beating the Villa goalkeeper. Jimmy Turnbull had come close to scoring between both those goals, driving over when in a good position, but he blotted his copybook in the final minutes of the game when he became physically involved with Hunter, the Villa left-half, after a challenge in front of the main stand, with players of both teams having to step in to separate the two players.

Seven days later, Jimmy Turnbull once again received his marching orders, this time for kicking out at an opponent, with the double dismissal earning him a six-week break from first team action, during which time United won three and lost three, only failing to find the back of the net on one occasion.

Sandy Turnbull scored his sixth goal of the season in the 2-0 home win against Chelsea on November 13th, but a run of five straight victories came to an end the following Saturday with the 2-3 defeat at Blackburn Rovers, a victory that cemented the home side's position at the top of the First Division, whilst also earning them record receipts of £1,200 from the 35,000 crowd in attendance. This defeat was the start of a period of inconsistency for Mangnall's team, which saw them win four, lose five and draw one of the next ten games, pushing them down towards mid-table, with the name of Sandy Turnbull failing to appear on the team sheet for four of those. But despite those absences, he still managed to find the back of the net on four occasions and receive favourable comments from the men of the press.

As United plodded away through their League program, thoughts constantly drifted across Manchester, to an area of wasteland just off Chester Road, almost on the banks of the Ship Canal. It was here that sooner, rather than later, the Clayton regulars would have to make their way in order to watch their

Sandy (seated, first from right) in United's first great team

favourites, leaving those odours and belching chimneys for a new home.

Tottenham were beaten 5-0 in the final First Division encounter at Clayton on January 22nd, a week after Burnley gained revenge for their dubious cup exit the previous season, with a 2-0 Third Round victory. With all the odds and ends being packed up ready for the big move across the city, United made the relatively short journey to Preston, where they lost 0-2, before travelling to the north-east to face Newcastle United, where they defeated the current League champions by the odd goal in seven, Sandy Turnbull notching two. He had obviously recovered from the cup-tie at Burnley, where he was forced to leave the pitch in considerable pain to a facial injury on two occasions.

Football in the early 1900's was a completely different game as to that of today. Obviously the biggest difference is the money that can be earned and, although those players of that bygone era were making more than many of those who paid their pennies to watch them on a Saturday afternoon, they were certainly not well off. Their playing kit was coarse and heavyweight, with the boots just as likely to maim as they were to produce a moment of individual brilliance. Injuries were simply an occupational hazard and, as you have read, Sandy Turnbull collected his fair share of those, more often than not limping off the field at the end of the game. He did, however, give as good as he got. Perhaps, at times, slightly more!

Comparisons certainly cannot be made between those Manchester United players who earned the club its first domestic honours and those individuals who pull on the red shirt (or whatever other colour it happens to be) today. Was Charlie Roberts a better club captain and a harder individual than Nemanja Vidic? There is, however, an eerie resemblance between Sandy Turnbull and Wayne Rooney in more ways than one!

February 19th saw the curtain rise on the new Old Trafford home, a venue considered the most modern in the land, with tip up seats and a playing surface akin to a billiard table. The setting was perfect. The result was certainly not. As on the previous Saturday, United shared seven goals with their opponents. However, on this occasion they could only manage the lesser amount, their first-footers, Liverpool, failing to be the perfect guests, notching four. But taking everything into account, it is fair to say that United were as familiar with the arena as their opponents, so home advantage, for once, could be discarded.

Watched by some 45,000 on a fine Mancunian afternoon, the occasion could not have asked for a better start than United christening their new ground by scoring the opening goal, with the honour falling to none other than Alexander Turnbull. With half an hour played, United were awarded a free kick and Duckworth sent the ball towards the Liverpool goal. Keeping his eye firmly on the brown leather sphere, Sandy threw himself forward, his head connecting with the ball, which flew past the outstretched hand of Hardy to put United in front. A few minutes later, it was 2-0. Hardy managed to stop a shot from Halse but failed to hold the ball, which rolled towards the feet of Homer, who gratefully accepted the opportunity to give United a 2-0 halftime advantage.

The second forty-five minutes saw Liverpool claw themselves back into the game with a goal from Goddard, the ball going in off the underside of the bar, but any immediate thoughts of a fight back were forgotten when Wall resorted United's two goal lead, surging past Robinson and Rogers, before beating Hardy at his left hand post from what looked like an impossible goal scoring angle. There was seldom time to draw breath as the pace was relentless as both teams pressed forward. But it was the visitors who made the breakthrough, with Goddard snatching his second of the afternoon when he shot across Moger and into the net. Liverpool sensed that they were in with a chance of at least securing a draw and within the space of a couple of minutes, they weren't simply on level terms, but in front, both goals coming from Stewart.

So, the first fixture at Old Trafford ended in disappointment, leaving United floundering in eighth place, seven points behind leaders Notts County but, as often was the case, they had two games in hand. Things failed to improve the following Saturday, as the visit to Villa Park brought a 1-7 reversal, a game that was to be Sandy's last until March 26th due to injury, but even then, he was only back for one solitary outing before missing a further three fixtures. In his absence, United ironically enjoyed a change of fortune; winning five, drawing one and losing one of the seven fixtures. The most noteworthy was a 5-0 victory over near neighbours Bolton Wanderers. The run took United up to third, but they were seven points behind leaders Aston Villa, so any hopes of following the cup success with a League Championship were highly unlikely - even more so as United had now played a game more than the team at the top.

Sandy rounded off his season with two goals in the final three games. Although outshone in the final fixture of the season by Picken who notched all four in the 4-1 victory over Middlesbrough at Old Trafford, it was good to see that he was back to his best, with the *Athletic News* informing its readers that, along with Meredith and Roberts, much of the game was devoted to 'exhibition football', showing 'some remarkable juggling'. 'Boro's McLeod, we are told, 'was helpless against Turnbull', who 'fed his partner (Wall) in beautiful fashion'.

The summer of 1910 saw a number of new faces arrive at Old Trafford, amongst whom were Hofton from Glossop, Dean from Eccles, Aspinall from Southport, Green from Chesterfield, Hodge from Stenhousemuir and West from Nottingham Forest. Of those new additions to the United playing squad, it was the latter, Enoch 'Knocker' West, who was to make the biggest impact, taking over the number nine jersey and to a certain extent Sandy Turnbull's mantle of the team's main goal scoring threat. He was also not simply to become a partner on the field of play - Sandy playing alongside him at inside left - they became firm friends off it as well.

West opened his United goals account on the first day of the 1910-11 season in the 2-1 win over Woolwich Arsenal, Harold Halse claiming the other, with Sandy Turnbull having to wait until the second fixture of the new campaign before claiming his first, but he was still playing catch up with his new teammate, as West also scored in the 3-2 home win against Blackburn Rovers. West's arrival on the scene seemed to act as something of an inspiration to Turnbull, not that he needed such a thing, but it began to look as if the duo had a personal wager, which perhaps they did, as to who would finish as leading scorer.

It was Sandy Turnbull who notched the solitary United goal in the 1-2 defeat at Nottingham Forest on September 10th, a game that attracted the largest crowd at the City Ground for some time, with the Forest directors rubbing their hands when the loose change was counted to the sum of £420, with a further £160 taken in season tickets. For the former, it might simply have been a case of having come to see United.

He made it three in three games, scoring the opener in the 2-1 victory over Manchester City the following week and maintained his place as top scorer with the only goal of the game in the next fixture against Everton at Goodison Park. Before long West was struggling to keep up with his striking partner as the goals continued to flow. Following that strike against Everton, he failed to find the net against Sheffield Wednesday and then missed the trip to Bristol City, but he was soon back in the groove, with seven goals in the following eight games. West in the meantime could only manage to increase his total by three, two of those coming in the 2-2 draw against Tottenham Hotspur at White Hart Lane.

Scanning through the match reports of the period, the name of Sandy Turnbull was never far from being that of United's 'man-of-the-match', whether he had notched yet another goal or not. Even in a no-scoring draw against Notts County, the first time in fourteen League games that United had failed to find the back of the net, or indeed suffered defeat, he was considered to be 'the pick of the bunch' or a 'shining light'.

He could also, however, make the headlines for all the wrong reasons. On November 19th, seven days after the draw at home to County, he was back amongst the goals with a double in the 3-1 win over local rivals Oldham Athletic. During the game, he was cautioned by the referee for making what were considered to be degrading remarks to the official who warned him that, should he repeat his comments, then he would be left with no alternative but to send him off. The game continued with no further conversations between player and official but, at fulltime, as everyone was leaving the pitch, Sandy slipped alongside the referee and said that he wanted to tell him that he had said the offending words again, but he had not heard him!

The 0-2 defeat at Sheffield United on December 10th left United in third place in the First Division, two points behind leaders Aston Villa, whilst also having played a game more. But by Boxing Day, three games later, they had climbed to the top, with a one-point advantage over the Midlands side, thanks mainly to a Turnbull and West inspired victory over Villa, although the 2-1 win at Sunderland and the 5-0 hammering of Woolwich Arsenal at Old Trafford also helped considerably.

Villa's visit to Manchester on December 17th was undoubtedly the match of the season to date and an eagerly awaited encounter between the current First Division champions and a team with aspirations towards their crown. The pretenders were a team that was growing in respect, with the Villa directors being reported as considering United to be "the finest in the country as to the conception of the Association game and its practical possibilities".

Two minutes before the interval, Sandy Turnbull gave United the lead, shooting through a forest of legs and just inside the post and, with United regaining possession almost immediately from the restart, he just failed to increase the advantage when his head was mere inches away from connecting with the ball in front of goal. He was also involved in United's second, his shot being deflected wide for a corner from which West got on the end of Wall's kick to nudge home.

His goal in the 2-1 win at Sunderland on Christmas Eve was strangely his last for some six games and perhaps more significantly the end of what could be described as a purple patch in front of goal, as he was to score only five more in the remaining four months of the season, despite missing only two games. Following the goal against Sunderland, his next would not come until almost a month later, on January 21st, and the 1-1 draw against Manchester City at Hyde Road, when he accepted yet another Meredith-crafted opening to give United the lead.

Despite his lack of goals, however, his presence in the team was essential and his contribution second to none, something emphasised by 'Harricus' in his report of the City encounter in the *Athletic News*. He wrote: "Wall was at his best in the first half, for Turnbull allowed him to rest after changing ends, and Turnbull is one of those players who seem to do as the spirit moves them. Apparently he is indifferent, but watch him closely and his seeming lack of energy is part of his programme, with intent to deceive the opposition. They forget he is playing, as it were, but he does not."

Despite the lack of goals from Sandy Turnbull and two consecutive 0-1 defeats in the final two fixtures of 1910, United maintained there push for the First Division title, and an unbeaten run between January 2nd and March 15th kept them three points ahead of an Aston Villa side determined to keep a hold of the crown. United had a one- game advantage over their rivals but all could well hinge on the meeting between the two at Villa Park on the penultimate day of the season.

A goal against Middlesbrough in a 2-2 draw on March 4th was Sandy's first in four games and it seemed to have rekindled his prowess in front of goal, as he scored in the following two fixtures, a 5-0 win over Preston North End and a 3-2 triumph over Tottenham Hotspur. Suddenly the nerves began to kick in as the games became fewer and the season rose to a crescendo. Notts County took both points with a 1-0 home win, in which United were poor, although 'Jacques' of the *Athletic News* wrote: "There was one Manchester forward, however, who played brilliantly. He was head and shoulders the finest inside man in the match – I allude to Turnbull, who all through the second half dribbled and passed superbly in an attempt to galvanise the line into life. He was laid out in a collision with Morley – both men were hurt – and he was also kicked on the head, but right to the end he was still the one man to threaten the Nottingham goal."

That same afternoon, Villa lost at Newcastle United, but then came a 0-0 draw against Oldham Athletic at Old Trafford and what was generally considered a fair result. It kept United in top spot, but with Villa involved in the FA Cup, United had now played two games more and held a four-point advantage.

A 'Knocker' West double saw Liverpool beaten 2-0 at Old Trafford, with Villa winning at Middlesbrough to maintain the challenge, but a 0-2 defeat at Preston did little to help their cause on an afternoon that saw United dismiss Bury 3-0. Easter weekend left the outcome still shrouded in mystery, as Villa defeated Sheffield United 3-0 on Good Friday, followed by a 2-0 win over Notts County twenty-four hours later. United could only draw 1-1 with Sheffield United on the Saturday and 0-0 with Sheffield Wednesday on Easter Monday. It was now, United in front by two points, but they only had two games left and one of those at Villa Park. Their rivals had three left to play and held more than a distinct advantage.

Villa indeed gained the upper hand with a 4-2 win in the crucial confrontation, but undid all their good work forty-eight hours later when they could only draw 0-0 with Blackburn Rovers, although it was a point good enough to give them the advantage at the top of the First Division. It all now hinged on the outcome of the fixtures of Saturday April 29th – United at home to Sunderland and Villa a few miles down the road at Liverpool. One point separated the two teams, with Villa also holding a .05 goal average advantage.

Strangely, there were only around 12,000 at Old Trafford on that final afternoon of the season, an afternoon that could see Manchester United crowned First Division champions for only the second time in their history. The rain undoubtedly put many off despite the events that threatened to unfold. The United players knew it was simply a case of win or bust so went about their task from the opening whistle and, by half time had stormed into a 3-1 lead, with United's left wing partnership of Turnbull and Blott giving the Sunderland right-sided pairing of Forster and Tait a torrid afternoon. Turnbull constantly supplied his left wing partner with exquisite passes and the former Southend United player, whose favoured position was on the opposite side of the field at either outside-right or right-half, was a constant thorn in the side of the Sunderland defence, with the crowd warming to what was his first senior outing of the season.

West headed home a Duckworth cross early on, only for the goal to be disallowed as the ball was judged to have crossed the dead ball line prior to the United right-half's centre. But it was the visitors who unexpectedly took the lead in the twenty-third minute, causing much anxiety amongst the sparse numbers around the stadium. Bridgett made the initial run forward, passing the ball towards Mordue. The Sunderland inside-right proceeded to send the ball into the United area where a number of his team mates lay in wait, and it was

Holley who pounced, sending the ball up against the underside of the bar and into the net.

With the wind on their faces, United went searching for an equaliser and the dual wing threat of Meredith and Blott soon had the Sunderland defence back-tracking. On the half hour, the Welshman was fouled by Milton near the goal line and, from the free kick, he dropped the ball menacingly close to the Wearsiders' goal where Turnbull leaped to head home. Ten minutes later, United were in front. Meredith, again in the thick of the action, swung over a corner kick. Such was the danger that Sandy Turnbull posed, half the Sunderland team seemed to be gathered around him. But the Scot suddenly began walking away from goal, taking his numerous markers with him, allowing West to move into the vacant space and score with something of a backward header. Halse added a third before the interval.

In the second half, it was almost all United. Halse scored with a shot on the run from a Meredith centre to make it 4-1, with the scoring rounded off when Milton put the ball past his own goalkeeper as it bobbled around a packed goalmouth. The crowd had cheered at halftime when the telegraph board showed that Villa were behind at Liverpool and they cheered even louder at fulltime, when the result found its way to Manchester – Liverpool 3, Aston Villa 1. Manchester United were champions.

During a close season in which manager Ernest Mangnall made only one addition, bringing in George Anderson from Bury in a £50 deal, Old Trafford staged the Players' Union Athletic Festival and it was reported that one of the funniest things ever to be seen at Old Trafford was the sight of Sandy Turnbull timing the sprints with a clock that he had carried from the dressing room!

The 1911-12 season kicked off in a rather unspectacular fashion for the Champions, with four draws, four defeats and four wins in the opening dozen games. Sandy found himself one behind 'Knocker' West in the goal scoring charts, while United were thirteenth in the First Division, six points adrift of Newcastle United and seven in front of bottom-placed Bury. Sandy was noted primarily for his actions in the opposition penalty area, but he was not adverse to rolling up his sleeves and giving his defenders a helping hand. He was also labelled in some quarters as being "slow", but this was something of a misjudgement by those on the opposite side of the touch-line, as there were not many forwards quicker off their marks when a half chance raised its head in front of goal.

December 2nd saw United travel to the north-east to face First Division leaders Newcastle United, a fixture that in the past had seen a glut of goals with score lines such as 5-0, 6-1 and 4-3. This encounter only conjured up five goals, but it gave out a clear indication to all concerned that the current champions were not going to give up their title without a fight. There was no 'Turnbull' to be found among the scorers in the visitors' perhaps surprising to some victory of 3-2, but as always he played his part, keeping the black and white striped shirted defenders on their toes. Perhaps even more strangely, the name of 'Turnbull' would be found amongst the United scorers on one occasion following his goal in the 2-0 win over Bolton Wanderers on December 23rd.

Sandy's return of seven goals from thirty appearances was his poorest season since he had made the cross town move from Manchester City. He had scored five in season 1908-09, but during that campaign, he had played in only nineteen games, compared to more than double that this time around.

United's drop from Champions to thirteenth was nothing short of a huge disappointment, but something was perhaps not entirely unexpected, as it was often considered that too much expectancy was placed on the shoulders of a select few. What was perhaps totally unexpected was the defection of manager Ernest Mangnall to Manchester City. But, then again, did the manger suspect that his League Championship and FA Cup winning side had achieved everything they could and that it was time for him to move on to another challenge? Mangnall, although classed as manager, was in effect the club secretary and his vacant position was filled by a similar office bearer in J. J. Bentley. The new man at the helm certainly had a footballing pedigree, beginning as a player with Turton FC, whilst at the same time finding time to pen match reports for the local newspaper, going on to become secretary and treasurer of the Lancashire club.

Hanging up his boots, he moved into accountancy and was soon to become secretary of Bolton Wanderers, going on to be regarded by many as one of the most influential figures in English football due to his involvement in the formation of the Football League. He was soon to pick up his pen in earnest once again, moving back into the world of journalism whilst continuing in his role with Bolton Wanderers but, when United came calling, like many before and after him, he found it irresistible and moved to Old Trafford. Many considered him out of his depth in the managerial role with United, but a look at the First Division table at the end of season 1912-13 shows a distinct improvement on that of the previous campaign.

Goals were also in short supply as season 1912-13 got underway or, more to the point, they were non-existent for both United and their robust inside-forward. The 0-0 draw on the opening day at Woolwich Arsenal was in reality an acceptable point, but losing 0-1 five days later against neighbours Manchester City was an early setback that they could have done without. Goals from Turnbull and Livingstone were enough to earn the first victory of the season, a 2-1 win against West Bromwich Albion, but five defeats in the following eleven games left United in fourteenth position, some eight points off the leaders – Ernest Mangnall's Manchester City.

The 2-4 defeat at Aston Villa on November 16th was Sandy Turnbull's last outing of the season at inside-left as, after missing two games, he returned to the side on the opposite flank, switching positions with West. Although it saw him back alongside Billy Meredith, this was only for one game, as the Welshman was to find himself dropped for the first time in his career. He did return to the side, but during this season, his appearances were to be few and far between.

But while Meredith's star was falling, that of Sandy Turnbull's continued to shine brightly, as the United programme editor described him as "the cleverest manipulator of the ball the game has known for a decade", whilst he explained that the player had been switched from inside-left to inside-right in an effort to help Meredith regain something of his old form. The programme editor continued: "In his own sphere, Turnbull ranks equal to Meredith and the selection robbed the latter of any grumble he might have had of being inadequately partnered."

At inside-right, Sandy continued to deliver, although his goals did not flow quite so frequently as in the past. Strangely, his goals, during this and in past seasons, were almost all solitary efforts, but on Boxing Day, he notched his first 'double' since November 19th, 1910, in the 4-2 win over Chelsea at Old Trafford. Twenty-four hours previously, the Londoners had been beaten 1-4 on their own ground. Against Chelsea, Turnbull in fact scored three. However, one of those, Chelsea's first, was past Beale, the United 'keeper! His double came from a twenty-five yard drive that gave Brebner in the Chelsea goal no chance and a header from a Wall centre that once again left the visiting 'keeper helpless.

Those victories over Chelsea had contributed to an improved League position, climbing to tenth, three points behind leaders Aston Villa. City had dropped to fourth and were due to host the return leg of this particular season's 'Battle of Manchester' on December 28th, when a victory for United could see them leapfrog their arch rivals. And leapfrog them they did, gaining revenge for their early season defeat, with a 2-0 victory, both goals coming from West in the opening forty-five minutes.

Goals, however, still managed to elude Sandy Turnbull, as he could only manage a meagre three in the second half of the season and on occasion his usual creditable performance and honourable mentions within the match reports were nowhere to be seen. Against Sunderland on March 15th his only mention from 'Jacques' in the *Athletic News* was due to a kick on the head seeing him seldom in the game and, as the final few games of the campaign approached, United were unable to claw themselves any higher than third, but had played more games than their immediate rivals, eventually finishing in fourth place.

He began season 1913-14 in good enough form, scoring on the opening day in the 3-1 win over Sheffield Wednesday and again the following fixture against Sunderland, clawing himself back into the spotlight and into the match reports of the national press. Unfortunately, Sandy Turnbull's star was waning; no longer twinkling brightly in the northern sky and his name was soon not to be one of the first pencilled in by JJ Bentley on his United team sheets. This, however, was not entirely due to his on-field performances being no longer up the standards expected by the man at the helm. A dressing room argument flared up between the two, coming on the back of the Football Association deciding to install a form of tax on each professional's wages, in order to assemble a relief fund to help clubs as they began to suffer the loss of players due to them entering the armed forces. A number of the professionals refused to pay, while the Players' Union refused to co-operate, and suddenly it was Manchester United who found themselves singled out, with Bentley's former source of employment – the *Athletic News*, where he was editor - quick to condemn the United players. Bentley suspended Turnbull, but his actions brought even more ill feeling into the dressing room, with the remainder of the players threatening to go on strike unless their teammate was re-instated.

By the turn of the year, Sandy was no longer a regular first-team choice. A report of the match against West Bromwich Albion on New Year's Day 1914 mentions: "The latter (Potts) played so cleverly that Turnbull cannot expect to regain his position for some time". Regain his position he did, against Bolton Wanderers, three days later, remaining in the side for the FA Cup tie against Swindon Town the following Saturday, where he was once again mentioned in dispatches as having a good game alongside his old friend Meredith. However, the cup tie brought something of a shock result, a last minute goal taking the southern-based side through and the end of a glowing career was now edging over the horizon.

Sandy Turnbull was to make only one more appearance in the red of Manchester United that season and that was on February 7th in his old inside-left position, away at Tottenham Hotspur, a game that would not produce any headlines, only a 1-2 defeat. On April 11th, Turnbull, along with George Stacey, was allowed to have the game against Manchester City as a benefit match but, due to injury, Sandy was unable to play, instead, accepting the plaudits of both sets of supporters from the touchline. City won the game 1-0, with the *Umpire* recording that the visitors received a more encouraging welcome than United when they took the field prior to kick-off but, while the result was perhaps not what Turnbull, or Stacey for that matter, had wanted, the takings of £1,216 certainly softened their disappointment. United finished season 1913-14 in fourteenth place in the First Division with everything at Old Trafford far from perfect. Their problems, however, were distinctly minor compared with what was bubbling away elsewhere.

On June 28th, 1914, Archduke Franz Ferdinand of Austria was assassinated by a Yugoslav nationalist, an event that was to in turn trigger off the First World War. Despite the undercurrent of increasing threat to world peace, the 1914-15 season kicked off as normal on September 2nd, with United losing 1-3 at home to Oldham Athletic. Sandy Turnbull was missing from that opening day line-up and indeed for the following two fixtures, a 0-0 draw against City at Old Trafford and a 0-3 defeat at Bolton, but he was back into the thick of things for the fourth match of the campaign against Blackburn Rovers, where two Enoch West goals secured the first victory of the season. Sandy claimed one of United's goals seven days later in the 2-4 defeat against Notts County and played in one more game before missing the next three. He then enjoyed a run of seven outings between the end of October and mid-December, but was then out of the side until April 6th when he returned for the 0-1 defeat against Oldham. Four days later, in the 2-2 draw against Middlesbrough on April 10th, he scored what was to be his final goal for United, and the following Saturday at Sheffield United, the final whistle finally brought down the curtain on not just his Manchester United career, but his Football League career at this level. His name, however, along with those of a handful of teammates, was soon to be on everyone's lips once again, as well as the front and back pages of the local and national newspapers.

On April 2nd, Good Friday 1915, Liverpool made the short journey along the East Lancs Road to face United at Old Trafford, a fixture that should, in reality, have seen the visitors secure victory without too much of a problem, as a look at the First Division table on the morning of the match saw United third from bottom, level on points with second bottom Notts County and only one point ahead of Chelsea who were propping up the table. Liverpool were five places above and six points better off.

United, rather unexpectedly as there wasn't the same intensity surrounding such fixtures then as there is now, won 2-0, with both goals coming from George Anderson. At the end of the season, United were still third bottom, one point better off than Chelsea and two above bottom club Tottenham at a time when only two teams were relegated. It was indeed a significant victory.

"A Moderate Game – Manchester United Get Two Points From Liverpool" proclaimed the headline above the *Sporting Chronicle* match report, while the *Manchester Football Chronicle* had the headline "A Surprising Display" above its report. 'The Wanderer', reporting on the match for the latter, wrote: "Personally I was surprised and disgusted at the spectacle the second half presented". While in the *Chronicle*, their correspondent wrote of the play in the second half "being too poor to describe". Neither they, or any of the other reporters present, voiced their opinions as to how the play was so dire, but the crowd were certainly not slow in making their feelings known, with many heard to comment amongst themselves that they felt the game was rigged. Especially after United had taken a 2-0 lead, when they did little in the way of attempting to increase it, happy to simply plod away, without putting the Liverpool defence under any form of pressure.

In the *Daily Dispatch* their correspondent 'Veteran' wrote that West "was chiefly employed in the second half in kicking the ball as far out of play as he could". So disgusted was the *Daily Mirror* with the proceedings that it simply carried the result and no report. Even the *Liverpool Daily Post* wrote "that a more one sided half would be hard to witness" and that Beale in the United goal went half an hour without touching the ball.

A missed penalty added to the drama. Taken by O'Connell, and not the usual spot kick exponent Anderson, the Irishman blasted the ball well wide of the post with the score at 1-0. It was a miss that even sowed some seeds of doubt in the referee's head as to the actual sincerity of the players involved, commenting later that it was "the most extraordinary match that I have ever officiated in". The match, however, was not going to be simply shrugged off as 'one of those games' and the rumblings of discontent soon developed into a full blown thunderstorm when a notice appeared in the *Sporting Chronicle* from a bookmaker, under the name of 'Football King', which offered a reward to anyone who could supply information on the events at Old Trafford a few days previously. It also appeared in the form of a handbill and read: "We have grounds for believing that a certain First League match played in Manchester during Easter weekend was 'squared', the home club being permitted to win by a certain score. Further, we have information that several of the players of both teams invested substantial sums on naming the correct score of this match with our firm and others. Such being the case, we wish to inform all our clients and the football public generally that we are withholding payment on those correct score transactions, also that we are causing searching investigations to be made with the object of punishing the instigators of this reprehensible conspiracy. With this object in view, we are anxious to receive reliable information bearing on the subject and we will willingly pay the substantial reward named above (which was £50) to anyone giving information which will lead to punishment of the offenders". The snowball was about to roll.

Within three weeks of the game, the Football Association had set up a Commission to look into the complaints that had been made and asked 'Football King' to come out and name the exact match he was referring to and also give his name and address, so that if there was nothing untoward about the game in question, the players of both sides could sue him for libel, whilst if he was not, then the Commission would look more thoroughly into the matter. 'Football King' remained anonymous, there were no claims for libel and the Commission continued in its investigations, interviewing the players of both teams, and it was not until December 23rd, 1915 that the final verdict was finally announced, when the *Sporting Chronicle* headlines proclaimed:

"Football Betting Commission Report – Eight Players Permanently Suspended"

The eight were L. Cook of Chester, J. Sheldon, R. R. Purcell, T. Miller and T. Fairfoul of Liverpool and A. Whalley, E. West and A. Turnbull of Manchester United. Others were thought to be involved, but those eight were suspended from taking part in football or football management and were also banned from entering any football ground in future. League football in its current format came to a halt in October 1915, by which time Sandy Turnbull could be found a couple of goal kicks, or so, away from his Old Trafford stomping ground, working for the Manchester Ship Canal Company. He did guest for Rochdale and Clapton Orient in the early days of the war, but even his contribution to the United cause was simply now nothing more than a memory.

In November 1915, he enlisted in the Footballers' Battalion of the Middlesex Regiment so, whether the outcome of the Commission's enquiry a month later had any real effect on him, we will never know. He had taken no part in the match itself, but was a firm friend of Enoch West, and he had also met Liverpool captain Jackie Sheldon, a former teammate, in the Dog and Partridge public house, a mere stone's throw away from the ground, prior to the game. He had little in the way of defence.

(Lance Sergeant) Alexander Turnbull's army records were destroyed during the blitz on London during the Second World War, making details of his time on the French battlefields of the First World War sketchy, to say the least. As a member of the Middlesex Regiment, he may well have been involved in the first day of battle at the Somme on July 1st, 1916, when 60,000 men died in that initial period of fighting. But we do know that if he was present on that horrendous day, he somehow survived, as he is recorded as having later joined the ranks of the East Surreys 8th Battalion, being with them in the spring of the following year as they waited to join the assault on the Hindenburg Line. Had he been 'excommunicated' from the ranks for the Footballers' Battalion due to his suspension from the game? Most probably not. His 'transfer' would more than likely have been brought about due to the depletion of the East Surrey's ranks, having suffered heavy casualties during the hostilities to date. It was a move that would cost Sandy Turnbull dear.

By some coincidence, the East Surrey's had a football team, and one of considerable note, while they are also remembered due to some of their men going over the top of the trenches on that fateful day at the Somme, dribbling footballs as they advanced across no man's land. Such was the strength of their noted team, it swept all before them to win the divisional championship and it is more than possible that, although banned from the game at home, Turnbull played an active part in the Battalion fixtures, as in one letter back to Manchester from the front, he spoke of having played in a game, but had not slept since as he had forgotten to ask permission from the FA!

One fixture that was recorded was the semi-final of the divisional tournament at Boeseghem, when the East Surrey's defeated the 7th Buffs 4-1. No teams or goal scorers are noted amongst the Battalion's records so, again, whether or not an A. Turnbull was involved is something we will never know. What we do know is that the final of the tournament was never played due to the Battalion being called into action of an entirely different kind, with disastrous consequences.

With the sun still to rise on the misty morning of May 3rd, 1917, the 8th East Surrey's advanced towards the village of Chèrisy, ten miles east of Arras, hoping to catch the German front line unawares. The village was captured by the relatively untrained soldiers and they reached the banks of the river Sensèe almost intact. However, on either side of the village, the units were not as successful and the isolated Battalion came under heavy shell fire. Within a couple of hours they were completely overrun when the Germans counter-attacked, leaving many either dead or captured, while a few were fortunate to retreat from whence they had come. Of the 500 or so 8th Surreys who attacked Chérisy for no gain, 90 were killed, 175 wounded and more than 100 captured.

At first, it was presumed that Sandy Turnbull was amongst those who had miraculously survived, as on the 18th May, the *Kilmarnock Herald* reported that "Sandy Turnbull, famous Manchester United forward, and a native of Hurlford, has been wounded and made a prisoner. He has been fighting for about a year". The information had been conveyed in a letter from a comrade by Sandy's wife Florence at her home at 17 Portland Road, Gorse Hill Stretford. The message to the Turnbull home read: "I am writing to try to explain what has happened to your dear husband, Alec. He was wounded and, much to our sorrow, fell into German hands, so I hope you will hear from him. After Alec was wounded he 'carried on' and led his men for a mile, playing the game until the last we saw of him. We all loved him, and he was a father to us all and the most popular man in the regiment. All here send our deepest sympathy".

As elusive on the battlefield as he was on the football pitch, there were hopes back in Manchester that one day, the family man and the former hero of both the City and United supporters would return. Sadly, it was not to be.

In another letter to the Turnbull home, this time in August 1918, Captain C. J. Lonergan of the 8th Battalion, who had returned to England after being held a prisoner of war, wrote: "It was a great shock to me to hear that my best NCO, i.e. Sergeant Turnbull, was still missing. Of course, I knew there was no hope of him turning up after such a long period. He was one of the finest fellows I have ever met. A great sportsman and as keen a soldier as he was a footballer. He had been hit through the leg early on in the fight. When I saw him his leg was very much swollen, so I ordered him back to the dressing station. He pleaded so hard, however, to be allowed to stay on until we had gained our objective that I gave way. Sandy was in command of a platoon. The men would simply go anywhere with him. Well, the end of it all was that, although we gained all our objectives, the division on our left did not. Consequently, the enemy got round our flanks and we had to get back as best we could. We came under very heavy machine-gun fire during the withdrawal. This was when I was hit. As I fell I saw your husband pass me a few yards away. I saw him get to the village which we had taken that morning. There was some shelter here from the bullets so heaved a sigh of relief when I saw him disappear among the houses. I knew he could get back to our lines with comparative safety from there. I never heard anything more from him. Those who were wounded all thought Sandy had got back. It was a bitter disappointment to me to hear that he had not been heard of. The only explanation I can give is that he must have been 'sniped' by a German who was lying low in one of the houses. It was a rotten bit of luck. I would have recommended him from Germany, but I had my doubts whether the German Censor would allow it to come through. However, I put his case strongly when I wrote from Holland and I do hope he will get the highest distinction possible. He certainly deserves it". The assumption that Sandy Turnbull met a fatal end as he attempted to get back to his own lines is one that we have to make.

There are two lasting memorials to A. Turnbull, the soldier: one in the British war cemetery in Arras, where his name appears amongst the 'missing', the other, a short walk from Old Trafford, on a war memorial by the side of Chester Road. Three years after his death, when he would still only have been thirty-six, he was posthumously pardoned by the Football Association for his part in the bribery scandal.

Despite his involvement in the events of Good Friday 1915, one cannot deny Sandy Turnbull his place amongst the Manchester United 'greats'. What he did was certainly wrong, if indeed he was guilty of the offence, but it must be remembered that he lived in a time of widespread poverty and the footballers' maximum wage. It must also be remembered that Eric Cantona, still hero worshiped from the stands today, assaulted a supporter during a game, while Roy Keane all but assaulted a fellow professional, again during a game. Of the trio, whose 'offence' was worse?

For me it was Turnbull's, the stocky built goal machine. Manchester United footballing legend.

Sandy Turnbull

Born: 1884 in Hurlford
MU debut: 1.1.07

		LEAGUE		FA CUP	
Season	Club	Apps	Goals	Apps	Goals
1902–03	MANCHESTER CITY	22	12	1	1
1903–04	MANCHESTER CITY	32	16	6	5
1904–05	MANCHESTER CITY	30	19	2	1
1905–06	MANCHESTER CITY	26	6	–	–
1906–07	MANCHESTER UNITED	15	6	1	–
1907–08	MANCHESTER UNITED	30	25	5	2
1908–09	MANCHESTER UNITED	19	5	6	4
1909–10	MANCHESTER UNITED	26	13	1	–
1910–11	MANCHESTER UNITED	35	18	3	1
1911–12	MANCHESTER UNITED	30	7	7	4
1912–13	MANCHESTER UNITED	35	10	4	–
1913–14	MANCHESTER UNITED	17	4	1	–
1914–15	MANCHESTER UNITED	13	2	–	–
	TOTAL	330	143	36	18

Give it to Joe

J. SPENCE

MANCHESTER U.

"Spence's standing at the club got to a point that can best be summed up by this straightforward formula:
Manchester United = Joe Spence;
and, hence: Joe Spence = Manchester United."

JOE SPENCE BY CHARBEL BOUJAOUDE

Mr. Soccer

It was the worst of times. The years that separated the two World Wars have long been forgotten by most Manchester United fans. And who can blame them? Nowadays, an occasional setback such as a draw, let alone a defeat, would lead to days of uproar amongst Reds worldwide. With that in mind, you should feel a certain degree of sympathy then towards our forefathers from the inter-war era when relegation was the club's default setting. If they were not busy going down, they were doing a good job trying to. Between 1919 and 1939, Manchester United spent nearly as much time in the Second Division as they did in the First. They almost ventured into the Third at one point as well. At other times they even went into the trouble of dabbling with bankruptcy and revolt. Trophies? Sure, you could see some, but first you had to take a short trip to that other club down the road. Yes, things were that terrible and it would be tempting – even if a bit impudent – to say a modest 'thank you' to Hitler for finally putting an end to United's dismal days! It would be, that is, if it weren't for the little matter of bombing Old Trafford and other such indiscretions.

Unsurprisingly, then, United fans of that inglorious era had to mostly look up to the Manchester skies if they wanted to witness any stars – there were hardly any that walked amongst them. Except, that is, for one player who shone so bright; one hero to chant about. His name was Joe Spence and the exact chant was "Give it to Joe". The memory of that name may have faded with time, however, back in the 1920s and early 1930s, Spence's standing at the club got to a point that can best be summed up by this straightforward formula: Manchester United = Joe Spence; and, hence: Joe Spence = Manchester United. Alternatively, you could refer to him as 'Mr. Soccer' as he became known to the city's footballing intelligentsia. That is what spending 14 loyal years at Old Trafford entitled him to, especially when superb levels of fitness and consistency allowed him to create both appearance and scoring records for the club. He was the only Red to be picked for England in a span of almost a quarter of a century. At his peak, standing at 5'8" and weighing 11 st, he was able to play brilliantly anywhere in the front line and he could make a round ball talk, 'thud' being the word it most commonly uttered. Add to that his cool looks, complete with curly front hair, and the Old Trafford masses simply worshipped him. He reciprocated with thrilling, carefree runs and breathtaking goals, over and over. No wonder whenever a long spell passed without him receiving the ball they would implore his teammates to 'give it to Joe'. This is his story.

Miner by Birth

Joseph Waters Spence was born on December 15th, 1898, in the small

Northumbrian town of Throckley, just six miles west of Newcastle. Not a common middle name, Waters, but it was actually his mother Hannah's family name. Until she married William Spence, that is. Joe's father was born in Scotland though that wasn't so far away considering that Hadrian Wall passes through Throckley itself. Having lost his father when young, William was forced into work as a miner even before he reached his teenage years. That was what led him to the area which had a booming mining community. Hannah, born in nearby Newburn, also hailed from a mining family whose children just had to be born males to be sent to the colliery.

The home Joe was born into was a typical mining house. The address, 62 Long Row, Newburn Hall, gives it away. It was indeed a long street with small houses packed adjacent to each other and inhabited by the colliery workers and their families. Joe's little corner in the world was a crowded one. In addition to his parents, obviously, there was his 3-year-old brother Thomas and two uncles: Daniel and Joseph Waters, after whom Joe was named. They were all miners; hewers, in fact, which, to be frank, is the worst kind of mining job you could have. In addition to burrowing deep underground – and sometimes crawling into a narrow opening if that's what it took – you had to pray the wall didn't fall in on you as you were digging out the coal. It was a job that hardened brave men.

With such a background, it was only a matter of time before Joe himself dived into the mining industry. He was 13 when he got his first gig at the colliery. No Xbox for him! Who needs that when you can get all the excitement and danger by digging for coal? Indeed, in 1910, a year before Joe got into the business, a record number of mining fatalities was reached. It was a tough teenage experience that added considerable strength to Joe's slender physique.

Even though he was still young, Joe quickly became a prominent figure in the local mining community, and it had nothing to do with efficiency or craftsmanship at the workplace. Instead, he became famous for his speed! The different mines in the area used to hold 100-yard races as a means of entertainment, though the events became a bit more entertaining when a gambling ring developed among the watching workers. In no time, Joe became the obvious representative from his mine as he competed against speedsters from other pits. Sure enough, he was a regular winner of these dashes, much to the delight of his co-workers, who had confidently placed wagers on his ability with colleagues of the other racers.

One-Man Team

Joe's childhood, however, was not all spent underground. He loved nothing more when not scouring for coal than scoring a goal. Black dust may have covered his face but it was football that ran through his veins. As it did with most young men in Tyneside at the time. Those parts have always been fertile grounds for footballers and have given us one Bobby Charlton and a certain Bryan Robson. Newcastle United, in fact, were enjoying their golden age when the game's popularity was reaching new levels. Our Joe, however, was a prodigy. There is a possible chance the term 'one-man team' was coined during Joe's first year playing schools football. Out of his team's tally of 49 goals, he personally contributed 42! I hazard that is also when the 'Give it to Joe' chant generated, for I can't imagine a more relevant instruction that the headmaster could have yelled out.

Outside school Joe was also wreaking havoc around the villages. At first he turned out for nearby Blucher Juniors, a local kids club, and later represented his town's team, Throckley Celtic. The mines had already endowed him with strength and made him staminally unchallenged. He was also so fast it appeared sometimes he didn't leave any speed for the rest of the forward line. And now on the field he was developing his footballing skills. At dribbling he was a master, he could shoot with either foot, and when he crossed his delivery was so excellent he could have worked for the Royal Mail. In fact, Joe was beginning to put a slight Beckham-*esque* bend on his crosses – a rarity back then with the old heavier balls, long before the influx of fancy foreigners who not only talked with an accent but crossed with an accent too.

The Suicide Club

In 1914, World War I broke out, but that most probably had nothing to do with Joe. It was called the Great War as numerous nations got sucked into it and the death toll started mounting. At first, Joe was too young to be involved but, at the age of 17, he was ready to fight for his country. From the mines to the trenches and a different sort of mines altogether. Around May 1916, Joe headed to Clipstone, Nottinghamshire, enlisting in the 115th Training Reserve Battalion. The 'training' part was to get him ready for first-team duty in the Machine Gun Corps, the swanky new way of fighting wars. These were the men who led from the front – where else for Joe? – and fired their machine guns at the enemy. 'The Suicide Club', if you like, and that is how it was dubbed: Great War statistics show that out of 170,500 British soldiers who served in the Machine Gun Corps, over 62,000 were killed or wounded. Sure beats the mines of Northumberland! By the end of November 1916, Joe had been transferred to the 'G' Battalion that was sent to France for action. As the war went on, the battalion became part of the Tank Corps in July 1917. These here were the innovative fellows, the first to use tanks in combat.

That is how Joe Spence spent his late teenage years. He may never have gotten the chance to win the World Cup, but he helped England win the World War. Also, though of a tad less importance, he helped his battalion win the

Army Football Championship. Even among the bullets Joe found time to kick a ball. He was later also able to make the odd guest appearance for Liverpool Reserves. That may be classified by Reds as the ultimate act of treason if viewed in isolation, but it was crucial in bringing him to the attention of Lancashire footballing circles, for soon after demob he was back home up in Northumberland.

Whisked to Manchester

The war ended in November 1918. Joe had done his part but his country no longer needed him. It was now time to get back to civil life. Only 'civil life' for Joe meant a return to the colliery. Unless he could find a gig doing the other thing he was good at – playing footy. He was fitter than ever, obviously, following his service, and he had kept himself sharp by turning up briefly for Newburn F.C., a town just five miles west of Newcastle. Fortunately, he was soon able to hook up with Scotswood F.C., distance to Newcastle: 1.5 miles. He was ever so closer to Geordieland.

An amateur team, Scotswood had neither a notable past nor a prominent future. *Now* was their moment in the sun. They had been invited to be part of an eight-team short league intended to keep the region's top clubs busy during the latter part of 1918-19, since competitive football had not yet resumed after the untimely end of the war. It was called the Northern Victory League and it included the Northeast giants Newcastle United, Sunderland, and Middlesbrough, all First Division clubs at the time. For Scotswood, this was their claim to fame but for one Joe Spence, it was his big break: the chance to parade his skills in the limelight and play his way out of the mines.

This league kicked off on January 11th, 1919, with Joe leading Scotswood's front line. He was soon amongst the goals especially in a 5-0 demolition of a team called Darlington Forge Albion when only the opposition goalie kept the score down. By late February, five figure crowds were descending on Scotswood's ground for the visits of Sunderland and Middlesbrough. Joe's exploits were alerting the talent spotters and it seemed only a matter of time before he was approached by a professional club. Towards the end of March, with Scotswood impressively third in the table, his big chance arrived… but not with Newcastle United! He may have been on their doorstep but he was whisked from right under their noses. Manchester United, the other pre-war giants, who won the championship twice and the cup once in the previous eight competitive seasons, were preparing for the imminent resumption of official league action. Manager John Robson had been scouting the country on a post-war recruitment mission to handpick a new team and had gotten word of a young scoring sensation who had been putting them away at a canter up at Scotswood. So he turned up to watch an encounter with South Shields on

March 22nd when the 'sensation' in question volunteered to put away a couple of goals, just for the occasion. He had now struck 14 goals in as many matches for his club. Mr. Robson offered Joe a contract right then and there, and the 20-year-old signed professional forms. He was now a First Division footballer.

There are different ways to celebrate such an achievement. Joe chose to produce the greatest ever debut in Manchester United's entire history, modestly speaking, of course. United were winding down their final season in the Lancashire Principal Tournament in which they participated during the four years of combat. On March 29th, 1919, Joe was picked at centre-forward. The visitors were Bury, the final score 5-1. Spence's haul: four goals! Wayne Rooney can keep his puny hat-trick, for *this* here was the most prolific debut by any United player before or since. When Joe added two more goals the following month he amazingly finished as the team's second highest scorer for the season. This was an impressive coup by Mr. Robson and his scouts. Scotswood were a decent team at the time and the peeved Newcastle scouts belatedly turned up to sign another forward, Tom Phillipson, who himself went on to become something of a scoring sensation at Wolverhampton Wanderers. Aston Villa stopped by too a while later and picked up George Harkus. But there is no denying that Manchester United had snatched the best of the lot.

Old China

Never before has a season been as eagerly anticipated as when 1919-20 kicked off on August 30th. Not only was this the first competitive kick since 1915, but also, after four years of fighting, it now meant that the safety and enjoyment of peacetime were back. Football was truly coming home.

Sadly, not all the footballers were coming home. So many had been left behind somewhere underneath a foreign field. More had found the four-year break too long to carry their careers over. At Old Trafford, the story was similar if not worse. Few of the pre-war stars remained, the team but a shadow of the title-winning outfit of 1911. Indeed, when Manchester United lined up at the Baseball Ground to face Derby County, as many as five players were making their debuts. One of them was called Joseph Spence. Despite a very brief cameo the previous spring, the directors had seen enough. The teamsheet read like this: Mew; Moore, Silcock; Montgomery, Hilditch, Whalley; Hodge, Woodcock, Spence, Potts and Hopkins. United took the lead after half an hour through Wilf Woodcock, appropriately enough considering he was the club's most hostile scorer during wartime football with 69 goals (conversely, he was rather docile in time of peace). A resurgent Derby, however, earned a deserved equalizer with eight minutes left.

Incredibly, four of United's debutants – Charlie Moore, Jack Silcock, Clarrie Hilditch, and Spence himself – were to form the backbone of the club until the 1930s. They were the Giggs, Scholes, and Neville of yesteryear, teammates on the pitch and great buddies off it. Charlie Moore, in particular, was Joe's best mate in the game. Joe may have earned the esteemed 'Mr. Soccer' title over the years but he was affectionately called by Charlie as 'my old china'! Professionally, they ran United's right wing. Off the clock, they were in charge of the fun department. Songs and jokes were there specialties, Charlie the one more in tune with the melody and Joe equally masterful in the front line and the punch lines. Their best work is immortalized in this famous anecdote that occurred on an away trip down in Portsmouth. Joe and Charlie bet their teammates that not only could they perform their singing act on a street corner, but they could also raise a shilling! In the event, they emerged with a nifty shilling and a half, though 3d of it came from a United director – out of pity perhaps or possibly in a desperate plea to get them to stop!

Legendary Crossing

With so many debutants, Manchester United made a slow start to the campaign, failing to win any of the first three matches. Then Spence started to demonstrate his scoring abilities. On September 8th, he notched his first league goal in a 3-1 win at Sheffield Wednesday then followed that with a brace in each of the next two games, both ending in victories over Preston. The first post-war Mancunian derby came up next, ending in a thrilling 3-3 draw. Not only did Joe provide a couple of assists, but he also scored an audacious goal that would have produced a million views had Youtube been around at the time. As the City keeper fannied about with the ball, Joe sneaked up on him, nicked the ball, and gleefully tucked it home. In the return fixture a week later, he grabbed the only goal of the game to give United their first derby victory since 1913. Joe's career had taken off.

While it seems odd that the same teams were playing each other on successive weekends, this was one of the changes that were implemented for the new season. It absurdly led United to play eight consecutive matches later on that season against teams starting with 'B'. Other changes that took place were the increase in number of Division One clubs to 22 for the first time and the instalment of Manchester United as firm favourites... for the drop! This, remember, was 1919 and not 1999. That United finished in mid-table was a refreshing surprise, for the club had no major stars. Sure, Spence established himself in the first team with a personally satisfying 32 league matches and 14 goals to finish as top scorer, but he was just beginning his career. An even bigger name, Billy Meredith, was firmly in the twilight of his. Meredith was the first superstar in British football but he was way past his best. Of course I am basing this statement purely on the fact that he was 45 years old! At least the Old Trafford faithful were lucky to have witnessed the two legends, Meredith and Spence, playing together up front for a couple of seasons. Neither was at his peak in that period (and this is no exaggeration – the first eight times they were fielded together the club couldn't score), but this short overlap insured that their collective careers spanned 45 years of league football as Meredith had made his bow in 1893 while Spence played on until 1938. Obviously the young pupil had picked up the odd fitness tip about longevity from the old master.

Second Season Syndrome

The old Welsh Wizard hung around Old Trafford for one more season. In addition to his words of wisdom, Meredith was also prone to playing the odd prank on said pupil, to build his character, Billy would surely claim. In his book "Back from the Brink", Justin Blundell tells of a particular incident when Joe, an avid dog lover, was forced to go on a frantic search. It turned out that Meredith was the brains behind the evil plan that saw Joe's whippet kidnapped, wrapped up completely in bandages, and safely stowed in the dustbin!

But Joe could use those light-hearted moments during his second season when the relative success of the previous campaign made way for struggle and disappointment. This phenomenon happens so frequently to players they should give it its own name! Of course it didn't help that the manager, Mr. Robson, had bought several new players in an attempt to restore United to the glory days. Apparently, this plan included constantly shifting Joe from centre-forward to inside-right or left before giving him a long run in the reserves. United finished even lower down the table! Joe's final total of 15 games would be the lowest throughout his Old Trafford stay, though his goal average remained admirable – first with the Stiffs and later after earning a recall. When he nabbed a brace in the ultimate match, a 3-0 win over Derby that pushed United six places up, he took his tally to seven league goals. In this mediocre campaign, this was all you needed to finish as United's top scorer (for a second year in a row), and three other players cottoned on and did the same.

A Splash and a Drop

Robson left Joe out of his initial team for 1921-22 then watched in horror as they fell 0-5 at Everton. Joe was promptly restored and, but for the odd absence, was to keep his place for the next 12 years. United were struggling from the outset that season, scoring just four times in the opening six fixtures. But come October, Spence sprang into life and personally undertook the task of solving that problem. Preston were hit; then Tottenham, home and away it didn't matter; then Manchester City. That local derby went City's way as Joe's solitary strike was overshadowed by a Barnes hat-trick. Conveniently, the fixture list provided an opportunity for revenge the very following Saturday when it was centre-forward Spence's turn to shine. It was the day he first rose to

1924-25. In United's promotion team (front row, 2nd from left)

prominence, coming up with a hat-trick of his own to singlehandedly silence the noisy neighbours 3-1. It turned out to be the last derby treble till the 1960s, and Spence completed it with another goal for the Youtube compilation. As the papers described it, Joe "was well covered when he received the ball, but with clever, strong footwork he literally forced himself into the goalmouth and lobbed Blair with a remarkable demonstration of enthusiasm". "Spence's Splash" was the headline. It was an early sign of things to come and when he struck against Middlesbrough in the next match, he set up a club record six-game scoring streak. Joe Spence had arrived.

By now Robson had had enough of managing a struggling United side and, citing health problems, he passed the job on to John Chapman. The latter's first task was to oversee another bad run at the end of the season. His promise of something new was spot on: Manchester United fans had not seen relegation for 28 years! For Joe the consolation was that a sustained run at centre-forward enabled him to finish as top scorer for the third campaign running, now with an improved tally of 15 goals. One of those strikes was a winner at Birmingham in February 1922 that gave United their only away victory in the middle of a 24-match stretch. Despite the disappointment of the drop, the Old Trafford regulars were definitely beginning to appreciate his efforts.

Joe with his wife, Alice

There is nothing like love to soothe the pain of relegation. Like every summer, Joe headed home to Throckley. Usually it was to see his family and friends, not to forget his beloved whippet, but this time he was attending to some matters of the heart. Joe Spence was getting hitched! The girl of his dreams? A 22-year-old Northumbrian lady called Alice Lown. Joe himself was only 23 but, as with the fashion of the day, not too young to embark on a life of marriage or the Second Division.

The Feted Position

Something had to be done to get Manchester United out of Division Two at the first attempt. The club was lacking a 'big name' personality and moved to obtain Frank Barson from Aston Villa. He was even promised his own pub once he led United back to the top flight. Barson may not have been the fastest of central defenders, but he could go from zero to 'complete lunatic' in three seconds! True he could play a bit, a lot actually, but he had a nasty streak that bordered on violence. Yet you couldn't hold that against him, much like if you ran into Popeye and noticed spinach in his teeth. It's what made him stronger. And, at that moment in time, it was exactly what United needed, especially as biographies of numerous Reds of that team, the likes of Hilditch and Moore, tended to include the phrase 'never once was he booked throughout his career'.

Manchester United made a brilliant start in the Second Division with a string of victories as if this was the life for them. Most indulgent was Joe at centre-forward with seven goals in the first nine outings. It should really have been eight goals but, just when he thought he had claimed a last-second equalizer at Sheffield Wednesday, the referee decided it was a good time to blow the final whistle while the ball was in flight! Still, Joe was earning a reputation as a tough performer with energy to burn. The apprenticeship in pits and wars was proving beneficial. Late goals were becoming his signature mark: a brace at Crystal Palace; a diving header against Wolves; a venomous volley versus Coventry. About the only way to stop him from running until the final whistle was to send him off! That aberration blighted Joe's record in the dying moments at Stockport County for "an alleged attempt to bring down an opponent".

Incredibly, the FA suspended Joe for five league matches, which was enough time for Ernie Goldthorpe, newly-signed from Bradford City, to establish himself at centre-forward, leaving manager Chapman with a dilemma. Spence had to be accommodated, the best solution being to move him to the right wing. It proved to be the turning point in Spence's career. From now on he occupied the number seven slot, spiritually at least, since there was no actual shirt numbering in those days. It would be a position in which he excelled, his adventurous sorties enlivening games and endearing him to United fans in the popular end, the 'Pop Side'. In effect, he inherited Meredith's role to insure that a United tradition of exciting right wingers continued and would in time include the likes of Delaney, Berry, Best, and Coppell.

Interestingly, Joe developed the 'Spence Style' of wing play. Yes, Joe had an individual dribbling technique that became his trademark over the years. He would approach every match with a three-step plan to test the opponents' left-back. The first time he received the ball, he would slip it past his marker and quickly take off to test his speed. Next, he would push the ball inside to test his man's weaker right foot. Finally, he would simply charge his opponent bull-like to see how he liked the rough stuff. Having analyzed all three attributes, Joe would then choose the most appropriate way of beating the poor fellow and repeat ad infinitum.

Thirty-sixth

Manchester United's promotion bid faltered by three points come the end of the season – the equivalent of a win and a half in those days and, coincidentally, what they wasted in their last two matches. Despite his switch to the flank, Spence still rattled in 11 goals, but perhaps he shouldn't have provided so many assists for Ernie Goldthorpe and Arthur Lochhead because they both ended up outscoring him by two goals.

The narrow failure wrecked United's momentum for 1923-24. They may have won the opening three fixtures but then they took the shortest route to a 14th final placement. Reds had been dreaming of a swift return to the top flight but, back in the real world, United were now the 36th best team in England! Never before had they sunk so deep, not even during the pauper days of Newton Heath, and only once in the future would they finish any

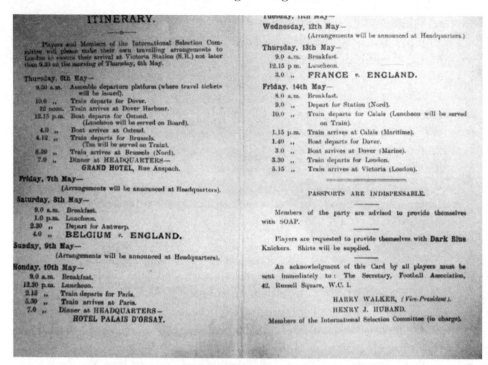

England itinerary given to Joe for his debut v Belgium.

lower. That is how bad this United team was, though you can't place any of the blame on Joe Spence. In fact, it was at times like these that his popularity soared among the Old Trafford masses, both for his hard work and his frequent tendency to entertain. Take April 12th, for instance, when Joe decided to relive his debut. He may have done it in wartime footy but now he was netting four spectacular strikes in a league fixture versus Crystal Palace. It has been done before and after, yet only on two occasions did a Manchester United player outscore Spence in a league match – when Andy Cole put five past Ipswich Town in 1994-95 and when Dimitar Berbatov matched him against Blackburn Rovers on a fruitful November afternoon in 2010.

Joe's goals reached double figures this season and he added another in a 3-0 friendly win against Hearts in Edinburgh. Joe had an old friend as a wing partner that day, 'old' in no way an exaggeration. Billy Meredith was 49 & ½ years old when he appeared for United, as a guest, I hasten to add, and not a trialist. Another highlight occurred on May 10th when Joe helped the Reds win the Manchester Senior Cup. It may have been a minor trophy, but the 3-0 thrashing of Manchester City in the final showed that United could compete at the top level. Only one problem, mind: they had to get there first.

A Curse Lifted

So what was it going to take to get Manchester United back into Division

Joe with the Football League XI in October 1926 (back row, 2nd from left)

One? The last time they were relegated, in 1894, it took 12 years to move up. Now, they were actually getting worse on a yearly basis since the war. So much so that the people connected with the club began to think that United were cursed! Even Joe had something to say on the matter. As Justin Blundell recounts in "Back from the Brink", Joe suggested 'the ground should be dug up to see if they could find the remains of a policeman or something of the sort that was perhaps casting an evil spell on the club's doings'!

Footballers have always been a superstitious breed and Joe Spence was a footballer. His peculiarity was that he always had to be the second player running out of the tunnel. Watch any newsreel of the time featuring United: first the responsible captain runs out, then there is Joe enthusiastically bouncing a ball, followed by some worried goalkeeper sporting that knowing look that he is in for a long afternoon ahead.

Superstitions aside, Joe was approaching his peak. He had been at Old Trafford five years now and had earned himself a benefit (against Rangers in April 1924 when he kicked off with a bandaged head but could not play!). In those days testimonials were awarded after five rather than ten years. Already he had amassed over 150 league appearances and notched 57 goals. He was raring to go. The whole team was, in fact. The defence, marshalled by Moore, Silcock, and Barson, epitomized catenaccio without even knowing it. Meanwhile, Joe was forming a Ronaldo/Rooney-type partnership with Tom Smith on the right side of the attack that was based more on telepathic understanding and similar sounding names rather than prolific marksmanship. At least they had the understanding going because they only contributed five goals each. Nonetheless, their creativity, added to a solid back line, resulted in a very memorable 1924-25 campaign. United, despite the obligatory mid-season slump, achieved second spot, which was a good thing because only the top two teams were let into the First Division at the time. Joe was ever-present, becoming the first United forward to do so since 1907. Promotion was confirmed on April 24th with a 4-0 demolition of Port Vale that was talked about for years after. Spence was the main orchestrator, scoring with a flying volley from Smith's centre and creating two other goals straight out of his 'dribble and cross' repertoire. He was now the star of Manchester United and would soon be performing at Division One grounds again after a three-year absence.

Joe with his shock of hair

And he would be a well-paid star too, the management having recognized his value to the team and decided to compensate him fittingly. Obviously, compared to what today's players earn, it was pocket change after you have thoroughly cleaned your pants. But back in the 1920s, the offer was over twice the national average, the United Board paying him £8… every single week! And he could bag another two pounds as a bonus on the rare occasions United won, and £6 a week in the summer just as a retainer. His wages never decreased, especially during the depression years of the near future, but they never increased either, remaining at a fixed salary throughout his time at the club.

With the financial climate of the time in mind, and with Joe being a generous soul, he would frequently send a fair size of his wages to his family back in Throckley. No wonder so many of his relatives regularly showed up in great force to matches at Old Trafford to provide support. In fact, it is they who should be credited with the sprouting of the famous chant for, whenever a United player had possession of the ball, they would loudly shout 'Give it to Joe'.

Cups…

There used to be a big hoopla made in regards to Manchester United's 26-year title wait that finally came to an end with the advent of the Premier League. It was just as well, for it allowed people to overlook an even longer drought of 41 years that went on from 1911 to 1952. It is fair to say that 1925-26 provided United's best chance of winning the championship during the inter-war era… despite finishing ninth! Well, in addition to representing the biggest two-year leap in the club's history (from 36th in 1924), mathematically speaking, ninth was the closest they got to first. Moreover, ninth was actually a misleading final position. United in fact finished joint sixth and, for most of the campaign, they basked in even dizzier heights while always keeping an eye on the very top. The problem was that, in this same season, United developed a serious case of cup fever. The longer it went on, the more symptomatic their league form became and, following a disastrous run of just four points in 10 games, United finally drifted out of contention in early April.

Throughout this relatively successful season, one Joe Spence ran rampant down the wing. In October he saw the birth of his only child, a baby boy named Joe Jr., but the sleepless nights were reserved for First Division left-backs all season as Joe, Sr. naturally, zigzagged his way past them to record seven league goals. He also had an enjoyable night in mid-November when he grabbed a hat-trick as United trounced Southport Central 9-0 in the Lancashire Cup. The League Cup it may not have been, let alone the mighty Intertoto, but at the time, this local competition commanded enough importance that first-teamers regularly participated in it.

Nonetheless, it was in a more famous knock-out tournament that Spence achieved fame in 1926. There is a reason I hadn't mentioned the FA Cup earlier in this story. United's league failings have been embarrassing enough in themselves there is no need to rub sodium chloride into the wounds! But this year United set on a cup run so enjoyable they sought to replay nearly every round. Joe played a big part in propelling the club into the semi-final by netting four goals, one of which was about the only thing he did in the victory over Tottenham having pulled a hamstring early on.

The run came to a halt at the semi-final stage when lowly Manchester City benefitted from their considerably superior luck (before going on to lose at Wembley and get relegated). But, amid the disappointment, Joe was able to glean not one but two claims to fame from this cup campaign. The 'Give it to Joe' chant was already a favourite at Old Trafford, but now leading figures of the Spence Fan Club went all the way and had it printed on banners to be waved about at Bramall Lane during the semi-final. Despite being misspelt (the ones I have seen actually say 'Give It Joe') the placards brought the song to national prominence, what with newsreel cameras being around and all. Consequently, the phrase stuck with Spence for the rest of his career. It brought him even more acclaim when it spread like a craze throughout the League and other supporters began using it whenever their team contained someone named Joe!

...And Caps

On a more serious note, Joe's exploits were alerting some important decision makers, namely the selection committee for the England national team. Since the war, only two United players had bothered the selectors, the last being Jack Silcock three years earlier. But Spence's star was rising and already he had been picked to play in a FA XI exhibition match against the Birmingham FA in December 1924. Finally, on Monday, May 24th, 1926, Joe got to run out in an England shirt, second behind the skipper, naturally, as superstitious beliefs dictated. And about time too: the international match was originally scheduled for May 8th as part of a two-game tour of Europe, but was postponed due to the General Strike, which was a waste of time and only served to make Joe wait a fortnight for his England debut and miss out on the cancelled second match.

The Belgians are obviously famous for their waffles, but a lesser known fact is that they provided the opposition for Spence's full international bow, not to mention the venue in Antwerp. The English FA, for their part, settled on providing the white jersey... and nothing else. The match itinerary that Joe received instructed him to bring along such toiletries as soap and toothbrush, but it also stipulated that he supplied his own navy blue shorts and white socks! As for the game, strangely, Joe had just as much experience as half his teammates since five other players were being introduced to the national fold. Yet it didn't matter when it came to spanking Belgium 5-3, thus recording England's highest away score for 14 years. Joe wasn't among the scorers but he did contribute heavily. In fact, this may have been an experimental line-up but, once the experiment was over, Joe was the only debutant to keep his place for the next match.

International Family

Joe Spence of England was now the man of the moment. Soon the Football League decided they couldn't live without him, picking him for their representative side against the Irish League on October 9th, 1926. The setting was Celtic Park, Belfast, but the scene was like in Manchester for Joe with high wind and rain showers – the plumbing in the Mancunian clouds obviously an old problem! Feeling at home – his middle name is Waters, remember - he opened the scoring after 28 minutes when he met Green's cross and fired in. After the Irish equalized, Joe's neat pass released Roberts who reclaimed the lead, which was all the Football League side needed to run up a 6-1 thrashing. How his United teammates missed his firepower that day. Yes, the league didn't stop for representative games at the time. In fact, the simplest way to ignite a club v country row was to announce an international match. On this occasion, due in part to Joe's inability to exist in two places at once, United fell 0-4 at Bolton. Incidentally, this defeat ended a remarkable run of eight consecutive outings in each of which United scored exactly two goals.

You know you're a hot commodity when your relatives become in demand. Bradford City figured they fancied a Throckley Spence for themselves, so they signed Joe's younger brother, William. Sporting similar looks and hairstyle, he unfortunately failed to prolong his career past a couple of first-team matches in 1927-28. Next of the closest kin was Joe's cousin from his mother's side, George Brown. The Huddersfield inside-forward was selected for England's next match on October 20th to form a right wing partnership with Joe. The international fixture versus Ireland was hosted at Anfield where Joe had 'previous'. A year earlier he had appeared there for United in a terrible defeat where the only consolation was that there was no vitriolic rivalry between the clubs yet to cause Reds fans death by embarrassment. In fact, the Kop breeders' classier grandfathers were moved to applaud Joe at one point when he sent a cheeky lob goalwards from the flank, only for Liverpool's custodian, Elisha Scott, to pull off a miraculous save. Coincidentally, Scott was Ireland's keeper for this year's international and Joe set about to seek revenge.

The Irish took a very early lead but, immediately afterwards, Cousin George netted on his debut. Ireland again went ahead. Soon after the break, however, came Joe's moment. Receiving Norman Bullock's pass, he skipped past McConnell and pelted goalwards at full speed. Scott ran out to block only for Joe to send a magnificent shot past him into the net. Joe Spence had scored for England. Ever the party poopers, the Irish again reclaimed the lead for the third time. There was only one thing left to do. Spence attacked down the right wing and sent in one of his bending crosses, which you can see for yourself on an existing Pathé newsreel. The pinpoint cross reached Bullock, who volleyed venomously into the roof of the net. An exciting encounter finished 3-3.

Boys of Summer

By all accounts, Spence was England's best forward that day. On a couple of occasions he forced Ireland's defenders into inventive goal-line clearances. In his own words, this match was his greatest honour in football. Yet, inexplicably, he was never to win a full cap again. It could be due to the selectors for whom tinkering was the pastime of choice. Take the Ireland match, for instance. Joe was one of only two players retained from the previous international and, if that wasn't enough, they made a further seven changes for the following one. Another plausible reason for his exclusion might have something to do with playing in a struggling United team, for no other Red Devil was called up for England duty after Spence for another twenty years! That was when Henry Cockburn got picked in 1946, and such a big fuss was made about it in town that Joe himself sent Henry a congratulatory letter wishing him good luck.

Exactly how bad was the Manchester United 1926-27 vintage? Well,

Spence running out second as superstition mandates.

they did eschew the dizzy heights of ninth place from yesteryear for a cosier 15th. And to achieve that feat, they opted for the lowest goal return in the division, but not the entire league, since Barrow and Bradford City mustered less. However, none of the blame could be directed at our hero Joe, who in fact enjoyed his most prolific season up to date. Alternating between right-wing and centre-forward, he netted 18 out of United's 52 League goals, which translates to an astonishing 35%. He also added one goal in the FA Cup and a couple in a friendly against Motherwell in April. Having just finished as runners-up in Scotland, they visited Old Trafford to demonstrate their League's merits and proceeded to get trounced 1-5. Joe certainly enjoyed the Easter holiday program as he rattled in five goals in three fixtures. His tally included four past Derby County in two games after which the Rams' directors entered into United's dressing room and told their visiting counterparts that they could depart the Baseball Ground with a 'fat' cheque were they to leave Joe behind! The United directors firmly rejected the offer.

The season may have finished but there was still some action in the summer of 1927. Manchester United announced late in March that they were embarking on a five-game tour of Switzerland. As a reward? Hardly. Although the directors might have privately held a faint hope that one or two of the players would get lost on the continent! The last time the club had travelled to Europe was back in 1908 when the players were pelted with rocks. However, with war veterans like Joe Spence in the ranks this time around, United were better prepared, only

Joe's bullets were now big, round, and made of leather.

It was a bonding and enjoyable trip for the players, at least as apparent from some existing photos. In one, just when you thought Joe could not get any cooler, there he was posing in suit and dark shades! Another group photo has the boys clad in their swimming shorts, with skin so pale you just knew the sun was going to be overworked that day. But one look at Charlie Moore's burgeoning belly gives you the impression that, if he were indeed a 'sportsman', he seemed less suited for football and more for sumo wrestling! There was no doubting the rest of the players' skills though, especially after they opened the tour with a 9-1 shellacking of FC Basle. The Swiss press was mesmerized. This is what one paper had to say following United's third win in a row:

"United did not disappoint anyone. Their team, composed of men of varying qualities though all equal, played for 90 minutes without ever relenting the rhythm, like a beautiful machine regulated to perfection. All the men knew their trade: incomparable control of the ball, which they moved with dexterity and rotated with ease; deep knowledge and marvellous application of the art of man-marking; and a perfect reading of situations – all attained with a natural ease so phenomenal it left the onlookers absolutely speechless".

Remember, United had finished 15th in the First Division! And by the time they played their last match of the tour, the Swiss papers were totally hooked: "The English professionals, impatiently awaited by the Berne public, left an excellent impression here. It is useless trying to find criticism in their play – Berne's players did nothing but defend". If the United players were gods in the eyes of their hosts, then Joe was Zeus himself. By the end of the tour host teams were borrowing players from other clubs, but that did not matter to Joe who continued to score freely. And by 'freely' I mean he was averaging two goals per game. He obtained one against Lausanne Sports FC with "a long shot that Schaer, who played a majestic game the previous Sunday, could do nothing about". The highlight, however, was on May 22nd when he claimed four goals against Servette Geneva. Obviously Joe truly loved his foursomes.

Centurion

Only one thought filled Joe's mind as 1927-28 commenced: to claim the club's records. On September 10th, champions Newcastle United visited leaders Manchester United. Leaders, yes, but only until this match was over. If you really, really want to know the score, Newcastle won 7-1. When your defence lets in seven goals, pulling one back is as redundant as an 'Open Sundays' sign on your local church door, yet Joe was able to glean a glimmer of consolation when he provided United's '1' in the result. He had now amassed 90 league goals, thus equalling the club record jointly held by pre-war heroes Joe Cassidy and Sandy Turnbull. He only needed one more week to nudge ahead with a brace past Huddersfield. From that day until 1953, a good quarter of a century later, Joe would remain United's all-time leading league marksman.

Then on October 15th, against Cardiff, with a header that had "all the strength of a kick", he reached a century of goals in all competitions, which meant the League and FA Cup back then. Apparently, not only was Joe aware of his milestone, it had also been preying on his mind. As soon as this tough encounter ended, during which a painful back injury had forced him to move out to the wing, he was quick to express his relief to the reporters: "Thank goodness that is over. Yes, that goal of mine late in the game was my hundredth for United". Up to that point unaware of this landmark, Joe's teammates rushed to congratulate him. One of the first to do so was debutant Billy Johnston, who had laid the pass for Joe to score.

A week later, no records threatened, he claimed a hat-trick against Derby County, just for fun. Or was it to produce arguably the greatest individual 12 minutes from a United player in history? That was all the time it took him to deliver his treble, starting it off with a tremendous goal, and the only debate was as to what was more 'tremendous' about it – that he got it from fully forty yards, or that he actually volleyed it! Next was November 19th when Aston Villa crashed 1-5 at Old Trafford. Joe's goal that afternoon meant that he was the first player ever to score 100 *league* goals for Manchester United. When he was in such hot form it was unwise trying to stop him. Just ask poor Jack Brown, Sheffield Wednesday's international custodian – he attempted to block a Spence scorcher and was left with a broken index finger.

Satisfied with the scoring records, Joe then turned his attention to the appearances total. When United defeated Everton 1-0 on March 14th, Spence was playing his 304th league match for the Red Devils. It was one more game than Billy Meredith had played, so Spence, if you're keeping up, had now represented United in the League more than anyone before him. A legend in his own lifetime! It was a record he proudly maintained until January 1966.

With his value ever rising, it was no wonder that Spence was a wanted man now. First he was back in the England fold, though only as 12th man for the Ireland game. Then Sheffield Wednesday came sniffing around for his signature. Let me explain something: the Sheffield Wednesday of that time was not the Sheffield Wednesday of today. In fact, they were destined to win the championship, no less, for the next two years, which made the inquiry even more flattering. However, the bid was firmly rejected – Joe Spence was not for sale. Adored in Manchester by fans and teammates alike, 'Mr. Soccer' was his label. And Joe lived up to it. With his shock of curly hair, he was coolness personified. Take a look at numerous team photos of the time. Joe always kept the same pose: shoulders slightly arched forward, head faintly tilted to his right. He sure liked that particular angle.

So, thanks, Wednesday, but no thanks. Spence was needed at Old Trafford more than anywhere else, and never more so than on the last day of the season. United were staring relegation in the face from so close they got cross-eyed. Two victories had moved them up from bottom spot, but they were still chilling in the drop zone when Liverpool came to town on May 5th. Only a win would do for the Red Devils and one man came to the rescue. His name? Joe Spence, the saviour of Manchester United. His miracle? A dazzling hat-trick so rare it has only been emulated two times in the best part of a century. And the outcome? United trounced Liverpool 6-1. It's a scoreline worth repeating, if not on the pitch then at least in writing: Manchester United trounced Liverpool 6-1. And you should have seen Spence's goals. According to one newspaper report, "all three were spectacular, two of them the reward of prompt decision and faultless marksmanship". When the last ball had been kicked that afternoon and the final tables were formulated, United had evaded the Second Division trapdoor by one solitary point.

Top scorer for the fifth time, had you not been keeping count, was Joe, this time with a career best 22 league goals. For a change, this did not constitute a new club record for that remained the possession of Sandy Turnbull, the scorer of 25 goals in 1907-08. But Sandy's tally came in a very successful side that won the championship. Spence's total, on the other foot, was achieved in a struggling team that evaded relegation by the width of one amoeba sitting sideways. In fact, in the entire history of Manchester United, only on one other occasion did the club's top scorer break the 20-goal barrier in a season during which United finished any lower that seventh in the table. That was Denis Law, by the way, a year before he was voted 'European Footballer of the Year'. If this doesn't prove Spence's pedigree then nothing will.

Barren Days

Ruud van Nistelrooy got it. Garry Birtles and Diego Forlan made their names off it. Every time Wayne Rooney got it, it made the national news. It is a phenomenon that every single striker fears and usually goes through at least once in his career: the barren run! And in 1928-29, it afflicted the one and only Joe Spence (Sr.). From the beginning of November until the end of the campaign, Joe could not score a single league goal. The only instance he shook the net during that period was in the third round of the FA Cup.

Yet there was no sign of what was upcoming when United kicked off the season in optimistic mood. Impressive victories against League giants Newcastle (5-0) and Huddersfield (2-1) had taken the Reds to sixth place. Meanwhile, Joe was again topping the charts with five strikes in 11 outings. But then it struck. Joe started hitting the woodwork; he missed a penalty; his lob that crossed the line against Leeds was not allowed by the referee, much to the dismay of the programme editor who banged on about it in two consecutive issues. In short, his form disappeared. And you know when Joe splutters, the team stalls. They stopped winning too, at least for a run of sixteen consecutive matches, enough to send them tumbling down to the bottom of the table and then further down.

Desperate times justified doing business with the devil. Or worse: Manchester United signed Tommy Reid from Liverpool. He was so cumbersome and big a centre-forward he instantly improved a winger's aim everywhere he went. This was just what Spence needed. He still couldn't score but he sure could cross, not to mention he could take corners better than Michael Schumacher. The partnership worked a treat. With a revitalized Joe providing and Tommy converting, United produced one of the most dramatic revivals the First Division had ever seen. After 27 matches, United had been three points adrift of 2nd bottom. By the end of the season they had risen to 12th.

United were again saved from the drop, Joe's reward being another benefit. These were awarded every five years back then and, conveniently for Joe, he had now completed a decade at his beloved club. He was already a hero to the Pop Side denizens, *the* hero, to be precise. No boos nor jeers were ever directed at him, unlike what usually befell many fellow forwards down the years. The Pop Siders sure could be cruel, but sometimes the criticism was deserved, for the typical United striker of the time was so average his shirt size was Xtra Medium. There was a downside for Joe, however, in that he did not have major silverware to show for his services. But, if you can call this a consolation, he did aid United to another success in the Lancashire Cup as Blackburn were defeated 2-1 in the final in May.

Bejewelled

On August 31st, 1929, it finally happened. At long last, Joe scored a league goal again. I would love to tell you that it was a stunning thunderbolt or a mazy dribble but, in truth, a scrambled effort from a couple of yards out was good enough for him. At least the days of outsourcing were over as Joe was back to providing his own goals now. The venue was St. James' Park where Newcastle United, as ever, were obliging (they did proceed to win 4-1 that day, but wait to see what happened in the return later on). It was the opening afternoon of a new campaign, which is always a good time to turn a new leaf. Joe was 30 years old now, a master on the wing, an experienced top flight performer. He was determined this was going to be *his* season. For the first time since 1924-25, he appeared in all 42 league fixtures, scoring 12 goals, and he picked up the 'top scorer' accolade out of habit. Joe was actually made captain for a spell this season but was only too happy when the extra burden was taken away.

The entire campaign was bejewelled with Spence displays. Exhibit A came on October 30th in the Lancashire Cup as United thrashed FA Cup holders

Bolton 6-1. Joe's contribution was a wonder goal: starting from the corner flag, he beat the whole defence and scored from point blank. Typical Spence – Ryan Giggs may have saved it for the biggest occasion but Joe wasn't as pernickety. On November 30th, his display which included a brace in a 4-2 win at Sunderland described as 'virtuoso'. What made up the reporter's mind was the quality of the goals. One was a thumping header following a left-wing cross, the other a customary raid around the defence topped with a cool finish. In December, Newcastle visited Manchester for the aforementioned return match and wished they hadn't: they were tonked 5-0 for the second year running. Joe Spence's name was on the scoresheet, as it invariably seemed to be whenever he faced his hometown club. This was his sixth goal past the Geordies in four seasons. Perhaps they shouldn't have overlooked him all those years ago.

Another team that Joe regularly excelled against was West Ham. On frequent occasions he was afforded a standing ovation by the more appreciative denizens of Upton Park. In the February meeting, he got all four sides of Old Trafford to stand up for him: one side per goal he scored that day. They may have seen Joe's 4-goal party trick one too many times, but this had a variety factor added: Joe performed his magic from the wing! An enchanted *Manchester Guardian* reporter picks up the story: "Then, too, there was Spence, the biggest worker any club could have. This was his match, for he scored all four goals, and they were four of the best one can expect to see in one afternoon".

The Slow Start

It is often when you are at your happiest, thinking nothing can go wrong and things will stay this good forever, that life slams you with a reality check, just as a reminder of how harsh it is meant to be. Joe's season of highs was immediately chased away by one of lows. Sir Alex liked to remind us time and again that Manchester United are traditionally slow starters. A case in point is 1930-31. United started so slow they didn't get their first draw until the 15th match of the season. They had already obtained their initial victory, mind, back in Game #13. But, yes, every single one of the first 12 matches was lost... all in the name of a slow start!

Still, as always, you could not blame Joe Spence for any of this. How could you, when the attack had scored 20 goals in 14 games? That is a better return than in the title-winning campaigns of 1992-93 and 2002-03. The defence, on the other hand, was effectively nothing more than a token gesture, offering the resistance of three or four randomly-placed training cones. Without exaggeration, Manchester United went down that season! After years of narrow escapes, they had used up all their lives, sometimes at a rate of three lives a year.

It was a shame that relegation blotted Joe's CV once more. On so many occasions he had been the club's saviour, but in this fateful year, his efforts were in vain, his six goals not enough. The big moan from the crowd was simply that Joe was not seeing enough of the ball, despite the Spence-specific chant. That was mainly due to him losing his productive partner, inside-right Jimmy Hanson, whose career was ended by a broken leg a few months earlier. But Joe wouldn't drop down without clutching a medal, even if it came in the minor trophy that is the Manchester Cup. One of his goals helped trounce Bury 5-1 in the May 9th final.

The Saving of United

It was not a sunny summer of 1931 in the life of Joseph Spence. He may have tasted relegation once before, in 1922, but back then he was still a relative novice, and at least the melody of wedding bells brightened some of the dark days. This time around the drop left a bitter taste in a player who had feasted on international recognition and crowd adulation from the Old Trafford terraces. Now at 32, he was in his right to wonder whether he would be playing top flight footy ever again. You could bring attention to Joe's harsher involvement in war, not to mention the endless days in the mines, but at least back then his meagre wages still trickled down the pit. Now, however, Manchester United had no money to pay him.

The only way matters would get worse was if he was missing from the starting line-up for the new season. Sure enough, his place on the right wing was filled by a new signing from Burton Town, no less, called John Ferguson. He had a reputation for supposedly delivering crosses on a sixpence. Only he wasn't able to demonstrate that at a poverty-stricken Old Trafford because the required coin was not readily available for him to aim at. When two defeats welcomed United to the Second Division, Joe Spence was welcomed back into the first team. However, he was selected at centre-forward as a replacement for big Tommy Reid, who had a soft spot for injuries. It had been years since he last played in this position, or this division, for that matter. Obviously, it took him a while to get the hang of it. Come November, it had all come back to him. He notched two goals versus Leeds, two at Oldham, one against Bury, two past Port Vale, one against Millwall, and another two at Bradford City. Ten goals in six consecutive fixtures. It was the most purple of patches of all his time at the club. Not bad for a 33-year-old!

Promotion, however, was not a topic of discussion this season. Not when the little matter of bankruptcy was threatening to blow the club into extinction. Yes, Manchester United were dabbling with their second financial crisis in 30 years. Back then, a Mr. JH Davies saved them. This time, Mr. James Gibson fortunately came to the rescue. But his decision to get involved hinged on one Christmas Day fixture against Wolverhampton. United, as a club and a community, had to show they were still alive. Joe marshalled his men for battle as the supporters packed the stands. Onto the field they stepped and stayed there until they had obtained a Herculean 3-2 victory, with Spence one of the scorers. Mr. Gibson had seen enough, which was just as well. United's exertions depleted the team for the return match the very next day. At least four Reds were given the sponge and cold water treatment before being sent out to the wolves. The Wanderers were only too happy to rack up a 7-0 revenge job on their way to winning the Second Division title. But Manchester United lived on. Joe returned to the flank, maintained his hot streak, and did what he does best: top the club's scoring charts for the seventh time with 19 league goals.

Farewell

And, so, the Joe Spence story continued. He may have been halfway into his 34th year, but, as he remained sharp and fit, why not carry on? At this age, interestingly, no other player in Manchester United's history was able to score as many goals as Joe had just managed the year before, until Teddy Sheringham pulled it off in 2001. And so Joe set off on a new season that would prove to be an emotional one for him and his thousands of fans. It was his fourteenth campaign at Old Trafford. Out of the original debutants in that first season after the Great War, only he and Jack Silcock remained. So much had changed since then, not least the managers – Joe was on his sixth! However, one thing had stood the test of time: the presence of Spence in the first eleven. For the time being, at least…

In the club programme, the editor described Joe as "fearless and robust". There was no mention of his flair, understandably at his age. But just because he was now a veteran, Joe was not going to just sit around conserving energy for yawning. He remained his usual ebullient self, both on the pitch and off it, boisterously declaring : "We're going to get to the top again". It was a prophetic statement, but would he still be around when it came true?

Joe started off well and had knocked in three goals by the time October 22nd arrived. It was a memorable afternoon for him, what with him becoming the first ever Manchester United footballer to appear in 500 league and cup matches. Five hundred outings for one club! You could count on one hand the number of men who had achieved this feat at the time. His teammates put on a show in his honour, the main entertainment being a 7-1 spanking of Millwall. One of the goals was set aside for him to celebrate.

A fortnight later, Joe was struck down with an injury that kept him out for seven games. Signs of wear and tear? He recovered shortly after his 34th birthday to notch a brace against Plymouth. In the return game a week later, he got another goal, and on January 14th, 1933, in an FA Cup tie against Middlesbrough at Old Trafford, Joe ("a little short on pace and wind but still the most aggressive of the forwards") headed his 168th United goal. It was to be his last for the club. New manager Scott Duncan, see, had promised the fans 'fresh blood'. He had plans for Mr. James Gibson's money, namely to replace United's older players with new – and preferably costly – acquisitions. Early in February, he couldn't apparently decide who he liked more, Neil Dewar of Third Lanark or Huddersfield's Ernie Hine, so he purchased both! Two new international forwards for a £12,000 outlay. I can't think of any other time in United's history when a new striking duo was so lavishly acquired. Free signing Joe was picked just one more time after that. On April 1st, 1933, a full fourteen years and three days since he made that four-star debut, he appeared in a 1-3 defeat away to Fulham. As the season wound down, the new recruits kept their places as Mr. Duncan tried to justify the heavy expenditure. The biggest shame was that Joe was only four goals shy of being top scorer again, surely a tally he might have pulled off had he been picked a few more times. And, to prove it, he did just that in the reserve team.

On May 3rd, keen United followers were saddened by an article in the local newspaper. Manchester United had issued their annual end-of-season transfer list, and the name of the club's longest-serving star was on it. Joe Spence was being released. After 14 exciting years, his clever dribbling and boyish enthusiasm were no longer to be cherished. But wait to see the statistics he was leaving behind, volume-sized and guaranteed to maintain his legacy for long after. Total games played: 510 – 481 of which were in the League. As I write, only Bobby Charlton, Ryan Giggs, and Bill Foulkes have played more in United's long history. Total League goals: 158 – a record at the time and only bettered by four others in the ensuing 75-odd years. Including the FA Cup, his total rises to 168. Once goals in the Manchester Cup, Lancashire Cup, War games and friendlies are taken into account, his tally approaches 200!

However, his greatest feat of all was the fact that he was Manchester United's leading marksman an impressive seven times. That was his specialty and no one has ever beaten it. Not Rowley, Charlton, Law, Best, nor Van Nistelrooy. And in these days of frequent transfers, it looks unlikely anyone ever will.

Bantam Joe

In the summer of 1933, Joe changed home for the first time in almost a decade and a half. A change of scenery, but not a change of division, as he crossed the Pennines to join Bradford City. It was strange for him to be a 'Bantam' having so often been the saviour of the Red Devils during the long years of poverty. It was just unfortunate for Joe that the days of prosperity came too late.

Bradford City, of course, had employed a Spence of their own before, Joe's younger brother, William, who represented them briefly in 1927-28. Six years on, they finally acquired the real deal. He may have been going on 35, but the Bradford City management took one look at him, noticed the talent, and

Joe with Bradford City (front row, 2nd from right)

implored him to lead the attack. "Score the goals" was the plea. It required a few matches to adjust, after that Joe was only too happy to oblige. On September 11th, he notched his first goal for the Bantams against Hull City. Then he scored in the next match. And the next. And the one after that. And the following one. And the subsequent. That was a six-match purple patch and patches, as you know, are Joe's area of expertise. The Valley Parade faithful loved it so much they demanded an encore. Mr. Spence responded with an even more impressive seven-goals-in-five-games holiday special. That included the obligatory goal against West Ham in an FA Cup meeting. In fact, Joe faced the Hammers three times this season and hammered them on each occasion.

November 25th saw Spence's first return to Old Trafford. Interviewed in the club programme, he expressed his joy at playing on the old ground again and meeting his old chums, promising them he would do his best. That prompted the programme editor to warn them not to 'give it to Joe' out of habit! And so it panned out: the Supporters' Club showed their appreciation by presenting him with a fancy cutlery set, the home team not so much, battling instead for a 2-1 victory. The winning strike, incidentally, was an own goal. Alas, it wasn't Spence scoring for United again but rather Barkus the fullback.

Despite Joe's goal frenzy, Bradford City did not stray anywhere near the promotion places. That was just not their scene. Their glory years, which amounted to one year really, happened in 1911. That was when they won their only major honour, the FA Cup. That was also the year Manchester United had last won a trophy, the league championship. They were last seen in the top flight in 1922 when they accompanied United hand in hand down to the Second Division. However, while United bounced back for another period of struggle in the upper tier, Bradford City opted to live out their misery in the lower reaches instead.

So, when this Spence-inspired campaign saw them finish in sixth place, it was actually their highest position for a dozen years. Yet the benefits were not only one way. There was something in it for Joe too. The Bantams quickly learned the most important lesson: when he is in such hot form, it is a good reason to give it to Joe. He benefitted to the tune of 24 goals – an unsurpassed club record in the top two divisions that still stands today. And if that was not enough, it was also a career best for Joe personally. Evidently, we had to wait till he was 35 years old to see his best, or however long it took for those fitness tips from Billy Meredith to come into fruition.

Speaking of old times, is it possible the Manchester United management wondered whether they had let Joe go too soon? Did the Red Devils miss him in their first Spence-less league campaign since 1915? You just had to look at the final table to find the answer. United did not finish above Bradford City. They could not be found anywhere remotely below them. But if you look all the way down in 20th place, just one spot above the relegation zone, that is where United languished. And they had to win their last match to avoid the drop. This was easily their lowest position during the Inter-war era. And if it was the lowest during the Inter-war era then it is a given this was the lowest in United's entire history. A measly eight goals was all that it took to be their top scorer, and Neil Dewar reached that total despite leaving for Sheffield Wednesday in December. Or, to be precise, running off with the director's daughter to Wednesday! And he still had time to finish as leading marksman for his new club as well that very season. Consequently, it remains inconclusive whether United struggled without Spence or was their season undone by love?

The Wrath of Spence

If there is one thing that is predictable in football, it is that football is unpredictable. There never is a repeat season. Have a look at 1934–35 as a case in point. At Old Trafford, the Gibson gold was beginning to shine through as Manchester United rose to fifth place. Bradford City, meanwhile, could not scoot fast enough down to United's recently-vacated twentieth slot, barely above the drop zone. See, Bradford City of the 1930s, much like Bradford City of a lot of other times, were a selling club. In fact, the supporters' biggest gripe was that the directors eagerly awaited a successful season only so they could

Joe in Chesterfield's colours.

get better value for their players. The accounts back this up. In a matter of a few years, the Bantams shifted as many as seven players up to the top division, a fact that ticked the manager Jack Peart off so much he nearly resigned in the summer of 1934.

Our man Joe was also transferred at the beginning of the campaign... to his old position on the right wing. Not too conducive for a prolific return from a 35-year-old, that wide berth. As a result, Joe struggled to match his first year's heroics, stopping on just five goals, only four of which were in the League. With so few strikes, he had to divide his goals wisely, but, knowing Joe, he used up seventy-five percent of them on two matches versus Newcastle United! You had to feel for the Geordies – no matter the division or the opposition, they could not escape the wrath of Spence.

All in all, it was a disappointing campaign. Joe had left his mark on the place, but the place hadn't left its mark on him. He was the kind who liked to attack, thus a team that spent every match struggling to come out of their own half was not his idea of fun. Come the end of the season, he packed his bags and his goalscoring record and set off. For footballers his age it would have been simple to just call it a career. But Joe's footy passion was as strong as ever, so he went with the other option old pros choose when they want to prolong their careers: drop down a division...

The Twisted Spire

Chesterfield is located in Derbyshire, just north of the city of Derby. There is a place where the River Rother meets the River Hipper. That is where you will find Chesterfield – the land between two rivers. Throughout history it made its name as a market town. By the 1930s, however, it had finally caught up with the Industrial Revolution. Railways, engineering, steel tubes – this town was now full of the stuff. And this town, incidentally, is where Joe Spence decided he wanted to live for the rest of his life. At 113 Brockwell Lane, to be precise.

The Spence family settled into the area in the summer of 1935. Joe Sr. was seeking employment. Coincidentally, the town had its own thriving mining industry, but those days were long gone for our Joe. No fear, though, for there was a football team about too, and that was why he moved here in the first place: to play for Chesterfield FC. Their home was the Recreation Ground, Saltergate, and they were nicknamed 'The Spireites', for no other reason than the fact the town is famous for the twisted spire atop the local church. Any fears that the dent was caused by a wayward Spence thunderbolt can be immediately dispelled on account of it having preceded his arrival by a few centuries. Yes, the place was old and the team itself, in fact, never hesitates to remind everyone that they are the fourth oldest league club around. Somehow, their concurrent propensity to dwell in the Third Division North was not broadcasted as loudly.

This year, however, Chesterfield were planning to do something about all the underachieving. In addition to Spence, his teammate Bauld too came from Bradford City, while others like Dando and Hasson also joined. And wait to hear Joe's wages: a whopping £5 10 shillings a week – more than the rest of the squad bar record signing Allan Sliman.

Champion Joe

Joe made his league debut for the Spireites in a 1-1 draw at Barrow on August 31st, 1935, at the age of 36 years and 259 days. Yet he wasn't the oldest debutant in Chesterfield's history. A whippersnapper named Jimmy Moore was 51 days older back in the 1920s. The speed was gone, but Joe had replaced it with experience to go with the celebrated trickery and guile. So, game after game, Joe hared down the wing – or expertly tricked his way, more likely – and provided crosses for the likes of Dando and Clifton to bang in. It was the best of times. They say the best form of defence is to attack. Well, this Chesterfield team mastered the art of defending! The goals flowed, there were hat-tricks galore, and the Spireites made it to February on just the one defeat. On February 1st, indeed, they gave the perfect illustration of their desire to entertain: Crewe Alexandra 5, Chesterfield 6! The scoreline needed the finishing touch of a couple of coolly-dispatched spotkicks by the ex-England international in the visitors' ranks. Earlier on October 12th, he had taken advantage of Southport's leaky defence to bang in his 200th club career goal.

By mid-March Chesterfield had risen to the top. And it was a good job they did. At the time you had to be the champion to get promoted, as did the winners of Third Division South, to be replaced

A paper cutting of Joe Sr and Jr.

by two teams relegated from Division Two. Spence and the Spireites pushed on and claimed the title on April 27th with a game to spare. Joe was back in the Second Division following what, results-wise, was the best season he had experienced as a player, despite his lengthy association with Manchester United. Speaking of the Devils, the Reds would not be awaiting their old hero in Division Two having themselves won that particular championship in this same season. Fear not, however, for they would very shortly be back! As for Joe, he did not miss any league outings, converting 11 total goals, including one in the Third Division North Cup. More importantly, he headed into the break with the first competitive medal of his career hanging around his neck.

In The Shadows

There was one thing Joe had not experienced since he arrived in Chesterfield: a run in the reserve team. Unfortunately for him, he got the chance to put that record straight for nearly half a season as 1936-37 kicked off. Of course, it was not always like that. In the pre-season practice match he was in the first team and on the scoresheet as the Stiffs were stuffed 5-3. A knock to Joe's 37-year-old bones, however, forced him to stagger off at halftime. The Chesterfield management was only too happy to stick new signing John Hughes in his place, especially since they had just handed Chester City £600 for his services. Hughes started off well and kept his spot.

You could forgive Joe had he wondered why should he be idling about in the Reserves, but he loved this game too much to give it up yet. Besides, by mid-December, the management themselves were wondering why Joe was in the Reserves. He should be in the first team, they reckoned. Obviously, Chesterfield sitting in 20th place had something to do with this sudden change of heart. So, on December 19th, with Spence recalled for his first league appearance of the campaign, the Spireites fought out a 1-1 draw with West Ham. Then Christmas Day proved a jolly good occasion for Joe when he unwrapped his appearance and found out it was his 600th in the league. This was a rare occurrence back then and the management showed their appreciation by inviting him to captain the side for the day. Yet Joe modestly refused the honour, possibly because it meant he could not run out second from the tunnel! A fitting opposition was provided by Aston Villa who dropped by Saltergate. Indeed, the mighty Villains were gracing the Second Division a mere five years after creating the still standing record of 128 goals in one season in the First. But Joe was celebrating his own landmark and he drove his team to their first victory in nine matches. This was, after all, a tough division which included, in addition to West Ham and Villa, the likes of Tottenham and Joe's personal whipping boys, Newcastle United.

Joe's spell in the starting line-up went on for another four matches during which he scored twice to help lift the Spireites up to thirteenth. However, that man Hughes was back soon to push Spence into the shadows. He only made three more appearances after that in this season, including a memorable one on April 3ʳᵈ. Not because Chesterfield lost 0-4 at home to Blackburn, but because Joe turned out at right-half for the first time in his life! A decimated squad had seen him and three other fringe players rushed into emergency action. By the end of the season, the majority of Joe's statistics had been formed in the Reserves (26 outings and nine goals). However, he was still not ready for retirement...

The Wizard's Last Spell

And, so, the Joe Spence story continued... still. He was now into his nineteenth season, curly bangs and all. Of all the footballers who had played in that first post-war season of 1919-20 throughout England, no one else was still kicking a ball for a living. That was because no one else had inherited Billy Meredith's formula for eternal youth. What also helped surely was that the extent of Joe's energy expenditure mostly amounted to gentle strolls in the second string.

Spot the difference!

Only once did he appear in the Second Division before the end of the year. At least this meant he was busy scoring for the Stiffs the day Manchester United stopped by the Recreation Ground and recreated themselves with a nice 7-1 rout of their indulgent hosts.

Early in 1938, however, Joe was set for an Indian, well, Winter, since the FA Cup could not wait till the summer. Chesterfield were having trouble negotiating a third round tie against Bradford City. For the replay, they postulated the best solution was to call on an ex-Bantam who was into his fortieth year and who had a prestigious international and cup pedigree. The truth was, apart from one run into the semi-finals with Manchester United in 1926, Joe's cup pedigree was anything but prestigious. Of course, he never mentioned that to the management, riding instead to the rescue like a knight in pyjama and slippers. His ex-teammates were so stunned to see Joe was still around they failed to stop him scoring his first goal in over a year. And good thing he did too for it earned Chesterfield another replay, which they finally won. Joe not only kept his place for the fourth round tie against Burnley, but he also netted in a 3-2 triumph. The lad from Throckley could still cut it! Mass hysteria was sweeping the town now, even the league form improving as Chesterfield put four goals past each of Coventry and Swansea. Then the fifth round tie versus Tottenham came around signalling Joe Spence's last moment in the limelight. Well, two moments, actually: the Spireites held on for a 2-2 draw at home before succumbing 1-2 in the replay. Nonetheless, Joe had been the unlikely hero of Chesterfield's best ever cup run. In fact, only on one occasion in the future have they gone any further – when Bryan Robson's Middlesbrough unfairly won the 1997 semi-final.

Coaching Days

You know it is time to call it a day when you have lost your last four outings. So, on February 26th, 1938, Joseph Spence Sr. played his last competitive match in the trip to Bury. Do you remember who the opponents were the day a young Joe first turned up at Old Trafford and grabbed four goals? That is right, it was Bury too. This was a fitting finale. Joe was as old as they came at Chesterfield, which specifically was 39 years and 75 days. I would quit too if I was that old. In reality, though, the majority of Spence's appearances this season had again come in the Reserves. He even played a few times for the third team. You get the feeling Joe would have turned out for Chesterfield's Ladies team, if they had one, just to get a game.

And so a lengthy career finally reached its conclusion. Joe had used his talent to the max. You should see the figures he was leaving behind. League appearances: 614, more than any other player in the country, and possibly the world, up to then… bar Billy Meredith! Joe simply had too much respect for the old master to overtake him. A record that he *did* claim for himself, though, was his participation in 19 of the 20 inter-war campaigns. And his final total goals: 211, not necessarily a record but astonishing for a winger.

Joe was not done with football, however. It was his first love and now he wanted to give back all he had learned. Yes, it was time for 'Joe to give it'. And where better than in his adopted town? The Spence family was already settled in Chesterfield, so Joe took up a position as a coach at Saltergate for £5 a week. With his experience and sense of humour, he had the credentials to excel in the role. You knew if his products did not make it, at least they would be the pranksters!

One lad who had already benefitted from Joe's influence was his young teammate Harry Clifton, a fellow northeasterner. Joe had passed on words of wisdom along with his crosses. Another was Joseph Spence Junior. Joe's son made it through the ranks with the Spireites as well as active service as a wireless operator in Burma during World War II. Soon after, Matt Busby nearly signed the flame-haired defender for Manchester United but, just as he was about to step into his father's famous shoes, the father himself advised him not to. Full-time football did not pay well, was his directive. Hence, Joe Jr. found employment in a bank before eventually combining it with a professional contract at York City. Rejecting United for the glory of the Third Division? Not something you would see a lot of today, that, but at the time, remember, United were just beginning to shake off the stench of the inter-war years. He spent four seasons with York where, to minimize unfair comparisons with his dad, he refrained from scoring any goals! He later turned out for non-League sides like Gainsborough Trinity, Buxton and Matlock Town. After his playing days were over, he remained in Chesterfield where he worked as a computer programmer. While his father was born a year into the previous century, Joe Jr. lived a decade into the new millennium.

Spence Sr. also left his mark on one Harry Roberts, and not just for footballing education. Apparently Joe's services also included housing accommodations. Harry had spent a part of the hostilities as a prisoner of war. An ex-soldier himself, Joe took Harry in and became a father figure to him as he embarked on a career in the game.

Apart from coaching, Joe also dabbled in scouting for the Spireites. Two of his discoveries were sold on to First Division clubs at a combined cost of £32,000 – a fortune for Chesterfield in those days. That was his last job in football, though not in life in general. A man has got to work; it's most probably why we were put on this earth. With that in mind, Joe Spence, famous footballer and ex-England international, obtained employment at the Tube Works – Chesterfield's pride and joy. The company would prove its mettle during World War II, supplying the British Army with most of its steel needs. A steely merchant himself, Joe joined the company in 1938, taking up a position as a clerical officer. He was so good at it he kept his spot for over a quarter of a century until retiring in 1965.

The Legend of Spence

I love Joe Spence! There, I've said it. From the very first time I saw his name in an old Eagle Annual when I was around ten, I have been fascinated by his persona. In my late teens, I had a shirt made with his picture printed on it accompanied, of course, by the slogan 'Give it to Joe'. My best mate gave me grief about it, saying things like: "How can you idolize a player you have never seen in action?" I asked him: "Do you believe in Jesus?" He nodded affirmatively.

I replied: "Have you ever seen Him in person?" He never mentioned Spence again. With Joe you just had to believe…

So how good was Joe Spence? Many regarded him as not only one of the best right wingers in England, but also as a centre-forward challenger to the might of Dixie Dean and George Camsell. The great Charlie Buchan - star of Arsenal, Sunderland and England - had seen his lionhearted and honest style of play up close as an opponent, and until his old age he would recall a couple of Spence goals that he considered among the best he had ever seen: "In each case, a short, sharp burst followed by an unstoppable shot!"

In his book, 'Forever a Babe', Tom Clare recalls the observations of his grandfather. The man began supporting Manchester United before the name existed, when they were still called Newton Heath, and he continued to do so until the mid-Sixties. Yet he measured every player up to Spence. Even the emerging George Best was not deemed of equal stature! Sadly, Tom's grandfather did not live to see George reach his peak, but you could see where he was coming from. To United fans who followed the club from around the start of the first world war until shortly after the second, Spence was *their* Best! The ultra-talented star; the ultimate entertainer; the master of the dribble; the one to turn to when they needed a moment of magic; the hero who carried the rest of the team week after week, season after season; the player they could hold up to the world. Yet Joe was more than that. If you take his scoring into consideration, you could even claim that Spence was their Denis Law! Except that 'The King' translated to 'Mr. Soccer' in 1920s speak. Just a glance at his scoring record justifies that claim. Between the two wars, Joe was United's highest scorer with 168 goals. Next was Tommy Reid with 67. In other words, you could take away a hundred of Joe's goals and he would still be United's top scorer of the inter-war era!

Iconic similarities aside, there is one player who has resembled Spence through several mirrors. There has to be. When you consider that around 850 footballers have represented United in its history, the chances increase that, at one time or another, a player would emerge who is more than just a symbolic reincarnation of another. A case could be made, for instance, for Billy Meredith and Ryan Giggs. Both Welsh; both wing wizards; wiry, lithe in appearance; and both enjoyed extraordinarily long spells at the club garnering respect and grey hair in equal measure.

Correspondingly, the player that most resembles a latter day Spence is one Wayne Rooney! As outlandish as that sounds, spare a thought for the telling factors. Both are Englishmen hailing, more precisely, from the north. Almost identical in height, they have the same type of physique – not the tallest body but abundantly strong with a heart to match. Looks? Though not exactly like staring into a mirror, there is an image of Joe from United's first post-war team photo in 1919 where he could be mistaken for the young Wayne who posed with the starting line-up before kickoff in the 2008 Champions League final. Even down to the glint in the eye! It was obviously around this time that their respective hairlines started going in opposition directions. But there are more similarities: They both made sensational United debuts; they could operate with equal enthusiasm all across the forward line; and they even tended to score freely against Newcastle United. Yet, more importantly, they both reached a stage where they were regarded as the talismans of their teams… at least, for Wayne, at times when he was not under the misbelief that the pate is hairier on the other side.

On December 31st, 1966, Joe Spence sadly passed away aged 68, a victim of pneumonia in Chesterfield Royal Hospital, having been admitted a week earlier after falling at home. On the same day, Manchester United played out an uneventful 0-0 draw with Leeds United. They could have used Joe that afternoon, for a moment of magical dribbling, perhaps, or a thunderous volley. But Joe's time was from long before then, from an era between the two wars. That was when he set the standards at Manchester United and challenged future generations to meet them, only a handful of players succeeding. "At one period", read his obituary, "it seemed each week as if he were playing the opposing side on his own". It was the time he created a legend at the club and earned himself a permanent place in Old Trafford folklore. He was the hero for whom the terraces reverberated with the chant: "Give it to Joe".

JOE SPENCE

Born: 15.12.1898 in Throckley
MU debut: 30.8.19
England: 2/1

Season	Club	LEAGUE		FA CUP	
		Apps	Goals	Apps	Goals
1919–20	MANCHESTER UNITED	32	14	1	-
1920–21	MANCHESTER UNITED	15	7	-	-
1921–22	MANCHESTER UNITED	35	15	1	-
1922–23	MANCHESTER UNITED	35	11	2	-
1923–24	MANCHESTER UNITED	36	10	2	-
1924–25	MANCHESTER UNITED	42	5	1	-
1925–26	MANCHESTER UNITED	39	7	7	4
1926–27	MANCHESTER UNITED	40	18	3	1
1927–28	MANCHESTER UNITED	38	22	5	2
1928–29	MANCHESTER UNITED	36	5	2	1
1929–30	MANCHESTER UNITED	42	12	1	-
1930–31	MANCHESTER UNITED	35	6	2	1
1931–32	MANCHESTER UNITED	37	19	1	-
1932–33	MANCHESTER UNITED	19	7	1	-
1933–34	BRADFORD CITY	41	23	1	1
1934–35	BRADFORD CITY	34	4	3	1
1935–36	CHESTERFIELD	42	8	3	2
1936–37	CHESTERFIELD	9	2		
1937–38	CHESTERFIELD	7	-	5	2
TOTAL		614	195	41	16

Gentleman Johnny

"[Playing under Matt Busby] gave me my playing philosophy,
which is to play attractive football devised to win matches.
We've got to remember that we are public entertainers"

JOHNNY CAREY

JOHNNY CAREY BY FRANK COLBERT

Retracing the Footsteps of 'Gentleman' Johnny Carey

The first of Sir Matt Busby's three great teams started to gel soon after World War II when he had taken over the reins at Old Trafford, together with his assistant, Jimmy Murphy. For the next seven years this very impressive United team was greatly influenced by their highly respected captain, Johnny Carey. In view of his gracious personality, this Irish-born skipper was generally nicknamed 'Gentleman Johnny' throughout the game and was often regarded as having come from the same mould as his esteemed manager in many ways.

For several years afterwards, led by Carey, the team entertained large crowds with their attacking football throughout the country while generally performing near the top of the league table. In 1948 Carey proudly received the FA Cup at Wembley after one of the greatest finals in the history of the game, and he subsequently also led United to a well deserved championship victory in 1952, the year before his rightly earned retirement.

Furthermore, he went on to win the highest personal awards in the game such as English Footballer of the Year in 1949 and Sports Personality of the Year in 1950. In 1949 he captained a Rest of Europe team against Great Britain in a celebratory game before 140,000 spectators at Glasgow's Hampden Park.

During his playing days Carey was often described by his colleagues with impressive superlatives such as 'a world class player', 'among the most complete and versatile footballers in history', 'an artist', 'a soccer genius', 'one of the greatest footballers of all time', 'a prince among contemporary footballers' and 'a Jack of all trades and master of the lot'.

In addition, due to his well respected character, 'Gentleman' Johnny was frequently labelled by his contemporaries as 'dignified', 'noble', 'gracious', 'oozing integrity', 'most generous of men', 'well mannered', 'a genial Irishman', 'a true sportsman', 'most modest of men' and 'like an honoured Roman Senator from the Forum'.

This therefore now begs the question: "Who then was this legendary footballing gentleman from Ireland, what was his background and how great was his impact on the beautiful game in England and Ireland during the days when football was really football?"

The Early Years

Johnny Carey was born in a middle class suburb in the south side of Dublin on February 23rd, 1919. Although he had been christened John Joseph Carey, soon after his arrival in Manchester at the tender age of 17, he would generally be known as Johnny thereafter. While attending the Christian Brothers School in Dublin, he developed into a very promising Gaelic football player from the age

A young Johnny with hair!

of 15 onwards. Shortly afterwards, he won Dublin championship medals and became a member of Leinster College's team.

In those remote years, and for several decades later, the two traditional Irish games of Gaelic football and hurling were the only ones passionately fostered by Irish school authorities throughout the Republic as a legacy of abhorrent British rule which would continue until 1921. Back in 1884, the Gaelic Athletic Association (GAA) was founded to control the organization of both extremely popular national games, Gaelic football and hurling. Two years later, this organization implemented a rule, thereafter referred to as 'the ban', which lasted for another 85 years. This law was specifically implemented to greatly discourage Gaelic football and hurling players not only from playing any 'foreign games' – such as soccer, rugby, or cricket – but also from attending such matches. From then on, any GAA players who were found to have flaunted this law were duly banned by the GAA from playing both hurling and football for up to 12 months.

In view of both of these unorthodox circumstances prevailing, Carey and his pals, typically, had no contact with any organized soccer games while growing up, either in their school or neighbourhood. However, by way of improvisation, the sports-minded young Carey eventually started to take part in impromptu soccer matches in his local public park, known as Herbert Park, from the relatively advanced age of 14 and onwards.

As a young teenager, he attended a staff get-together dance at the English-owned company where his father was working. Startlingly, soon after his first dance on the floor, he was quickly informed by a nearby official from his Gaelic football club that he was duly being permanently suspended by the GAA from playing Gaelic football in future... purely for having attended an 'English' dance! In the words of the young teenager, "after the initial shock, I did not worry. That dance made my decision for me. I thought it only right that I should be allowed to play any game that I choose".

From there, events now moved quickly for him as he concentrated on the 'foreign' game of soccer instead of Gaelic football. First he played for the famous Dublin junior soccer club, Home Farm, where 'I went as a goalkeeper but they played me at outside-right'. Then he moved to St. James Gate, also in Dublin. Amazingly, after playing a mere six first-team games in which he scored six goals, he would soon be heading across the Irish Sea to Manchester United in November 1936. As a raw 17-year-old, he was about to embark on a hugely impressive career in a game in which he only had a few years' experience.

His astonishing transfer was initially sparked off by the Reds' legendary Dublin scout and ex-player, Billy Behan, who wrote to Manchester United's manager Scott Duncan about a promising Bohemians centre-forward named Benny Gaughan. Duncan went over to Dublin to see for himself and was happy with Gaughan's potential. As a result, arrangements were made to sign the player, and Louis Rocca, United's chief scout, was due to go over shortly afterwards to complete the deal. Meanwhile, however, Scottish giants Celtic had stepped in with a better offer and Gaughan soon went to Glasgow instead while Rocca was on his way to Dublin. When he arrived on Saturday morning to find Gaughan had already left for Celtic, he was naturally most disappointed. But the persuasive Behan asked him to stay on in the city to have a look at another youngster the next day - the 17-year-old playing for St. James Gate, named Carey.

According to Behan, Rocca agreed to have a look at the lad and thought him a great prospect despite his lack of experience. Carey was playing against Cork Athletic and scored in the first minute – only his sixth game for St. James in just two months of League of Ireland football. At that time, he had started to study as a civil servant. Ironically, it would be another 33 years before he would eventually pursue this career with the Treasurer's Office of Trafford Borough Council, after initially completing a hugely impressive career as a soccer player, and subsequently as a not unsuccessful manager.

While describing this same game in Dublin, Rocca states: "It was a poor game but there was something about the inside-right which took my fancy. A meeting of the St James' directors was called there and then. We talked for hours and eventually I got Carey's signature for £200, which was a League of Ireland record fee. No greater Irish player crossed the Irish Sea to make a name in English football". That same evening, Carey's father gave Rocca a real homely Irish welcome that lasted well into the early hours of the morning.

Interestingly, a few decades later, while being interviewed about his childhood years, Carey recalled how he had started to develop his powers of concentration and to sharpen his wits on tennis courts in Dublin from the age of 12. He recounted how he frequently acted as a ball-boy in big tennis tournaments such as Davis Cup games, sometimes on centre court at Fitzwilliam (the Dublin equivalent of Wimbledon), to make some pocket money. In his own words, "the ball-boy must always carefully follow the game, point for point, otherwise he might be throwing back the balls to the wrong end of the court". He then went on to recall one particularly amusing incident when he was 'stumped' by the international tennis star, Baron von Cramm - at that time Germany's Number One and one of the greatest players in the world - who sent him to the pavilion to collect some 'spotted dog', which turned out to be a plateful of currant cake to sustain the German during his game!

Apparently, Carey's definite determination came from swimming, or alternatively was brought out by that sport, when on one particular occasion his father entered him for a 100 yards race, even though he could only swim 40. Unusually, the officials had to delay the start of the next race to allow Carey to finish - but finish he did. As a result of a few similar incidents such as this, his determination soon became a feature of his play on the soccer field. With Carey having suddenly arrived at Old Trafford for the first time as a raw 17-year-old, we can only speculate on how overawed he must have been. In total contrast with the mere few years of 'the foreign game' of soccer which he now had under his belt, all the other United recruits whom he would be competing with had been playing the game ever since they had first started to kick a ball as kids in the streets. In addition, they invariably enjoyed the considerable advantage of constant coaching during this period.

Carey Arrives at Manchester United

Many years after his United debut, Carey recalled to Busby an amusing incident which happened to him as a raw 17-year-old just arrived in the foreign city of Manchester. In the words of his manager, Matt Busby, in his autobiography, 'My story': "When the shy Irish boy arrived in Manchester for the first time he was surprised, but flattered, to be apparently greeted by newspaper placards announcing "United's Big Capture"! Johnny bought his Chronicle and his News only to be brought down to earth with a bump when he read,"Manchester United have signed Ernest Thompson, centre forward of Blackburn Rovers, for £5,000.

"The story occupied a lot of space, and having read the whole account of the negotiations, plus full details of Thompson's career, Carey saw in a very small type at the foot of the report the announcement 'United have also signed a junior from Ireland. His name is J. Carey'. Johnny told that story against himself, but he had the last laugh - Thompson, despite the big transfer fee, played no more than 20 first team games for United, while J. Carey, the 'junior', stayed to complete an illustrious career during which he achieved the sort of success which entitled him to be remembered as one of the finest footballers ever to wear a Manchester United shirt. Carey stayed to play hundreds of games, as he became one of the great footballers of all time. He was at Old Trafford, Carey, when I arrived, and I quickly made him club captain. That was how much I thought of his wisdom and ability, and as a player he was an artist". As so often in the future, Busby's judgment was sound and the Irishman would go on to have a very impressive career subsequently as a hugely influential and mature captain at the peak of the English first division for some eight years.

Looking back through all those years, one can only speculate how overawed any other 17-year-old would have been when arriving at Old Trafford for the first time with only a few years of soccer experience under his belt. However, subsequent events at Old Trafford would prove that the mature Dubliner quickly found his feet and grasped the opportunity with both hands.

He soon made rapid progress at United, initially making his debut in the third team, then playing a few games in the second team, before breaking into the first team at the start of the next season, 1937/38 - a mere six months after his arrival at the club. When he started off in the first team he had to initially compete for his place with the future English international, Stan Pearson, who had made his debut in November. On days when the ground was heavy Carey was picked to play in the team and when it wasn't he had to give way to Pearson. Eventually, both players played in the team together. Back in October, the promising centre-forward Jack Rowley had made his debut and he would go on to be United's top goalscorer for several years. Carey's first team debut had been on September 25th, 1937, at inside-right in a 1-2 defeat to Southampton at Old Trafford. It was only a month into the season and United's fans were already extremely frustrated by the team's poor performance.

In 1985 Alec Shorrocks, in his book on Busby's first great team at Old Trafford, titled 'Winners and Champions' recalled the words of a Manchester daily newspaper on the following Monday after Carey's impressive debut: "The only bright feature of the game from Manchester's point of view was the play of Carey, a black-haired Irish youngster at inside-right. He was the one man on the side who used the ball thoughtfully, and for forty minutes he played so well and so ardently that he created the illusion that United were winning. Carey, at all events, did not deserve to have so disheartening an introduction to the Football League".

A local reporter wrote: "The lad looked a useful forward - maybe he could score goals as well! Those who saw the game were unanimous in their view that he has the makings of a valuable player. His footwork at times would have done credit to an experienced player". He scored his first goal for United in his third outing, in a 3-2 victory against Nottingham Forest on December 28th.

At Old Trafford, Carey soon discovered that he had come to an unglamorous Second Division club whose background did not impress or instil confidence in a new arrival such as himself. Although manager Scott Duncan's team had gained promotion in 1936, they would be relegated the very next season. At that early stage, Carey's hair may have been black but soon after the war it would start to thin quickly and the sight of his bald pate as he led out his teammates was the first thing that regularly started to get the United fans jointly shouting out his name.

Only six weeks after his United debut, he played his first game for the Republic of Ireland. On November 7th, 1937, at the tender age of 18, he appeared at inside-left in a 3-3 draw against Norway in a World Cup qualifying game in Dublin. In those years there were, in effect, two Irish teams, chosen by two rival associations. Both organizations, the Northern Ireland-based IFA and the Republic of Ireland-based FAI claimed jurisdiction over the whole of Ireland, and they selected players from the whole island. In this, his first season, Carey helped United to gain promotion to the first division as runners-up, together with players such as Jackie Rowley, Stan Pearson, Tommy Bamford, Harry Baird and fellow-Dubliner Tommy Breen. He had scored four goals in a total of 16 league appearances (23 in all competitions) for the first team. In the FA Cup, however, the team was eliminated by Barnsley 0-2 in the 4th round.

Having returned to the first division again, the 1938-39 season proved to be very ordinary for the club, and their interest in the FA Cup ended after a replay in the 3rd round at the hands of West Bromwich Albion by a convincing scoreline of 0-5. At this stage, Carey and Jack Rowley were fixtures in the team with 32 and 38 league appearances respectively and Carey, who scored six league goals from the inside-right position, played a total of 40 games in all competitions during the season.

The last game of the campaign for the first team was a 2-0 win against Liverpool. Giving an impressive performance that same day for the opposition in the right-half position was the Scottish captain, Matt Busby, who would go on to become United's next manager immediately after the war. United finished the season in 14th position in the league. However, despite a poor season back in the top flight, there was much reason for optimism in the club due to the fact that the reserve team, which now contained several promising future stars, had won the Central League championship.

Carey at War

Having played three games in the league at the start of the 1939-40 season, United found themselves in 10th position in the league, on a total of three points, but the 2-0 defeat at Charlton on Saturday 2nd September would be the last game in England before official Football League games were suspended for six years due to the outbreak of World War II. It was also Allenby Chilton's debut but he would have to wait six years for his second game!

Shortly after war was declared on September 3rd, the Football League competition was abandoned. Conscription was originally started in May 1939 for all able-bodied British males between the ages of 18 and 40. The Football League was soon replaced with regional competitions in which clubs could use guest players from any local military establishment. At the start of the war, some United players were now returning to their places of birth to await their call-up notices. However, Carey and Rowley in particular were still able to fit in a number of appearances for United's first team before joining the army.

Shorrocks goes on to remind us that: "In the early fifties, Carey had an impressive reputation of being the quintessential captain who was thoughtful, consistent and a genuine sportsman. However, over ten years earlier, while playing in a War Cup game against Blackburn at Old Trafford on May 4th, 1940, a less mature and impulsive Carey was uncharacteristically sent off the field together with an opponent."

In the words of the *Manchester Evening News* correspondent Don Davies, writing under the non-de-plume of 'An Old International', "this week my cue is villainous melancholy with a sigh like Tom O'Bedlam. Carey, of Manchester United, our black-haired gentler version of the incomparable Doherty, was requested by the referee to accompany the Blackburn player, 'Guest', to the dressing room, presumably for conduct unbecoming of sportsmen and gentlemen. With three minutes only remaining of play in a brilliant match, United were winning handsomely. Then our eyes fell upon two of the gladiators who were mixed up in a private scuffle. Carey and Guest were soon identified and arraigned as being the culprits.

"An Irish fan coming away from the match described them, in his Irish

Johnny Carey,
captain of Manchester United

accent, as 'two poor craythurs that couldn't do anybody any harm - a couple o' game cocks breastin', wan against the other' and he voiced the feelings of many. Carey and Guest had transgressed, beyond doubt, but they were shocked, as we were, when the blow fell". By all accounts the referee's decision seemed unjust, and most reports were fulsome in their praise for Carey's display of football skill that day - after all he had scored one of the goals in the 2-1 victory.

In Old Trafford's last game on March 8th, 1939, United beat Bury 7-3 with Carey and Rowley both scoring hat-tricks. In October 1940, when a United team containing Carey and Aston played against Manchester City in a Northern Regional game, there was much evidence that the old rivalry between the arch-enemies still existed despite the war clouds now hanging overhead! Then on March 11th, 1941, Old Trafford was suddenly bombed by the Germans who were concentrating on the nearby industrial areas of Trafford Park and Salford Docks, resulting in extensive damage to the main stand, dressing-room and pitch.

Playing conditions in those dark days were often very exacting for players, especially during mid-winter months. With poor drainage and under-soil heating totally unheard of, most pitches often became very bare and muddy, especially around the goalmouth, between the months of November and February. Football boots were made from pure leather, extended up to the ankle and had very hard toe-caps, causing some serious injuries to the unlucky victims of a hard kick. Footballs were also made of pure leather and, just like the boots, would soak up any moisture in wet conditions making it very heavy to head them. Before each game, generally, the fans' first inkling of team selections came from a chalk board which was carried around the pitch prior to kick-off. In total Carey had played in all three games in this his last season before the advent of World War.

Originally, when World War II loomed on the horizon, the youthful Carey had found himself in the unusual position that his native country, Ireland, had declared itself neutral, as was the case previously in World War I. However, the highly-principled Dubliner soon volunteered for service with the words 'Any country that is good enough to give me my livelihood is good enough to fight for!'

During the war years the Football Association and Football League arranged fairly regular international games, mostly against Services teams, with Carey playing many times for Ireland. In addition, several players on United's books would continue to turn out for the club in regional matches.

Shorrocks tells us that in the words of Carey: "While subsequently waiting for the actual call-up to arrive I went to Metrovicks, the aircraft factory in Trafford Park. I got married during the year after the war had started and then I was called up and I served in the army in North Africa and Italy. I was there for three and a half years before the war finished and I was eventually repatriated. During the war, I remember being selected for Ireland thirty days before the game and everyone said that this was a record because they didn't usually select teams thirty days before a game. They did this because they didn't know whether I would be able to get home, or not, since I was in Italy at the time. Actually, I don't think I managed to get home for that particular game.

"Eventually I managed to re-start my international career, because I was first capped in 1937 against Norway for the Republic of Ireland, and I more or less stayed in the team until 1953 when I retired. I won caps for both Eire and Northern Ireland because, at the time, Northern Ireland felt that it had the right to choose players from the whole of Ireland, so they also picked players from the South like Peter Farrell and Con Martin. I suppose there were five or six of us from the South who played for Northern Ireland. I got seven caps for them and twenty-nine for Eire. As a professional, of course, I was obviously prepared to play for both. In September 1946, I played against England on a Saturday in Belfast for Northern Ireland and also against them again on the following Monday for Eire. I got two fees, so I was alright!"

While serving in Italy during the war Carey played part-time professional soccer for a few prominent Italian clubs and the popular player received the amusing nickname from the locals - 'Cario'. He received a number of offers to stay on in Italy as a full-time professional after the war as a result of many generally impressive performances but decided to turn them down. During part of his time in Italy he served in the Queen's Royal Hussars and was in the same unit as the Preston North End and England legend, Tom Finney. In Carey's own words, "It was great fun. I had a job as a sergeant coaching and training all the football-minded personnel in the unit". Sadly, however, the war had robbed the football world of the opportunity to see Carey in his prime years.

On February 3rd, 1944, England beat Scotland 3-2 at Villa Park in an exciting game in front of over 66,000 fans. The general consensus was that the man of the match was Scotland's captain, and right-half, Matt Busby. One of Scotland's goals was scored by the Glasgow Celtic right-winger, Jimmy Delaney, who a few years later would become a star in Busby's FA Cup winning side.

Between 1939 and 1942, prior to going to Italy, Carey had also played a total of 112 war-time games for United in regional league games and scored 47 goals in total. During these years, he once scored four goals in one game, and he went on to score three hat-tricks in other games, as well as the only goal of the Lancashire Cup Final against Burnley on May 17th, 1941. In addition, he guested for other clubs including Cardiff City, Everton, Liverpool and Middlesbrough.

On February 19th 1945, following a clandestine approach by Louis Rocca, United acquired the impressive 35-year-old ex-Liverpool player, Matt Busby, as their new manager. Prior to that he was a physical education instructor during the war and played eight games for his native Scotland in this period, including many as captain. At one stage he was asked to take a British Army football team to entertain the football-starved troops in Greece, Egypt and also Italy where he came across his old friend, and sometime first division opponent, Jimmy Murphy. Busby soon invited the ex-Welsh international to be his assistant at Old Trafford as soon as he would be released from army duties. However, Busby himself would not be de-mobbed until September 1945.

At the end of that season, United found themselves in thirteenth position in the league table having won six, drawn nine and lost eight games. The good news, however, was that Carey was finished with his Service days and had returned to the team permanently. Both the defence and midfield were playing reasonably well and Busby knew that, although the goals were still lacking up front, he could still look forward to the return of quite a few forwards such as Rowley and Pearson to greatly improve the scoring rate.

Soon after, the war ended in August 1945, but it was still deemed too early for official football to resume. Another season of regional competition was arranged since teams were not yet prepared. United, for instance, found themselves with a bombed stadium and some players were missing from the league team. In United's first league game of the season, they were beaten 3-2 at Huddersfield. Goalkeeper Crompton would make his debut in September and would be the only player in that eleven to become a regular in the star-studded and successful team for the next six years.

On October 22nd, the 36-year-old Busby at last started his official duties as manager at Old Trafford. On that autumn morning, dressed in the obligatory 'demob suit', Busby soon started to realize the considerable size of the job now ahead of him as he surveyed the scene at Old Trafford. He had inherited a League club without a functioning stadium, United had an overdraft of £15,000, there was nowhere to train at Old Trafford except on the cinder track car park, and its club offices were a mile from the stadium. The newly installed manager immediately donned a tracksuit and took part in training out on the pitch with his players, something which was totally revolutionary in those distant days. In the words of Carey, "when I joined United before the war, Scott Duncan, wearing a business suit, was typical of a soccer manager. But here was our new boss playing with his team, demonstrating what he wanted and how to achieve it. It was unheard of in those days. Matt was ahead of his time".

When Busby picked his first team for the forthcoming game at Maine Road against Bolton Wanderers on October 27th, he used the guidance of both club secretary Walter Crickmer and coach Tom Curry. Having won this exciting game 2-1, before a crowd of 30,000, the team was now sixteenth in the table. Johnny Carey, who was home on leave and playing his first game for the team for two years, scored the team's equalizing goal.

Busby's decision to make him captain for that game was justified apparently due to the fact that he had a great game. Both manager and captain had taken to each other immediately. However, any hopes that Busby had of building a team around the Irishman at that early stage were soon thwarted when the popular Carey was told to return to Italy after the game, leaving Busby with only a faint promise of an early demobilization. Nevertheless, Carey had enough time to squeeze in another game and played a major part in United's 6-1 victory against Preston North End on Saturday November 3rd. As a consistent scheming inside-forward, he knitted the team together and was an influence behind almost every goal. In the words of a local reporter, "The most commanding figure of all in the team was Johnny Carey, an influential player both on and off the field". Even the Irish Football Association selectors found it difficult to prize him away from his Service responsibilities in Italy. They had selected him a month before he was due to appear for Northern Ireland against England in Belfast on 15th September but found even then that he couldn't get leave to play.

Nearly thirty years later Busby described his new potential captain as follows: "Of all the players, I knew only one, and him only slightly. He was Johnny Carey, a tall, quietly-spoken yet loquacious Irishman of commanding presence". Soon afterwards he started to realize that "Johnny Carey was a natural captain, who had the instinct for transmitting my wishes once the players were on the pitch, which after all, is one of the qualities needed, but not always possessed, by captains. A skipper doesn't actually need to be psychic, I suppose, but it helps if he is, and a good understanding of his manager's likes and dislikes goes a long way towards achieving the same results".

Eamon Dunphy, a United reserve player from the early sixties, describes Carey the captain in his book, 'A Strange Kind of Glory', as follows: "Busby had soon recognized that his new captain stood for something by which Manchester United wished to be known: something that was noble rather than feckless, dignified rather than coarse. He was neither militant nor one of the boys. But that was not what was required of him. The Irishman provided leadership which was symbolic of the ethos that the manager had sought to inculcate into his football club from the beginning. In addition, Carey was loyal and decent, his behaviour always impeccable. He played the game graciously".

In Jim White's book, "Manchester United – the Biography", the author adds: "Busby was impressed with the way Carey carried himself. He was serious, old for his years and chastened by his war service. Maybe, in the way he dressed and also in his refusal to engage in the earthy language of the training ground, he reminded Busby of himself (although Busby never went as far as to

A left-footed clearance for the cigarette cards.

become, like Carey, a teetotal non-smoker). Busby didn't see any significance in the fact that the rest of the lads considered their captain to be somewhat stand-offish". Interestingly, although White labelled Carey a non-smoker, he apparently forgot to mention that Carey was a pipe-smoker, coincidentally just like his manager.

Carey once recounted that "Being captain of the team didn't exclude me from criticism, however. Matt would say 'How about getting the ball up to the forwards quicker, you fellows at the back want to take the lace out of it'. I asked Matt afterwards if he really thought I was doing too much on the ball. His answer left me in no doubt 'Yes' he said, then he explained how I was slowing down the game and giving opposing defenders time to pick up forwards. 'I want you to give an exhibition of first-time kicking'. Here was another example of Matt's psychology. He didn't stress the things I was doing wrong; he gave me something positive to do".

Full-scale repairs to Old Trafford didn't start until February 1946 and, despite optimistic forecasted dates for its completion, it would not be ready for its first game until August 1949. In February 1946, Busby signed Glasgow Celtic's right winger, Jimmy Delaney, for £4,000 despite advise to the contrary due to the player's advanced age (30) and his not inappropriate nickname 'Brittle-bones'. The popular goalscoring winger would make his debut in August against Grimsby Town at Maine Road.

On February 2nd, Carey was the first United player to play in the Victory Internationals when he took the field for Ireland against Scotland at Belfast's Windsor Park. As further proof of his versatility, he was picked to play at centre-forward but appeared at inside-left due to injuries to other players. In front of a capacity crowd Ireland lost to Scotland 2-3 but he was adjudged to have been the 'the best forward in the game'. On April 13th, 1946, Busby moved Carey to right-back because of several injuries in the team. As a result of his hugely impressive performance in his new position, he remained there not only for the rest of the season but also for the remainder of his career, barring injuries.

In the eyes of many experts at that time, Busby's inspired decision to move Carey backwards gave him a fullback of world-class standard. In Carey's own words, "I used to play at inside-forward before the war against Busby and, when he became manager, I can remember him saying 'You know, I've never pictured you as an inside-forward but as a wing-half or even a full-back'. I replied that 'That's probably because I never got up into the opposition's penalty area'." Coincidentally, Busby's first meeting with Carey was in a war game at Windsor Park while playing at centre-half for a British Army team, in direct opposition to his future club captain, at centre-forward for Ireland. This encounter convinced the manager that Carey was 'something more than a great footballer'. Carey further explains that: "Actually, as an inside-forward I did tend to operate a lot in midfield. Certainly it was an inspiration on Matt's part to convert myself and Johnny Aston into fullbacks – we were both really inside-forwards. As fullbacks we were the ball-players and supplied the finesse and Henry Cockburn and John Anderson were the strong players and did all the work. It just worked out that way, though it was contrary to the general pattern of the way defences operated at that time".

Based on his own personal experience at Manchester City as a player, Busby had learned how beneficial it could be for a struggling inside-forward to move to the backline where he would be normally facing the opponents' goal. However, Busby had faced opposition from United chairman Harold Hardman when he tried to find a more suitable position in the team for his somewhat struggling Irish inside-forward.

In the opinion of his outside-left Charlie Mitten, "I always thought that Carey looked very awkward initially, leggy like a bloody colt. He needed time to develop his strength. But Busby knew that he could get more out of Carey and duly moved him back nearer his own goal. First he tried him at wing-half, and then put him at fullback, where he blossomed into a world class player. He eventually made his name as a right-back of course, but he learnt his skills up front. He was also a good goalkeeper and a good centre half. You never saw John wildly kick a ball - he always did something sensible with his passes. John's re-positioning had repercussions for years afterwards - he would still be captain in 1953".

Having soon settled down at fullback, Carey's innovative defensive play, scrupulous fairness and clean tackling won him much respect from his colleagues as well as opponents. He quickly developed a reputation of invariably coming off the field after a game with spotlessly clean shorts due to the fact that, instead of diving into the tackle to win the ball, he alternatively would usually jockey his opposing winger with the ball out to the corner flag, thereby rendering him virtually harmless.

In his autobiography titled 'After the Ball', United's star of the sixties, Nobby Stiles, states that his uncle Tommy played for St. Pat's local team at wing-half, in front of his dad, who was a fullback and who tried to model himself on 'the great Johnny Carey of Manchester United and Ireland'. "Look at Carey", Nobby's dad once said to him, "at halftime and at the final whistle. Look at his shorts. On the muddiest day they will be shining white. He has such balance he always stays on his feet. You cannot make a tackle while you're sitting on your arse". Later in the book, Nobby adds: "Apart from my father making the point about Carey's balance and the important explanation for his immaculate shorts, no-one ever taught me how to tackle. It developed naturally".

United had been knocked out of the FA Cup in the 4th round by Preston North End by an aggregate scoreline of 3-4, the FA having decided to run the ties on a two-legged basis that year. During this season, left half-back Henry Cockburn made his first team debut in January and Carey made four competitive appearances.

At the end of May 1946, Jimmy Murphy, who had now finished in the services, arrived at Old Trafford to take up Busby's offer of the assistant manager's job. To this very day, Murphy is still recognized by many football experts as being Busby's best ever signing. In addition to the Welshman's hugely successful coaching of three great United teams over the next 25 years, he was in many ways the main influence behind the legendary Busby Babes. However, his greatest contribution to United was probably his tireless work as caretaker manager immediately after Munich, despite great personal grief and loss. Amazingly, this huge unprecedented effort not only ensured the survival of a totally shattered club but also eventually resulted in it resuming its place at the peak of English football just over five years later. Truly, he can be described as the rock that the Reds' foundation for continued success was built on. Coincidentally, both Carey and Jack Warner faced each other in the number 4 position in an international at Ninian Park before 40,000 spectators where the host country Wales lost by 1-0 to Ireland.

League Football Returns

The Football League now resumed again for the first time on August 31st, 1946, and during the previous season Busby had used an extraordinary number of players while trying to find a settled side. In addition to the many players who played informal games at Old Trafford during the war, he was also giving a chance to several others who had originally made their debut before 1939 such as Pearson, Rowley and Carey. In view of the dilapidated condition of the bombed Old Trafford stand and dressing rooms, Manchester City had agreed that United could play their home games at Maine Road on alternative Saturdays for the next two years, while United reciprocated by allowing their neighbours to use their home pitch for reserve games.

During the season there would be debuts for Johnny Aston, Johnnie Morris and Charlie Mitten in the months of September and October. By the end of the new season Busby had now found a reliable formation which would consistently keep United near the top of the ladder for the next six years. Regular goalkeeper Crompton was a non-spectacular but very consistent and courageous custodian and a fitness fanatic. Carey now played regularly at right-back and was partnered on the left by Mancunian Johnny Aston, who was soon an England international. The half-back line consisted of Warner, an effective passer of the ball, the six-foot tall and powerfully built Allenby Chilton, and the diminutive but dogged Henry Cockburn, both of whom were also England internationals. The free-scoring forward line regularly consisted of Jimmy Delaney, creative Johnny Morris, the prolific goalscoring duo of Jack Rowley and Stan Pearson, together with the speedy Charlie Mitten at outside-left. Delaney had been signed to supply the ammunition, together with Mitten, for the English international inside-forward trio of Morris, Rowley and Pearson.

With reference to Jimmy Delaney, the author Geoffrey Green recalls in his book 'There's Only One United' that Carey the Irishman, with his dry Irish wit, soft brogue, and pipe, has since said that when he himself wanted a breather he would work the ball up the right wing and give it to Delaney. In his own words: "That done, I could rest for five minutes while 'Baldie' waltzed round the place for a time!" Conveniently for Carey, he failed to mention that he himself was just as bald and probably looked even older than his winger.

United's first game of the new season was against Grimsby Town at Maine Road where they won 2-1 in front of 40,000 fans. Only three of the United players (Stan Pearson, Johnny Carey and Jack Warner) had taken part in the same fixture exactly seven years before, just as war was about to be declared. The team started off the season playing open attractive football which attracted big crowds of up to 60,000. However, injuries to key players, including their first choice goalkeeper, Jack Crompton, eventually started a decline in form and they dropped to 17th in the league table after 13 games. Nevertheless, in November, form started to pick up again and, having finished the season with 11 victories in 12 games, they were runners-up in the league with Carey making 31 appearances (33 in all competitions) for the first team. In the FA Cup, United were eliminated in the 4th round by Nottingham Forest by a scoreline of 0-2.

On September 2nd, 1946, Jimmy Delaney and Carey were both chosen in opposition for a Scotland versus Ireland game at Windsor Park. However, unfortunately for Carey, he had to withdraw due to an injury. Startlingly, later in the same month, Carey played two international games for different teams, both of them against England within three days of each other. In the first game, the Northern Ireland XI (IFA) lost 2-7 on the Saturday at Windsor Park and, in the second game on the following Tuesday, the Republic of Ireland (FAI) were defeated 0-1 in Dublin. On November 27th, he was one of seven Republic-born players in the IFA eleven who drew 0-0 with Scotland thereby helping his team to finish as runners-up in the 1947 British Home Championships.

A keen United fan, Tony Quirke, who was attending St. Bede's College in Manchester in the late forties, recalls that Carey was the school coach at the time. In his own words: "Johnny Carey was a very quiet and gentle man who had one key phrase for us budding footballers, 'Go to meet the ball'. Sir Matt's son, Sandy, was also at St. Bede's then and Carey spent quite some time coaching him as a centre-half in those days". Coincidentally, several years later, after Carey became manager of Blackburn Rovers, the young Busby played on the fringe of his first team for three years.

Towards the end of 1947, a settled United team was starting to show consistently impressive form which was now pulling in considerably improved attendances again at Maine Road of around 50,000. As a result, there was growing hope of some silverware coming to Manchester at the end of the season. This new increased optimism would eventually prove to be justified when United finished as runners-up in the league and also worthy FA Cup winners.

Early in the New Year, however, Carey was to receive a huge personal honour, in keeping with his considerable status in English football. As Shorrocks recounts: "At the end of March 1947, Manchester United were delighted with the news that Carey had been included in a squad of fifteen players from whom a Rest of Europe team would finally be chosen to play a Great Britain eleven at Glasgow's Hampden Park on May 10th, 1947. This memorable game had been arranged as a welcoming showpiece of the Football Association to celebrate their re-joining FIFA after they had been excluded in 1928 on the question of 'broken time' payments for amateurs. Nearly twenty years and a world war later it was time now to forgive and forget. The quality of continental football was a mystery to most British fans at the time but the immense popularity of soccer, together with the Moscow Dynamo visit the season before, guaranteed excited interest all over Britain. In the words of Carey:

"At the time there were competitions in the newspapers to let the readers give their opinions on which players should represent Great Britain and I was very pleased to see that a lot had voted me into that side. When the time came to select the side, though, it was found that I wasn't eligible to play for Great Britain, but I was qualified to be considered for the European team. I thought to myself 'Well, that's it. I'll never get into that side'. Then I was very surprised to learn that I had been picked for the Rest of Europe squad of fifteen players. I was also notified that I should go over to Amsterdam and then to Rotterdam where there would be a trial match against a Dutch team.

"The Great Britain side was announced a month later and consisted of Swift (England), Hardwick (England), Hughes (Wales), Macauley (Scotland), Vernon (Northern Ireland), Burgess (Wales), Matthews (England), Mannion (England), Lawton (England), Steel and Liddell (both Scotland).

"There was only a little difficulty with the language in that team. Many could speak some English and I could speak a little Italian because I'd been over there during the war. Some days later we stayed at the Marine Hotel in Troon before the game and I will never forget one of the waitresses complimenting me on my command of the English language!

"I was absolutely amazed when just before the practice game the president of FIFA came over to me and said 'We want you to be captain'. It was a tremendous honour for me and we beat Holland 2-1 in front of a crowd of 60,000. I can remember all the players, particularly our small goalkeeper Da Rui. My word, I was surprised how small he was, only about 5 feet 5 inches, but very agile. I thought he might be struggling because there were some big fellows knocking around in the Great Britain team like Tommy Lawton and Billy Liddell.

"As expected, the Great Britain players, on a fee of £20 for the match, overwhelmed the Rest of Europe side 6-1, after leading 4-1 at halftime, in front of a massive 134,000 crowd. So we didn't know much about continental players, and this was the problem with the Rest of Europe side. We were a mixture and, while we were all fairly good players, we weren't together as a team. The whole thing was a beautiful spectacle though, and such a convincing win for Great Britain. Britain, and England in particular, were masters in football in those days and it wasn't until 1953 when the Hungarians came over that we were shown what it was all about". Significantly, the Great Britain captain, Ronnie Burgess, commented after the game that "If ever I admired the play of the strong Irishman, I did that day. Although he was unable to hold much

Johnny Carey and the legendary 1948 Cup winning team

conversation with his teammates, he led them with wonderful skill, setting a superb example".

Lifting the Cup

By December the Salford-born halfback, Johnny Anderson, had established his place at right-half for United at the ripe age of 26, taking over from Warner. In the third round of the FA Cup, United were drawn away to Aston Villa. Unexpectedly, the home side scored 13 seconds after the kick-off! At that time, Johnny Carey thought that Villa's early goal was the worst thing they could have done and in his view, "Fancy taking the liberty of scoring so early. We settled down to it and set about them, and the football which we played was out of this world. You know, it was an extraordinary thing about this 1948 team - when the chips were down we could step up our game and destroy the opposition in ten minutes. The passes flew - everybody played all out and we could transform a game where we found ourselves a goal down to one where not long later we were leading by several goals. It happened in the Villa game and it happened in many other matches as well".

In Shorrocks' 'Winners and Champions', one spectator at the game had this to say: "After Villa delivered that lightning rapier thrust in the opening seconds, the first United player to get a touch of the ball was Jack Crompton, the goalkeeper, as he fished it out of the net. While he was doing so Carey put his hands on his hips, looked around at his fellow players and gave them a wide, courageous Irish smile. It was as if to say, 'Now my lads, let's show them...'. There, indeed, was a much needed tonic. There was captaincy. It was a smile that was to take Manchester United up to Wembley's Royal Box three months later to receive the Cup itself from the hands of King George VI. United duly came back with a vengeance and were leading 5-1 at half-time. Despite a great second half comeback by Villa, United eventually ran out convincing winners by 6 goals to 4!"

The first United player to be voted "Footballer of the Year" in 1949.

Shorrocks tells us that: "In the next round, John Aston recalled how a Liverpool plan to re-position their star outside-left and Scottish international, Billy Liddell, had failed miserably. Matt Busby had played with Liddell in his Liverpool days, and United's defence, and John Aston in particular, had been well briefed. In the words of the left-back, 'They put Liddell at outside-right against me because Carey always used to have a good game against him, and Johnny had caned him once or twice in league games. Liddell was a smashing bloke and always gave you a good tussle. Anyway, in that game they thought that they would play him on me. Bloody easy, he was - I was surprised how easy'". United finished 3-0 winners, with goals from Rowley, Morris and Mitten. In the 5th round United found themselves paired with the FA Cup holders, Charlton Athletic, at Leeds Road, Huddersfield (City needed Maine Road for their own cup tie). On a muddy pitch in incessant rain, Charlton conceded an own goal by Bricknell minutes after the kick-off. Thereafter, United continually battered the Charlton goal with goalkeeper Sam Bartram virtually standing alone between United and a consolidating second goal. Eventually, on 85 minutes, Mitten headed in a Delaney cross to bring the final score to 2-0.

In the next round United had a convincing 4-1 win over Preston North End with goals from Pearson (2), Morris and Mitten. A Manchester newspaper reporter wrote: "Johnny Carey steadied the defence in typical fashion and constantly supported the attack. He impressed the crowd with his calmness and strength". In the semi-final against Derby, United were pressed hard for most of the second half but their defence held firm, largely due to Carey playing 'his usual immaculate game'. Many press reports lauded both Carey and Pearson for their 'great contribution', with the latter scoring a hat-trick in a 3-1 victory.

There was soon great excitement amongst soccer fans when they realized that United, who were generally regarded as the most entertaining team in England, would be paired in the Cup Final with a formidable Blackpool team containing the two Stans from the national team - centre-forward Mortensen and the legendary Matthews, in search of his elusive first cup medal. During the weeks before the eagerly-awaited game, Carey found himself surrounded by a pile of letters from all parts of the UK with requests for tickets for the final, but with little hope. In the month prior to the big game, the United players published a brochure to commemorate the final. In the publication the gracious Carey wrote as follows: "Players who have been fortunate - and I know that I have - to pick up a variety of honours in football, all agree about the thrill of leading out a team at Wembley. April 24th, 1948, will certainly be a red letter day for me, not, I hope, from any notions of conceit, but because I am deeply conscious of the great privilege it will be to walk out at the head of such a grand set of fellows as ours, and alongside as worthy a set of opponents as Blackpool. What effect the so-called 'Wembley nerves' may have on all of us remains to be seen. We expect to be impressed by the vast arena and by its roaring multitudes, its elaborate ceremony, its formal introductions and so forth; but once that is over and done with, and the boys feel the ball at their toes, I am hoping we shall be able to forget where we are and give of our best.

"That is all we want. We know that the coolest heads will win, and one thing that should help to put us in the right frame of mind is the knowledge that we shall be following 'The Boss' - Matt Busby, a football manager second to none. No-one can better appreciate his grasp of strategy or his uncanny gift of sizing up our opponents than I, the skipper, whose responsibility it is to see that his instructions are carried out on the field, and I take this opportunity of thanking 'The Boss' on the boys' behalf, for all that he has done for our well-being and our comfort. We should like to thank our directors and the staff too, for their kindness and help which has contributed largely to our success. Special praise and thanks also to our supporters for their encouragement on all occasions. As for the boys themselves - their loyalty and co-operation have been an inspiration, and I, for one, am confident that it will be there at Wembley. Here's to a fine game and may the best team win".

In his book, 'There's Only One United', Geoffrey Green tells us that: "The morning of April 26th, 1948, dawned fine and sunny. It was as if that smile of Johnny Carey was still shining all over the world". Certainly it had helped to illuminate Manchester United themselves, for here they were on that April day poised to face Blackpool in the Cup Final, without having played a single tie on their own ground. On the eve of the final Matthews was the first recipient of the newly inaugurated Footballer of the Year trophy. Coincidentally, at the end of the next season he would be succeeded by Carey. Unfortunately for neutral soccer supporters both of these star players would not be paired against each other at Wembley as they were positioned on opposite wings. The line-ups in the final were:

Manchester United: Crompton; Carey, Aston: Anderson, Chilton, and

Cockburn; Delaney, Morris, Rowley, Pearson and Mitten. Blackpool: Robinson; Shimwell, Crosland; Johnston, Hayward, Kelly; Matthews, Munro, Mortensen, Dick and Rickett.

Blackpool scored from a dubious penalty after 14 minutes. Thereafter, an extremely exciting game ebbed and flowed and, after 45 minutes, Blackpool were leading 2-1 with United's lone goal having come from Rowley. At halftime, Carey egged his players on with the words 'Don't panic. Keep playing the football we have been doing all season; play it the way the Boss wants'. In the words of Busby from his book 'Matt Busby's Manchester United scrapbook': "It was skipper Johnny Carey who, during the ten-minute break, provided the necessary inspiration for his team-mates. He urged them: 'Keep on playing football as you have been doing - the goals are bound to come'. His utter confidence stoked the rest of the team, and we drew level for the second time by scoring one of the 'brainiest' goals I have ever seen, scored by Jackie Rowley".

In an exciting second half, United went on to get an equalizer from Rowley again after 20 minutes. One of the features of the game was a royal battle on the wing between Carey and Blackpool's left winger Rickett. Further goals from Pearson and Anderson brought the final score to an emphatic 4-2 victory for United, thanks as much as anything to Carey's leadership. For many decades later, the match would be recognized as the most exciting and entertaining Cup Final in history and, while he was presenting the cup to Carey after the game, King George's remark to the United captain was 'I thoroughly enjoyed the game'. Immediately afterwards, while his teammates were parading the trophy around the hallowed Wembley pitch, the proud captain was interviewed and replied with the words "I am very pleased to be taking this cup back again to Manchester after a period of forty years". While the cup was being presented by King George, Carey happened to drop the lid on the ground. Coincidentally, on the next occasion that United also won the cup final, in 1963, Carey's eventual successor and fellow Irishman, Noel Cantwell, actually threw the trophy up into the air in another extreme show of excitement.

As thrilled as Busby must now have been at his triumph coming so soon, he let others do most of the celebrating. He knew that there was a long way to go. In the words of his skipper "He never used a superlative about something that didn't deserve it. Very occasionally after a game he would come and say 'Well done, skipper' which meant more than a thousand pounds. You had to win his heart. I don't suppose he did it more than four or five times in seven years. I always tried to play in such a way as to make him say it". A few days later, Carey said to his manager: "I always thought I would give my life for this medal. Now it's happened so quickly I just cannot believe it".

United's FA Cup victory was all the more impressive in view of the fact that they had scored 22 goals in six games and all against first division teams. In addition, all matches were played either on a neutral venue or at an away ground and, en route to the final, they beat both the reigning league champions as well as the FA Cup holders, while winning every tie by a minimum of two goals.

In Busby's biography, 'My Story', he later described the many impressive qualities of his great '48 Cup winning team. He concluded with the words: "These then are the men whose combined talents were welded into a team good enough to win the FA Cup in 1948. Some, like Cockburn, Morris and Pearson are still in the game. Others, more is the pity, will never again delight the football enthusiast with their artistry - unless persuaded to forsake, temporarily, their well-earned retirement for an occasional exhibition match. It is a tragedy that great footballers must, like more expendable beings, grow old, because some, alas, can never be replaced". United finished runners-up in the league once again, with Carey making 37 league appearances, 44 in all competitions.

Champion Carey

The traditional Charity Shield match in 1948 between FA Cup winners United and league champions, Arsenal, was played at Highbury and resulted in a 4-3 victory for the Londoners. Four months into the new season, United were in fourth place in the table but were not as impressive as they had been the previous campaign, despite a high goal-scoring rate. As a result, the fans were eagerly awaiting a return to true form by a team which was basically the same as that which had played so impressively at Wembley the previous April.

However, after they started to again make good progress in the FA Cup in 1949, inside-right Johnny Morris suddenly had an altercation with manager Busby, prior to the sixth round game against Hull City. Despite being a key member of the attack, the youngest member of the famous '48 team was soon afterwards transferred to Derby County. Unfortunately, a few months later, Morris' absence would generally be regarded as the main reason behind the team's subsequent defeat in the FA Cup semi-final to Wolves. Although United lost by an obvious offside goal in the replay, typical of Carey's disciplined team in those days, they accepted the result without a word of protest and were the quick to congratulate the opposition at the end of a great game.

A few days before that replay, it was announced that Carey had been voted 'Player of the Year' by the Football Writers' Association. Impressively, he had polled some 40% of the votes and only one fewer than the combined total votes of English legends, Raich Carter and Billy Wright, who were in second and third place respectively. He was clearly a very popular choice. United's quietly spoken and modest captain was rated as one of the best fullbacks in the game. Unfortunately, however, against all expectations, he was unable to lead out United in the Cup Final at Wembley for the second year in succession.

On Friday, April 29th, Carey attended the Football Writers' dinner in London where he was presented with the much-coveted trophy. Afterwards, both he and manager Busby caught the overnight sleeper train up to Newcastle where United's proud captain helped his team to a 1-0 victory over the Tynesiders. This victory resulted in the team now moving into second place in the table before their last game of the season against the newly-crowned champions, Portsmouth. Their subsequent 3-2 victory in a great game secured runners-up place once again for the third year in a row. Ironically, at Derby County on the same day, their rivals Stoke City were beaten 1-4 largely thanks to a hat-trick from the home team's recent signing, Johnny Morris. During the season, Carey had played an impressive total of 41 league games, 50 in all competitions.

While playing in an international game against Spain in Dublin Johnny was uncharacteristically given the greatest run-around of his otherwise hugely impressive career by the opposition winger, Gainza. His reputation as an international fullback was blunted, but only momentarily, after that game. However, his reputation for sportsmanship reached new heights due to the fact that not one foul was given against him in that same gruelling encounter.

United went nine games undefeated at the start of the 1949-50 season and, in January, found themselves in second place, only a few points behind leaders Liverpool. Eventually, with a dozen games remaining, their recent impressive run was starting to give many fan's visions of a league and cup double. However, a well below par performance in a 6th round FA Cup replay against Chelsea soon ended their cup run due to a 0-2 defeat.

A 7-0 annihilation of Aston Villa shortly afterwards in the league fuelled further optimism of becoming champions at last and, with 10 games remaining, they were now leading by 4 points. Unfortunately, due to a sudden bad run of form, they won only two of those remaining games and finished up in a disappointing fourth place, having been runners-up on the three previous seasons. In hindsight, a sudden loss of form from the usually reliable goalscorers – Rowley, Pearson and Mitten - together with the loss of the injured Crompton, had been significant.

During the season, Busby had introduced goalkeeper Ray Wood in December to replace Crompton, who had a broken wrist. Stockport-born wing-half Jeff Whitefoot became the youngest player ever so far to make his first team debut for the club at 16 years and 105 days. In due course, Whitefoot would go on to succeed Carey in the right halfback position before eventually signing for Nottingham Forest where the Irishman would become his manager in 1963.

On September 21st, 1949, Carey had captained the Republic of Ireland when they became the first 'foreign' team to beat a star-studded England team on home soil, by a convincing scoreline of 2-0. In the words of the skipper, "the personal high spot for me was skippering the Irish team that beat England 2-0 at Goodison Park. That day England included such great players as Tom Finney, Wilf Mannion, Billy Wright, and Neil Franklin (in addition to Carey's club mates Aston and Morris), and they were stunned by our display. They could not believe it back home, and most Irish people thought the announcer had made a mistake when the result was given on the wireless". Carey was also voted 'Sportsman of the Year' at the end of the season in which he had made 38 league appearances for United, a total of 43 in all competitions.

Earlier in 1950, the club had been invited to do a six-week close-season tour of the USA, and they duly sailed to New York on May 2nd aboard the Queen Mary. The *Manchester Chronicle* had commissioned Carey to write a regular series of articles for the paper, which would give to its readers ongoing accounts of the team's experiences on the trip. While en route to New York, the skipper described games between the team and the crew in table tennis and darts. The players also joined the passengers' table tennis competition where Jack Crompton beat Stan Pearson in the semi-final, and Carey himself in the final.

After the legendary liner had docked in New York, Carey enthralled his readers back home with stories of the typical warm receptions which they normally received, and the food and neon lights they came across, and they even met Louis Armstrong. In the words of the skipper, "the traffic and bustle are tremendous. I think it is because they are six hours behind England and they are trying to catch up with us!"

Soon Carey started to unveil some unusual news. In a column headed '3,500 pounds a year does not tempt us', he described how he had received a telephone call in New York telling him that an "agent would be contacting me and some of the United players to persuade us to play football in Colombia, for a generous salary and expenses". Carey was however skeptical of the whole business and added: "None of the United players would consider such a proposition because it would mean 'finis' as regards our future in the game in Britain". The ever sensible Carey was referring to the fact that, at that time, Colombia was not a member of FIFA. However, one United player, winger Charlie Mitten, found it impossible to refuse a salary which was several times his present one, just one part of a lucrative package. Significantly, at the end of his season in the sun, a homesick Mitten refused to sign a new contract for his new club and soon returned to Manchester with his family hoping to continue his career at Old Trafford. However, he was soon fined and suspended by the FA for six months, at the end of which he was reluctantly transferred by United to Fulham.

Due to the team's erratic performances in 1950-51, Busby used 23 players in total while gradually introducing young 'Busby Babes' to replace a few of the old guard. In mid–November, after five happy and relatively successful years at Old Trafford, Delaney decided to return home north of the border because he felt that, being now in the autumn of his career, Scottish football would suit him better. Interestingly, he would still go on to appear in cup finals in both Northern Ireland and Eire. As a result, he completed a personal record of having won three cup medals, together with a runners-up one, in four different countries.

Unfortunately, the recent loss of both wingers Mitten and Delaney would prove significant for the club. Despite an impressive late flourish in the second half of the season, United finished as runners-up once more – on this occasion to Spurs – for the fourth season in the last five. In addition, they were beaten in the 6th round of the FA Cup by Birmingham City 0-1. Carey played a total of 39 league games, 43 games in all competitions, during the season. Goalkeeper Reg Allen made his debut in August and reserve centre-half Mark Jones did likewise in October.

As Geoffrey Green relates in 'There's Only One United': "The new season of 1951-52 started off on a high note with Jack Rowley scoring three hat-tricks in three weeks and a total of fourteen goals in seven games". New signing Johnny Berry from Birmingham was starting to quickly impress at outside-right after his debut in September. Mitten's place on the left wing was eventually filled by Mancunian Roger Byrne who, eighteen months later, would go on to succeed the retired Carey as a highly influential skipper of the quickly emerging Busby Babes. By the end of the season, Byrne had scored an impressive seven goals in the last six games. He would soon go on to become the first of the modern fullbacks, innovatively doing overlapping runs down the wing. In addition, Busby Babe Jackie Blanchflower made his first team debut in November.

Earlier in the season, Carey was moved to the right halfback position to make way for Tommy McNulty at right-back. With five games still remaining in the season, United were level on 48 points with both Arsenal and Portsmouth. However, in United's second last game of the season, which was played at Old Trafford, they were duly crowned champions after beating Chelsea 3-0, a game memorable for a Carey goal which symbolically won the championship for United. Carey, having received a square pass from full-back McNulty, strode ahead with the ball at his feet and shot from thirty yards. The ball hit the back of the net and rolled out as far as the penalty spot. It was such a tremendous goal that the fans were still cheering well after the game had been re-started.

For decades afterwards, the modest Carey would happily recall the event: "Because time was quickly running out for me, I really wanted to win a championship medal. We were left with two home games at the end, one against Chelsea on the Monday and the other against Arsenal on the following Saturday. Chelsea's form was unpredictable at that time. After going a goal up, we were struggling a bit and the ball came to me. Because I was unchallenged I just kept going. When I reached their penalty area, I took a shot with my left foot and it soared into the top corner of their goal. The crowd gave me a terrific ovation, but I suspect that it was more from relief than anything else".

In truth, however, Carey's memory was clearer than that, as Nobby Stiles recounts in his autobiography of an aeroplane meeting between the two. It was soon after the 1966 World Cup final and Nobby's famous jig on the Wembley pitch. On the flight to Dublin, Nobby soon started to discover that his new-found fame apparently made him a bigger celebrity than another famous passenger. He was startled to find out that it was 'one of the men who had done so much to make United's name synonymous with football of the highest class'. Nobby went over to Johnny and told him how much he admired 'his critical goal against Chelsea that won the 1952 championship', as he himself sat on the wall above the scoreboard end with his brother, Charlie. "I'll tell you how I did it, Nobby", Carey said. "I dragged it inside the defender and then, after dropping my shoulder and going the other way from him at the halfway line, I took it on and then shot with my right foot into the top corner". "That's exactly how I remember it, Mr. Carey", Nobby said before adding: "But then who would forget something like that. Would you?"

Carey was proud of the title success and in his own words: "Winning the championship is a fantastic prize - it is won over forty-two games in comparison to the FA Cup, which is at the end of only six games. If it is all down to one game - the luck can go with you or against you - that's why we find all kinds of teams getting to the actual final. In contrast, the team which wins the First Division Championship has really earned it, I can assure you."

Alf Clarke, the chief football writer for the *Manchester Evening Chronicle* at that time, commented that, although he had been watching football for many years, he had never seen such a tribute as that which had been accorded to Johnny Carey by the supporters when he scored United's second goal. They rose to the United captain who later told Mr. Clarke that he would always remember their gesture. Remember, he certainly did, and the crowd's gesture of affection for this genuine world-class player visibly affected him. As a result of United's league win, 'Gentleman' Johnny Carey now had the distinction of becoming the first non-UK player to captain both an FA Cup-winning team as well as the first division champions from the same club, albeit in separate years.

David Meek reminds us in his fascinating book titled 'United Legends': "Like Busby he had an aura of dignity that marked him out as someone special. His contribution to the 1952 championship prompted a glowing tribute from the *Manchester Guardian* who accorded him and Busby the rare honour of a glowing mention in their esteemed leader column".

That article read: 'After an interval of 41 years, Manchester United had regained the championship of the Football League. The title has never been better earned. Not only has the team, in the five years before this one, finished second four times and fourth once in the League and won the FA Cup, it has been captained, managed and directed in a way that is a lesson to many others. J. Carey, the captain in this period, has been a model footballer - technically efficient thanks to hard work, a fighter to the last, without ever forgetting that he is a sportsman, a steadier of the younger and of the inexperienced, an inspirer of the older and tiring, and at all times the most modest of men, although he has won every honour open to him.

'Matt Busby, the manager, has shown himself as great a coach as he was a player, with an uncannily brilliant eye for young local players' possibilities, whether in their usual or other positions, a believer in the certainty of good football's eventual reward, and a kindly, yet when necessary, firm father of his family of players.

'Between them they have built up a club spirit which is too rare in these days, a spirit which enables men to bear cheerfully both personal and team disappointments and to ignore personal opportunities to shine for the good of the whole team.

'Moreover, by eschewing the dangerous policy of going into the transfer market whenever a weakness develops, and giving their chances instead to many local citizens on the club's books, they have made it likely that this club will persist, since the club today is a Manchester one, not only in name, but in fact as far as most of its players are concerned.

'Manager and captain could never have brought about this happy state of affairs had they not had through these years such full authority and support from the board of directors as must be the envy of many other officials in all parts of the country'. It was a very *Guardian*-esque tribute but nonetheless well deserved, and United themselves knew that they had been given exceptional service by their model player.

Geoffrey Green, who was also a highly respected writer for the *Times*, paid tribute to Carey as follows: "No man in the United side at this period was more deserving of praise than the captain Johnny Carey, a model captain and among the most complete and versatile footballers in history.

"At first glance, with his thinning hair and thoughtful expression, he looked older than his true age. But there was no doubting his maturity. From the moment he led out his side, you got the impression that he was bringing out a pack of schoolboys who were to be put through their paces under his supervision. Not that he was overbearing, on the contrary. Yet there was something in his measured, stately tread that engendered an instant feeling of respect and authority. Carey, the most generous of men and of opponents, earned his plaudits to the end".

The United regular line-up at the end of the season was: Allen; McNulty, Aston; Carey, Chilton, Cockburn; Berry, Downie, Rowley, Pearson and Byrne. Although United were now league champions at last, they had been knocked out of the FA Cup by a scoreline of 0-2 in the 3rd round by Hull City. Carey had played 38 league games, 42 games in total in all competitions, during the campaign. A total of six players (Carey, Chilton, Rowley, Pearson, Crompton and Cockburn) who had now won championship medals, had also won FA Cup medals in 1948. Four of them, including Carey, were signed before the war and were still keeping their place in the team on merit. However, they realized that their days were numbered with the hugely promising Busby Babes on the horizon.

Carey was also given the chance to play in goal after Jack Crompton had been carried off concussed at Chelsea in December. He had actually done that before: "I had played in ten different positions for Manchester United and the only position which I was not selected in was outside-left. I played in goal because Jack Crompton had a very bad bout of flu which only became apparent after we had reached Durham on our journey to Sunderland. So I played the whole game in goal. We couldn't get a replacement because the kick-off was at 2 o'clock. The doctor didn't see Jack until about ten o'clock so that left only four hours to send to Old Trafford (for a replacement). So Matt looked at me and said 'You'll have to play in goal'!

"We drew 2-2, which wasn't at all bad, and I was very pleased with myself. I couldn't do anything about the first goal which was an own goal by Allen Chilton - a real rocket header into the bottom corner of the net, miles away from me. I admit that I was responsible for their second goal which was over a crowd of players. So there I was, very pleased with myself, until coach Tom Curry brought me down to earth. His words to me after he entered the dressing-room at full-time were 'If it had been a load of hay going through the goal you wouldn't have got two handfuls of it!'"

Carey's Farewell to United

In June 1953, a transition in players was quickly happening at Old Trafford with so many impressive incoming young players soon to be labelled the Busby Babes. At the end of the season, the fans could look back at a campaign which on the surface looked disappointing due to a 5th round FA Cup exit to Everton with a scoreline of 0-2, in addition to an 8th final position in the championship. However, a team which was now in transition could look back on impressive debuts for future Busby Babes stars such as David Pegg, Johnny Doherty, Eddie Lewis and Billy Foulkes (in November and December), together with Dennis

Viollet, new star-signing Tommy Taylor, and the outstanding Duncan Edwards (in March and April). As a result, the foundations of an even more exciting team were now being steadily built.

Carey had been asked to go and watch Taylor playing for Barnsley, and he later recalled: "I was very pleased when Matt signed Tommy. He had previously asked me to watch the Barnsley versus Leicester game at Filbert Street to keep an eye on the young centre-forward called Taylor. I reported back to Matt and told him I was very impressed, and I felt he would be a good goalscorer for Manchester United. Matt turned around to me and said that I was the ninth person to recommend him. My prediction was right of course as Tommy would go on to score a hugely impressive 131 goals in 191 games for the club, as well as 14 goals in 19 appearances for England, before his untimely death in the Munich Air Crash in 1958".

When Taylor arrived off the train in Manchester to sign for United, he was met by the genial Carey and Busby together with a posse of press photographers. Interestingly, Carey quickly noticed that the very humble Taylor was carrying a brown paper bag under his arm containing his football boots which the captain quickly grabbed out of view of the pressmen.

Manchester United's supporters were now preparing for Carey's sad departure because of an article by the *Manchester Evening News* correspondent, Tom Jackson, at the end of the season which stated: "There is an odds-on chance that this will be Johnny Carey's last season as a player. Within the next few days, the Manchester United captain, who has achieved every honour in football since he started his career as a junior at Old Trafford in 1937, is due to decide whether or not he will re-sign for next season. Carey, the most popular captain in United's history, has of course been offered terms for 1953-54 but he told me today 'My future as a player hangs in the balance. I am not getting any younger and I don't intend to become a has-been in the game which has been my life'. United, anticipating that he might not be available as a player next season, have already offered him a job on their coaching staff knowing that the considerable qualities which had made him such a great player as well as his considerable influence were suited for management. It is also known that several foreign clubs would value his services as a coach".

The news was no easier to bear when Johnny Carey made his decision that he was ending his career as a player in May. He was now retiring after seventeen seasons with United because "I do not feel capable of playing the United brand of soccer for another season".

On May 23rd, 1953, the *Manchester Evening News* duly made the following announcement: "Johnny Carey, Manchester United and Eire captain, and one of the greatest footballers of all time, today announced his retirement as a player. The United captain, who has been one of the most versatile footballers in the game, said: 'My 17 seasons at Old Trafford have been very happy ones, and my thanks are due to the directors, manager, secretary, players, trainers and other staff for their help. The encouragement I got from my supporters and the Press has enabled me to get the most out of my ability. To them also my warmest thanks'".

In Stephen Kelly's fascinating book, 'Back Page United', he relates a tribute from the esteemed journalist, Tom Jackson, as follows: "So Johnny Carey, the man who has always lived up to the title of 'Soccer's first gentleman', has played his last game for United. Soccer will be indeed all the poorer without this modest, almost self-effacing Irishman who has proved such a wonderful inspiration to the team he has captained throughout all their great post-war years".

Carey's last game for United was on April 25th at Middlesbrough, and he had now played a total of 32 league games, 38 in all competitions, during that season. In total, despite a gap due to the war, Carey had played 306 league games for his beloved United, 344 in all competitions, and had scored 18 goals. Carey's last international game for the Republic of Ireland was appropriately in Dalymount Park, Dublin, in a 4-0 win against Austria on March 2nd, 1953. It had been fifteen years since his debut, also at the same venue, against Norway. Despite a six-year gap due to the war, he had played a total of 29 games for his beloved country, many of them as captain, scoring three goals in the process, and had appeared in seven different positions.

There was soon much speculation about what he would do next. However, just before the new season began, Second Division Blackburn Rovers made an announcement that they had appointed him as their manager.

David Meek further reminds us in his book, 'Legends of United', that "Matt Busby parted company with Carey somewhat reluctantly but told him that he had all the necessary qualifications to become a full manager and urged him to try his luck". He would go on to lead Blackburn to third place in the table at the end of his first season. Typically, he had absorbed himself fully into his new job at Blackburn although he also maintained his close connections with Manchester United simultaneously. His retirement was another one in the breaking up of the great 1948 team and he had been the first of the group to make his debut way back in 1937.

On Carey's retirement in the summer of 1953, the United directors took the unprecedented step of inviting him into the boardroom to convey their appreciation for his great service to the club. The minute which recorded the tribute said it all about his contribution to Manchester United: "The Directors expressed their deepest regret at his decision to end his playing career and unanimously agreed to put on record their great appreciation of his long and loyal service. By his outstanding personality as a true sportsman, the honours he had won as an international and in club matches, he has covered his career

Hard at training! Carey (centre) with Aston, Cockburn, Rowley and Crompton.

with glory and set a shining example to all who follow him".

In his book titled 'Father of Football - the Story of Sir Matt Busby', the author David Millar gives us further proof of the high esteem with which Carey was held by Busby when he relates that, "although it was only three years since he had his last benefit, nevertheless Busby decided that he was entitled to three-fifths of a second one".

In later years while looking back at his retirement, Carey recalled: "At the time when I retired I knew deep down I could have played for another two or three years. I was thirty-four when I finished playing but I was very fit and Matt would have liked me to continue at Old Trafford. But I looked at the tremendous career I had, and the six years that the war had taken a lot away from it, but from 1946-53 I'd had seven years at the top and I'd set a standard and I felt that the only way I am now going is down.

"I also felt that it wasn't fair for all the people who looked up to me and wanted to tell everybody what a good player I was. I didn't think that I was going to enjoy playing Second or Third Division football. I looked at United and thought 'There is no way I can keep my place in this team, except maybe on reputation, and I didn't want to keep it on that basis'.

"In 1953 United were so well equipped that you could see the club bounding with talent. Duncan Edwards, Roger Byrne, Dennis Viollet, David Pegg, Liam Whelan and Jeff Whitefoot were all there by then. The whole club was all geared up. Unfortunately there wasn't a position for me at the club. Jimmy Murphy was there doing a tremendous job and Walter Crickmer and Les Olive were there on the administration side".

"What Matt wanted was for me to stay as a player and do a bit of coaching with the youngsters, and to gradually work my way into that side of the club's activities – but, rightly or wrongly, I decided that I would try my luck and see if I could make my name as a manager, and, as it happened, I went to Blackburn Rovers where I had six tremendously happy and successful years".

Geoffrey Green further adds: "Thus, after eighteen seasons, the knot was cut, and his going had about it the departure of some honoured Roman senator from the Forum. Busby himself also felt the break deeply. Both religious men of the same faith and of similar outlook on loyalty, service and integrity, they were more like brothers than manager and player. They shared, too, the same feel for football, seeing in it 'a game hurting with conflict, yet passionate and beautiful in its art'."

About thirty years later, as the charismatic pipe-smoking Irishman looked back on the great 1948 team, he said: "I used to enjoy watching our attack because I was standing at the back and could see all that they were doing. The forward line was tremendous and they could all really play. Opposing defenders realized that they didn't have to mark just one or two of our forwards - all United's forwards needed watching. Sometimes it would be Charlie Mitten who'd get three goals, sometimes it'd be Jack Rowley or Johnny Morris or Stan Pearson, and, while Jimmy Delaney didn't perhaps score as many as the others, he instead made lots - they were all pretty formidable.

"As players we weren't perhaps as showbiz as players are today. We were just professional footballers in a very successful team. Our wages were modest and fixed, with a minimum and maximum amount. However outstanding you were you got the same as every other player in your team in those years. We enjoyed our football tremendously, more so than now. I don't think today's players get the same enjoyment from playing. They have so much more pressure on them. But, make no mistake, they are ten times more fitter and better organized.

"The crowds were marvellous and tolerant and they were also there to enjoy themselves. There was always pressure in our day, of course, but we were playing for the team and not so much for the money. Football in our day was more entertaining, possibly because we made more mistakes. There were more goals for the simple reason that goalkeepers weren't as good as they are today. And Matt Busby always encouraged flair. Sometimes it went wrong and he was always watching in case it did go wrong, but he always gave you authority to express yourself on the field. If I had to make comparisons between all the post-war sides at Old Trafford, I'd have to say that I don't think that the 1948 side was nearly as good as the 'Babes'. When the 1948 side played, having regard to the conditions and facilities of the time, we were outstanding and everything which we achieved reflected that, but we couldn't have lived with the Babes. We had six or seven really good players but the Babes had eleven and many more besides. They had power, strength, ability, skill, not just in certain places, but everywhere".

When looking back at his illustrious playing career under the legendary Busby, Carey commented: "This experience was invaluable to me. It gave me my playing philosophy, which is to play attractive football devised to win matches. We've got to remember that we are public entertainers". He then went to Blackburn with the best wishes of all at United.

Carey the Manager

When Carey started his management career at Second Division Blackburn Rovers in 1953, the Ewood Park club now anticipated that he would bring to the hot seat the same shrewd and thoughtful skills that he had used as a player. He soon started to achieve some relative success and brought the club into the First Division at the first time of asking. Within three years, he also took over an additional role as the manager of the Republic of Ireland team from another former fellow Irish international, Alex Stevenson. His first game in that position was against Spain on November 23rd, 1955. Unusually, many years later, inside-left Arthur Fitzsimons would recall that, in the week before the game, he received an introductory letter from Carey. The manager had actually posted the same letter to all the players who had been chosen by the 'Big Five' (the team selection committee). It contained the letterhead of his new club, Blackburn Rovers. Innovatively in those days, Carey had also outlined his team tactics in that same letter which preached a philosophy of a type of total football which he described in his own words as 'all up, all back'. Typical of his often-quoted general tactics to "fizz it about", it instructed that "we must try to play quick accurate football, with the ball kept on the ground". He went on to elaborate: "Try to keep the ball moving, by every player moving into open spaces", obviously reminding his players of the oft-used adage that 'the ball travels quicker than the man'.

Typically in those distant days, the Irish team played all their home-based weekend games on Sundays. Their players, who unfortunately all played for their Football League teams the previous day in England, would then promptly head for the overnight boat from Liverpool as soon as possible, arriving somewhat sleepy-eyed in Dublin on the morning of the game. For this reason, by way of explanation, Carey's letter went on to state: "It is unfortunate that we cannot get together for a few days prior to this important match, so that we could pool our ideas, and get some teamwork into our play. We shall, however, have a pre-match talk at the Gresham Hotel (in Dublin) on the morning before the game".

Probably Ireland's greatest performance under Carey's management was in a World Cup qualifying game against England in Dublin on May 19th, 1957. These two arch-rivals were two of only three countries in the group, with one team due to qualify for the 1958 finals in Sweden. Ireland had already been convincingly beaten in the first leg at Wembley by a 1–5 scoreline.

Disappointingly, however, in the 88th minute of the second leg at Dalymount Park, they were deprived of a victory which would have resulted in a play-off, the equalizing goal being scored by Atyeo. This star-studded England team contained four Busby Babes – Roger Byrne, Tommy Taylor, David Pegg (on his debut), as well as Duncan Edwards – in direct opposition to club-mate Liam Whelan. Amusingly, the somewhat introverted Whelan decided during the game to nutmeg Edwards on two separate occasions in front of his home supporters. Sadly, all five United stars would lose their lives nine months later in the Munich Air Crash.

At that time, Matt Busby's son, Sandy, was a reserve player under Carey's wing at Ewood Park. Some time previously Busby had decided that, rather than risk accusations of nepotism from United fans, it would be prudent to transfer his son away from Old Trafford. As a result, he felt that Sandy's best chances of developing his career would alternatively be better served under Carey, his former captain now managing at Ewood Park.

On February 7th, 1958, shortly after Carey heard about the Munich crash, he quickly headed for his former manager's home. In the words of Sandy Busby: "Me mam was in a state of shock. She was just sitting on the sofa upstairs and no-one could get any sense out of her. All of a sudden, 'Uncle' Johnny came running up the stairs screaming 'He's alive, he's alive'. As soon as me mam heard me dad was alive she was right". Carey said: "After the crash I went to see them and I kept in touch with Jimmy Murphy and we discussed one or two things, but really there wasn't very much I could do, much as I wanted to help".

Carey's impressive early achievements at Blackburn soon attracted the interest of one of the more glamorous First Division clubs, Everton, in 1958. In the manager's own words at the time: "I've accepted the post of manager at Everton because it's a challenge I feel must be met. If I hadn't taken it, it's likely all the rest of my life I'd have wondered just how I would have gone on and how I'd have tackled the job of raising the team to its one-time greatness". Unfortunately, he found out the hard way a few years later when he was the cruel victim of a shocking dismissal by the club chairman, John Moores. Interestingly, however, the team which he built was to win the championship a mere two years later.

On Carey's arrival at Goodison, the team had been close to the basement of the First Division. In his first two seasons he had resurrected them to sixteenth, and then a remarkable fifth in the table - their highest position since the war. In addition, he had brought some fine players to Goodison, including Alex Young and Jimmy Gabriel. However, despite being in an impressive second position in the league shortly afterwards, the team suddenly had a bad run in his third season when they suffered eight defeats in a row. Soon Chairman Moores started to make an approach to the ex-Everton player, Harry Catterick, who at the time was impressing as manager at Sheffield Wednesday.

Having attended a meeting at London's Cafe Royal, both Carey and Moores were travelling together in a taxi back to their nearby hotel when the manager was suddenly informed of his sacking by the chairman, despite having over two years still to go in his contract. Generally known as the 'Quiet Man of Football', Carey philosophically said: "I had been at Everton before Mr. Moores arrived, and he wanted a manager appointed by himself. I think he wanted a tough manager, someone to crack the whip. I'm afraid that's not for me".

The revolting manner of his sudden sacking would however shock not only Carey himself, for obvious reasons, but also his former mentor Matt Busby, who was disgusted by the action. The following day, Carey sat in the directors' box at Goodison Park while Everton beat Cardiff City 5-1. The cheers from the crowd on his appearance told Moores what the fans thought. "I know in my own mind that I was never a failure," Carey responded.

A few days later he quietly attended a league game at Deepdale between Preston North End and his old club, Manchester United. It was his first "layman's" view of a football match since he started to play the game when he was 17, back in his native Dublin. As he settled down on his seat and lit his pipe, he joked: "I haven't decided yet which is the biggest headache - being a manager, or not being a manager".

For the moment he was just one of the masses... or so he thought. Shortly afterwards, the crowd spotted him. Then came the handshakes, warm smiles and a steady procession of autograph hunters. He said: "I will try not to get tensed up, but just enjoy myself. I'm afraid it's hard to switch off a habit of years and to relax completely to enjoy the play as a spectator". However, the game had no sooner started than he was sucking nervously on his pipe, his eyes on every move, his cool football brain analyzing every player - old habits die hard.

In his recent autobiography entitled 'John Giles - A Football Man', the author, and ex-United winger, describes meeting Carey for the first time prior to his own international debut as a starry-eyed 19-year old in 1959: "Jackie Carey, the manager, gave us the team talk. This in itself was an awe-inspiring moment for me, because Carey was an idol to me - captain of the United team which won the FA Cup in 1948, and the league in 1952, captain of the Rest of Europe against Great Britain in 1947, and Footballer of the Year in 1949. Jackie Carey was 'The Man'. His instruction was to 'fizz it about' - basically sound advice aimed at getting a bit of urgency into the game. It was just about all any manager could do in the circumstances, addressing a bunch of players, some of whom had never met one another before, coming together only on the morning of the match. His aura was enough to inspire me and no doubt the other lads felt the same".

Giles and his teammates were about to face a Swedish team which, as the host country, had been runners-up to Pele's Brazil in the 1958 World Cup finals only the previous year. Giles continues: "In fact all day I had to stifle the urge to address men like Noel Cantwell (future United captain) and Carey as Mister! Cantwell did everything right, coming to each of us with a few words of encouragement. 'Settle down'... 'Enjoy it'... 'Get on the ball'. It wasn't the words he said that mattered, it was the fact that Noel Cantwell was talking to me. That was enough". Remarkably, Ireland went on to beat their esteemed opponents in that game by a scoreline of 3-2 with Giles among the scorers in a notable debut.

Not surprisingly, a short time after his sacking at Everton in 1961, Carey was again working, have been appointed manager of Second Division minnows, Leyton Orient, while still managing the Republic of Ireland. Not long later he was affectionately nicknamed 'The Quiet man of the Orient'.

Impressively, in his first season at his new club, he led them to promotion to the First Division in second place, behind a quickly emerging Liverpool under the legendary Bill Shankly. "We want Carey; we want Carey" was the chorus echoing around Brisbane Road on the afternoon of the last game of that season. It was one of football's greatest fairy tales. Only a year after Orient narrowly escaped relegation to Division Three, he had now ingeniously steered them on a shoestring budget into the glamour of the First Division, thus becoming their idol. He had taken them off the floor into the same division as the glamour teams, all of whom they would have memorable exchanges with in the following season. Unfortunately, however, they were soon relegated the next season after a dismal run.

In 1963 he took up a position as manager of Nottingham Forest, then in the First Division, at a salary of £3,000 a year, with Dave Sexton as his assistant manager and Tommy Cavanagh to crack the whip as his coach. Coincidentally, almost ten years later, 'Cav' would arrive at Old Trafford as a coach with Sexton's predecessor, Tommy Docherty.

Elsewhere in his autobiography, Giles talks about the absurdity of the Irish selection committee, known as 'The Big Five', who astonishingly, with no soccer expertise whatsoever, picked the Irish team. In Giles' own words: "Though it now seems completely mad, for a long time, the Big Five was accepted as normal. Looking back, I feel that Jackie Carey had the stature and respect from his great playing career to try to change the system. He would have known how wrong it was when he didn't pick the team, but he had to make the most of whoever was selected, leaving him at times in the Gresham Hotel in Dublin on a Sunday morning, talking to players, some of whom he had never met before, hoping they might be able to 'fizz it about'.

"Eventually, it seemed that Johnny had become disillusioned with the Ireland job. His managerial career in the real world had gone into decline after a promising start at Blackburn. So the FAI had ground him down until there wasn't much leadership coming from Johnny, and I quickly realized that there was no belief or confidence in the squad".

Giles then goes on to emphasize the absurdity of the amount of authority which the Big Five had by looking at the World Cup qualifier against Spain in 1965. Remarkably, this Irish team contained a core of four championship-winning Manchester United players in goalkeeper Pat Dunne, full-backs Shay Brennan and Tony Dunne, together with captain Noel Cantwell, filling in efficiently at centre-forward. In addition, the team included world class players Giles up front and Sunderland's Charlie Hurley at centre-half.

Carey's team astonishingly beat a highly-rated Spanish XI in Dublin in the first leg 1-0, thanks to a Cantwell header. But an injury-hit Ireland succumbed to a 1-4 defeat in the second leg and now faced a play-off at a neutral venue to decide who would qualify for the finals in England in 1966.

However, the subsequent story doing the rounds at the time was that, rather than use a toss of a coin, or have a lottery, to decide the venue for the play-off, the Big Five soon relented and settled for Spain's preference of Paris... shortly after they had been presented with a few crates of very expensive Spanish wine! As a result of their subsequent narrow 1-2 defeat, one can therefore only speculate in hindsight how Carey's star-studded team would have alternatively fared while playing on familiar territory in England during the World Cup finals had they qualified.

Soon afterwards Carey decided to relinquish the international job with the inevitable words "I just have not the time these days to fulfil these international duties, as well as looking after the club". Carey had found the clash of loyalties between his club, Nottingham Forest, which was enjoying a highly successful season, and his country too exacting.

Those five years at Forest were surely Carey's most successful in football management, taking the team to the First Division runners-up position in 1966-67, just behind Manchester United, as well as reaching the FA Cup semi-final. It was a double triumph for the famous Busby/Carey combination. Unfortunately, in 1968, after a run of poor results, he was asked to resign. One of the main reasons for his dismissal was surely his inability to make effective use of the legendary, but notoriously disruptive Scottish international left halfback, Jim Baxter, whom he had signed in 1967 for the princely sum of £100,000. Typical of the Irishman, he left Forest with the best wishes of all at the club, and with his reputation intact.

When subsequently reflecting on the pricey purchase, Carey reflected: "Transfer deals are one of the worst perils facing a football manager". Shortly afterwards, in 1969, he found himself back again at Blackburn Rovers after a sixteen year gap, this time as administrative manager. Soon afterwards, when the team started to struggle, he changed roles with the manager, Eddie Quigley, for a short while before his early retirement from management in his beloved game. His only reaction to his last sacking was: "It's nothing to worry about. I regard it as all part and parcel of the game. If your club gets relegated you expect to get the sack, so this decision did not altogether take me by surprise. I can't really complain, for the club have honoured my contract, although I do feel that time was my enemy. I took over as team manager in October after being administrative manager and did not have a lot of breathing space".

In the mid-sixties he reflected on his managerial career in the following words which could also have been attributed to his benevolent mentor Busby: "Apart from the worries of looking after the team on the field, the manager has many problems to face. Footballers are human. They have private lives and private worries the same as everyone else. Often these worries affect their play. It is the manager's job to do all he can to share his players' troubles and, if possible, to find a remedy for them. The fact that players get more money now makes the manager's job harder rather than easier". These words go to emphasize the calibre of the man that was the genial Johnny Carey.

In the summer of 1971 he decided to end his relatively new career as a manager after sixteen years. Despite a lack of real success as a football manager, his dignified image remained intact. David Meek goes on to tell us: "He went with head held high, too. He had never compromised his principles, or his philosophy, concerning the way the game should be played". Geoffrey Green recalls: "On a few occasions in the early seventies, Carey, who was a very popular figure in British football and on the continent, had been one of the favourites to take over as United manager, in addition to Don Revie, Jock Stein, Ron Greenwood and Jimmy Adamson. Sadly for United fans, due to unknown reasons, there would be no return to his beloved Old Trafford for 'Gentleman' Johnny Carey, and the Reds were soon relegated to Division Two."

It might appear, considering his relative success as a manager, that Carey sometimes got a rough deal. He was, however, never a manager in the style of Revie, Docherty or Clough. He was in a sense a 'front man' - the genial father in the Busby mould who presented the right image for a club, possibly relying more on respect than on ability.

Carey's career as a manager was somewhat shorter and far less successful than that of Busby, both of whom could in many ways be said to have been 'cut from the same cloth'. In addition to being highly respected in soccer circles for several decades, they both possessed a deep knowledge of the game and always had a great influence on players under their command. Also, just like Carey himself, Busby was never given to fiery team talks such as the 'hairdryer treatment' in the dressing room, and he held his after-match post mortems only on the Monday after the game on the training pitch where no swear words or profanities were allowed. In addition, according to a few of his long-serving players in the sixties, the charismatic Busby lost his temper only on a few occasions after his team's defeat. His dressing-room team talks were calm, collected and analytical, in the manner of his original team captain, Carey.

However, probably the one marked difference between both managers was that the Scotsman could invariably rely on the oratorial skills of the passionate Jimmy Murphy in the dressing room to quickly add the 'fire and brimstone' to his own initial team talk, after he himself had left the room. Busby could invariably rely on the fiery Welshman to provide the proverbial 'iron fist in the kid glove' of their hugely successful partnership, when required. In the absence of a fiery streak in Johnny Carey himself, we can, in hindsight, only speculate how much more successful he would have been if he also had a Murphy-like character as his assistant to crack the whip for him when required.

After retirement he decided to work for a local textiles company and later took up a rather modest job as a civil servant with the Sale Borough Treasurers' office near Manchester, where he remained until his death at the age of 76 in 1995.

In the mid-seventies, Tommy Docherty brought him back to the game as a part-time scout when he became manager of United, but golf had become his main occupation by then and he had now become an enthusiastic and competent player. Carey remarked at the time: "Saturdays are devoted to golf now, but I still think that football is a terrific game. I perhaps wish that players would accept defeat with a little more grace and I would like to see the players allowed to express themselves more, but at the end of the day, football is super, the best game in the world". Interestingly, at one stage of his retirement, his wife commented: "Sadly, he hasn't been to a game since he finished playing". He replied: "Since I left management I haven't been there (Old Trafford) all that much. There was always this standing invitation but one didn't want to impose" – a typical reaction from the somewhat reserved and humble Irishman.

Looking back then over Carey's vastly impressive career in football, one can generally only admire and wonder at his tremendous personal achievements in 'the foreign game' of soccer which he took up by chance, so relatively late in life. Despite this huge initial handicap, he not only made the grade extremely quickly at Old Trafford but also, despite losing seven years to the war at the peak of his career, he still had another seven years as a hugely influential captain of a very successful United. Even more notable, however, he was also generally regarded by the experts as one of the greatest players, and most highly respected people, in British football with the well deserved nickname of 'Gentleman' Johnny Carey.

Carey Tributes

In view of his considerable status in the game both as a Manchester United captain and as a manager, there have been many tributes paid to Johnny Carey, both during and after his playing days. However, although his manager Matt Busby can be considered to be a bit biased, there can be very few, if any, people who knew him so well and so intimately. Four years after Carey's retirement Busby wrote his autobiography titled 'My Story' in which he included the following tribute:"Having spotlighted most of the personalities in the 1948 Manchester United team, I have deliberately left until last the greatest of them all, that prince among contemporary footballers, United's captain and right-back, captain of Eire and the Rest of the World against Great Britain, Johnny Carey.

"He achieved the sort of success (after 17 years at Old Trafford) which entitled him to be remembered as one of the finest footballers ever to wear a Manchester United shirt. People who know me will vouch for the fact that I never indulge in idle adulation, but I am certain that Johnny Carey was one of the truly great players of all times.

"I first met him in Belfast, at Windsor Park. Johnny was playing for Ireland; I was in the British Army Team. He played centre-forward - I was directly opposing him at centre-half. That first meeting convinced me that Carey was something more than just a great footballer. His every action suggested that he was a thinker, a student of the game prepared to go to any lengths to achieve his goal - soccer perfection.

"When I became manager of Manchester United, one of my first jobs was to appoint Carey as club captain. As soon as I had settled in, and really knew my players, it was obvious that only one man could be skipper: that man was Johnny. I think it was proved in later years that the decision to give the captaincy to Carey was one of the wisest moves I made during my early years at Old Trafford.

"It is difficult to do honour to a soccer genius through the medium of the written word, because ability such as Carey possessed has to be seen to be appreciated to the full, it must unavoidably lose some of its lustre when related after the moments of greatness have passed. That is why I believe the most satisfactory method of paying tribute to the brilliance of Johnny Carey's football is to describe a single incident which emphasizes so perfectly his command of the game, his artistry, his genius. The occasion was a Coronation Cup game between Glasgow Rangers and Manchester United, the incident a precision pass over right-back Carey's head to the Rangers' outside-left.

"It was the sort of ball to get a full-back into trouble - just a little too high for a headed interception and perfectly placed for the winger to break away towards goal with the defender caught on the wrong foot. Carey looked beaten, but, swinging around until he had his back to the man who had passed the ball, Johnny caught it on his instep, juggled it on his foot for a couple of seconds, flipped it over his head, turned around and placed a perfect pass to one of his United colleagues. The crowd - and about 98 % of them were Rangers enthusiasts - stood and cheered their spontaneous approval. They could not help themselves, because they had seen for an instant a spark of genius - they had seen Johnny Carey.

"I mentioned that Carey was a thinker, and at times he seemed so completely engrossed in this football business it caused some to imagine that he was aloof, yet beneath the quiet exterior lays a sense of humour as sharp as it is unexpected. It is sometimes stated that a really great footballer can play in any position, and Johnny Carey provided evidence to support that theory. For United he turned out in ten different positions - for some reason or other never getting around to playing at outside-left. A real Johnny-of-all-trades… and master of the lot! What a pity there are not more of his type in soccer today."

In the late sixties the chief soccer writer of the *Irish Press* described him as follows: "He always was what the sports writers call an unruffled player. He never lost his temper, never aimed to flatten an opponent, never blustered with the referee".

Geoffrey Green recalls in his book 'There's Only One United': "Here indeed was a man who had been one of the outstanding footballers of his times, an architect of the constructive defence and almost as great in his way as Stanley Matthews, the destroyer of defences. At first glance, with his thinning hair and thoughtful expression, he looked older than his true age. But Carey never encouraged any exploitation of his personality. For him the game was one thing; personal triumphs at best were an irrelevancy. And in defining his art there is some temptation to use only negatives. He was not audacious (though he did possess an audacity of thought). He was not a showman, nor magnetic in an obvious, vulgar sense. Yet there was nothing negative about his craftsmanship. If he rightly won his place among the greats as a full-back, he must rank as the finest all-round player who ever took the field. After all, ten different positions in the immaculate United side, and seven for Ireland, was a fair enough recommendation of anyone's ability".

Green further reminds us: "Many memories remain of Carey, the artist. His exact anticipation; the smooth, unhurried positional play that carried him to the right place at the right moment with no more show than if he were taking a quiet stroll on a summer's evening; his exquisite balance; the way he measured his clearances, with the ball always used to the best advantage of the colleague in front of him. And if sometimes he broke the accepted canons of a fullback by beating his opponent in the dribble near the danger zone, well never mind, it was something that could be excused in him, because he was above the lesser mortals. For, in effect, he was a fullback who combined the constructive ability of wing-half with the footwork and intelligence of an inside-forward, and as such he mastered the arts and graces of the game".

Eric Thornton, in his book titled 'Manchester United - Barson to Busby', states: "Johnny Carey, the play-anywhere star, the brilliant scoring forward who became the master defender and the perfect reader of the game in a memorable career, was one of the kingpins in Busby's early building plans. The Irishman was one of a flush of aces in Matt's manipulative hand, always a great favourite with the Old Trafford crowds, and has plenty to look back on with pride".

In his highly recommended book entitled 'The Insiders Guide to Manchester United', the ex-Busby Babe John Doherty described Carey as "something of a genius who could play brilliantly wherever the manager wanted to put him, and his stature in the game was demonstrated by his selection to captain the Rest of the World against Great Britain shortly after the war. John was blessed with superb touch with both feet. He was magnificent in the air and he could chest the ball with total assurance. Against that, amazingly enough, he had no pace at all, yet no matter where he turned out, speed was never an issue, his pure ability and shrewdness getting him through every time. Indeed, the older he got, the cleverer he showed himself to be, always endeavouring to remain goalside of the ball so that he wouldn't be exposed.

"In the Coronation Cup in 1953 (the year of his retirement) he played at centre-half, and there were plenty of neutral observers who reckoned that he proved himself to be the best centre-half in Britain. This situation illustrated graphically that having Carey in the United side was like having an extra half a dozen players on the staff. He was known as 'Gentleman John' but, in some ways, that was a load of rubbish. He pulled more shirts and took more people by putting his foot in than anybody, but he was discreet about it! I remember him once saying to me 'Son, you don't jump up to head a ball face on. You jump up sideways and you protect yourself with your elbow'. Of course he was not doing it to hurt people, merely to look after himself. John was a genuinely nice man, a quiet character who smoked his pipe and saw football as his job, going to work at Old Trafford as routinely as other men might go to their office. He was a wise old sage too. After my senior debut against Middlesbrough, I was in a hurry to get away when a United fan asked me to sign a programme. I said: 'Can't stop, got a bus to catch'. On the subsequent Monday, Carey drew me to one side at training and said that he had seen me refuse to sign. I mentioned my bus but he replied 'Son, there'll come a time when nobody asks you for your autograph, so sign 'em all while you've got the chance'. That was sound advice. He knew that the supporters are the people who pay your wages, and that you should offer them courtesy - typical of the man known as 'Gentleman John'!

"I made my debut when Johnny was captain and I can't recollect him ever getting annoyed, not even if someone had kicked him. He seemed to stroll through games. If he were playing to-day he would be described as laid-back, then we just thought that he was unflappable. The big thing of course was that he was a great player and as captain his influence was immense. He was a thinker not a shouter".

In Wilf McGuinness' autobiography titled 'Man and Babe', he lauds the United captain whom he saw in action at the end of his distinguished career: "The right-back and captain was a softly-spoken Dubliner Johnny Carey, the cream of footballers. He was such a smooth operator who always seemed to have plenty of time and it seemed that no-one could get past him. Even if he was up against a flyer, he was able to get his body between his opponent and the ball, and he never looked like he was committing a foul, even if he was. Gentleman John, as he was called so aptly, exuded class. He never flapped no matter what the situation and he was a stylish, straight-backed, all-round performer".

Sir Stanley Matthews also had something to say about Carey in his autobiography, 'The Way it Was': "No mention of the forties could be complete without including the talents of Johnny Carey. He wasn't known for his pace, but he more than made up for it by an astute and intelligent use of the ball and uncanny sense of positioning. Johnny, who was balding in his twenties, always appeared to be older than his actual years. In a way, that was appropriate because even when young he used the ball with all the guile and cunning of the most experienced professional. He still had a few years left at the top when he decided to retire and the temptation to carry on must have been a strong one. But two considerations weighed heavily on his mind - a reluctance to carry on in the public eye for a day longer than he could guarantee a flawless performance, and a concern that to stay longer would deny similar privileges to the youngsters coming through the ranks at Old Trafford. By retiring with his reputation at, or near, its meridian, he escaped the jibes of those who take delight in chivvying flagging football warriors, however eminent. His leisurely gait when playing as a forward prompted teammate Henry Cockburn to say 'Johnny's pace deceives opponents. He's actually slower than he looks'!

"I played against Johnny many times. Although I had much the better of him when it came to speed, his astute sense of positioning which he used to force me wide and into a position where it was difficult to make a telling pass made him a tricky adversary. As a manager, he was not motivated by financial reward. His enjoyment remained the same as it had been as a player - simply the thrill and excitement of being involved in a game he loved".

In his highly recommendable book, 'Roger Byrne - Captain of the Busby Babes', Iain McCartney quotes Matt Busby regarding an interesting incident from a close-season tour of the US in 1952 that illustrates the big influence which Carey had on Byrne. United were facing Atlas Club of Mexico in Los Angeles: "Atlas were a tough, tough lot. Seeing how things were going, I told Johnny Carey to instruct the team to keep their heads, keep together and keep calm. This he did, but Roger defied him and was sent off. I was annoyed about this. I did not like Manchester United players being sent off, especially abroad where club and national reputations suffer more than any individual reputation. So I told Roger that he must apologize to Johnny Carey or I would send him home the next day. I would give him two hours to do it in. No more than fifteen minutes later Johnny Carey came to see me to say 'Roger has been to apologize'. Carey's eventual successor, and captain of the legendary Busby Babes, had learned a valuable lesson from not only his manager but also his great mentor".

In his autobiography 'Manchester and Beyond', the legendary United centre-half of the late fifties and sixties, Billy Foulkes, describes his original skipper and role model as follows: "Johnny Carey was one of the classiest operators, whether at right-back or right-half, it has ever been my privilege to see. When I played behind him for the first time, making my senior debut against Liverpool at Anfield in December 1952, he looked like an old guy: prematurely balding, a bit stooped, shorts too long for him, he didn't seem anything like the popular idea of a professional athlete. But he didn't take long to open my eyes, just strolling through the action, intercepting and prompting, always cool and always in control. He was superb in the air, just flicking balls unerringly to the feet of teammates, and I left the pitch thanking my lucky stars to have played alongside such a master. I learned so much from that guy in the course of just one game. I admit that I was worried after we conceded our goal, but Johnny told me to keep on doing the simple things well and we would prevail - and so it proved. Afterwards the captain came up to me and asked my age. I told him I was 20; he looked me in the eye and declared, in that soft Irish brogue of his: 'I think you'll do well'. That's all it was, nothing over the top to turn a young fellow's head, but it made me feel eight feet tall".

Jimmy Hill, the renowned BBC commentator, sang Carey's praises in 'Great Soccer Stars': "How well Carey would have fitted into the modern game, where inside-forwards came back and fullbacks pushed up! For Carey was both of those in his time, and every other position as well. He was among the best all-rounders football has known, or is ever likely to know".

In 'Legends of United', David Meek states: "The most influential player in those early days was undoubtedly Johnny Carey, arguably the last of the great Corinthians in professional football. 'Gentleman John' had an easy-going, pipe-smoking demeanour, and was always calm and collected, even in later life when he was a manager. He had an aura of dignity like Busby - a giant among giants, a legend, Busby's on-field lieutenant, the embodiment of his manager's philosophy. Johnny Morris grins: 'They called him Gentleman John, and that was appropriate provided he got the ball'! Carey lived with the Mitten family for a time initially after crossing the Irish Sea as a youngster, and Charlie himself remembers: 'He was a terrible inside-left in the A team when he started, colt-like, but he became a brilliant fullback. He was a good ball-player, as we all had to be'. Morris stresses that the captain knew how to enjoy himself: 'Travelling home from games he was always in charge of the sing-songs on the bus. He livened up plenty after a game'."

In another chapter from 'A Strange Kind of Glory', Eamon Dunphy describes his fellow Irishman as follows: "The man was cool, well-mannered and intelligent. He dressed impeccably, read the more serious newspapers, and trained hard. A devout Catholic - Carey didn't swear - Johnny was what people thought of as a model pro. He was a leader, similar in many ways to Busby who made him captain of the side. However, he was not too popular in the dressing-room because he was not 'one of the lads'. He was quiet and distant. When more exuberant spirits like Mitten, Cockburn or Aston started messing, Carey's manner would indicate disapproval. He had short arms and long pockets; he was careful with his money - a fault according to the dressing-room code.

"Busby knew the score. He wanted Carey's poise to be the hallmark of his team. Carey's character was a plus in his manager's book, a desirable counterpoint to the inevitable raucousness of dressing-room life. He became the leader Busby was looking for. Perhaps, more than any other player, Carey confirmed Busby's belief that the qualities of character and intelligence, sensitively nurtured in the right environment, were indispensable to a football club".

In his 1948 autobiography, "Football from the Goalmouth", the famous Manchester City goalkeeper, Frank Swift, who appeared for England against Ireland, wrote: "I must pay tribute to the Eire captain, Johnny Carey, who was the man of the match. Johnny nearly started the game at centre-forward when Welsh cried off shortly before the kickoff. He played the first half at right-half and finished up at left-back when Hayes was injured. He seemed to get better and better as the game went on". It is surely significant that "that lovable Irishman", as Swift refers to Carey, was chosen as the best player in that game which featured such esteemed English players as Lawton, Wright and Finney.

In Stan Liversedge's book 'Epitaph to a Legend', he asks the question: "And what of Johnny Carey, the genial Irishman who was born to be a leader - and those were the words of Busby himself. I remember meeting Carey many years later, when he was working in local government at Sale, and he didn't seem to have changed a bit. He still possessed that air of authority which characterized just about every move during his playing days. You could see what Busby meant".

Manchester-born Eddie Lewis, who was a very promising teenaged centre-forward at Old Trafford in the early fifties, also sang the praises of his soon-to-retire club captain, Carey, on several occasions. Coincidentally, in 1962 he also played briefly under him at Leyton Orient during their promotion year. In the opinion of the charismatic Eddie, his new boss's management style was more similar to a Dave Sexton-type character than a more extrovert Docherty or Ferguson. Prior to his recent untimely death in Johannesburg, Lewis recalled fond memories of Carey's oft-used exhortation to his players in the dressing-room before a game to 'fizz it about' in order to keep up the tempo of the match.

In addition to his well deserved personal awards received during his playing career, Carey was elected to the Caltex Hall of Fame in Dublin in 1964 - the most coveted honour open to Irishmen in the field of sports. United's chief scout of the forties, Louis Rocca, made the statement that "no greater Irish player crossed the Irish Sea to make a name in English football". It surely still firmly applies to 'Gentleman Johnny' Carey, the somewhat reserved, but determined, 17-year old who initially crossed the channel in 1937 on his way to Old Trafford with just a handful of top level matches in "the foreign game" of soccer under his belt.

Sadly, they don't make them like "Gentleman" Johnny Carey anymore in the beautiful game of football.

JOHNNY CAREY

Born: 23.2.19 in Dublin
MU debut: 25.9.37
Ireland: 29/3   Northern Ireland: 7/-

| Season | Club | LEAGUE | | FA CUP | |
		Apps	Goals	Apps	Goals
1937–38	MANCHESTER UNITED	16	3	3	1
1938–39	MANCHESTER UNITED	32	6	2	–
1939–40	MANCHESTER UNITED	2	1	–	–
1945–46	MANCHESTER UNITED	–	–	4	–
1946–47	MANCHESTER UNITED	31	2	–	–
1947–48	MANCHESTER UNITED	37	1	6	–
1948–49	MANCHESTER UNITED	41	1	8	–
1949–50	MANCHESTER UNITED	38	1	5	–
1950–51	MANCHESTER UNITED	39	–	4	–
1951–52	MANCHESTER UNITED	38	3	1	–
1952–53	MANCHESTER UNITED	32	1	5	–
TOTAL		306	17	40	1

The Gunner

"The specific reason we watch United is for those precise moments when the team scores. That is when we spontaneously explode in celebration of a goal. And Jack Rowley personally made United fans burst with joy over 360 times!"

JACK ROWLEY BY CHARBEL BOUJAOUDE

The Gunner

You cannot write a book about Manchester United legends and leave out the greatest goal-scorer of them all, name of Jack Rowley. He arrived at Old Trafford in 1937, soon started scoring, and did not stop thereafter. By the time he left, some eighteen years later, he had outscored any United player before him or after. Now the history books might not back this claim up – a look at the club's top strikers' list shows Bobby Charlton and Denis Law ahead of him – but there is a mighty good reason for that. Jack lost seven competitive seasons to World War II when more pressing matters meant that footballing feats were not deemed official. However, Jack used that opportunity to demonstrate what might have been had war not interrupted his career. He travelled the land in search of goals, plundering them much like the allied soldiers plundered their nazi foe. Jack in fact did both – he was an anti-tank gunner in the army – and his dual role earned him a suitable nickname on the football fields: the 'Gunner'. It had nothing to do with those fancy dans down in London and everything to do with striking fear into the hearts of opposition players. And if defenders feared him because he invariably embarrassed them, statisticians had their own reasons for hating him: they had to keep updating his scoring records every week or so!

So what was Rowley's secret? When you talk about a player who has rattled in more goals than Charlton, Law, Best, Van Nistelrooy and the likes, there has to be something special about him. And there was. First and foremost, he could shoot straight and he could shoot hard, and in this simple game of football, sometimes that is all you need. 'Hard' is a misleading description here, simply because it does not give full credit to the magnitude of power in his left foot. An erstwhile teammate from the forties, Johnny Morris, once said: "If you put a ball on the 18-yard line for Jack and he let fly, the keepers never saw it". They did not fare much better were he to shoot from thirty or even forty yards either. Long-range rockets were in his repertoire too, which was fine by the keepers because it meant he was not close by to barge them into the net along with the ball. Aggression was one of his favourite on-field pastimes for he was fearless, storming into aerial battles to head home with ferociousness to match that in his left boot.

Jack could play almost anywhere across the front line. Attacks consisted of five men at the time and, though he started his career on the left wing, he made his name later on at centre-forward as well at either inside-forward slots. Yet no matter where he was selected, he took to the pitch with the strongest desire to score. He played always to win; be it an international match, a cup final, or merely a friendly. That is how he became the highest goal-scorer in Manchester United's history.

Rowley Power

Jack was born in Wolverhampton as John Frederick Rowley. In retrospect, it is a good thing he opted to go by 'Jack', if only because the Manchester United FA Cup-winning XI in which he made his mark already boasted a couple of Johns and a couple of Johnnys. His date of birth was October 7th though there is some confusion over the exact year. Earlier publications tended to state 1920, but recent sources have preferred to go with 1918 instead. Though he is long gone now to clarify the matter, Jack – who should know best – did once mention that he was eighteen years old when he had a hernia operation in 1936, so this would identify 1918 as his most accurate year of birth.

Either way, there is a hint of divine interference with Jack's arrival on earth. When the Great War ended, it heralded peace in the world and two decades of mediocrity for Manchester United. They spent their time either rattling around the bottom of Division One or larging it in Division Two altogether. It was feasibly in view of this that the gods sanctioned the birth of Jack Rowley to save the club. Indeed, it would take until he grew up and joined United for them to return permanently to the top flight and eventually attain Cup and League glory.

Divinity apart, football was in Jack's genes, passed down to him and his brothers from his father. Rowley Sr. had a spell at Walsall and kept goal in the local leagues until an advanced age. You could imagine him keeping in shape by having his sons take shots at him, which in turn helped hone their shooting powers. This would explain why two of them became lethal marksmen in the Football League. Jack, of course, would achieve international acclaim with England and legendary status with Manchester United, but his younger brother Arthur did not do too badly either. In the colours of Fulham, Leicester, and Shrewsbury, Arthur carved a niche for himself as the highest ever scorer in Football League history, no less. His total is a staggering 434 league goals. It is doubtful Jack could have surpassed that tally even if he had his seven war seasons back, but he did amass 208 league goals of his own throughout his career, bringing the combined Rowley brothers' total to 642 league goals! From just two siblings!

In different circumstances most of these goals could have been scored in the name of Manchester United. At the age of 14, Arthur joined his elder brother at Old Trafford and appeared for United in unofficial matches. Unfortunately the war put paid to any professional contract. Arthur did however leave a mark at the club when he scored for the Reds in a wartime league match at the age of 17 in 1943.

While United reaped the benefits of one Rowley at least, spare a thought for Wolverhampton Wanderers. They had both brothers on their books as youngsters but let them go. Spare no sympathies though, for Wolves have only themselves to blame for making the same mistake twice. And then they had the nerve to complain later when Manchester United snagged Duncan Edwards from right under their noses.

It was with his hometown club that Jack began his career. He had initially played for a local team called Dudley Old Boys but, once he finished school, he joined the ground staff at Molineux at the age of fifteen. Due to his speed and powerful left foot, his best position was deemed to be outside-left, and that is where he spent a large part of his early career. The manager at the time was the haughtily-titled Major Frank Buckley, who had risen up the army ranks during the Great War. Buckley, as a matter of fact, was a former Manchester United player, though the Major's minor role with the Reds was restricted to three matches as understudy to Charlie Roberts in 1906-07. He was also something of a revolutionary figure whose methods were indirectly integrated into those of younger managers such as Messrs Busby, Shankly, Revie and Clough.

However, Buckley's biggest direct contribution to United was not giving Jack the opportunity to make the breakthrough at Molineux. Jack was constantly kept in the reserves and was even loaned out to a local outfit called Cradley Heath in October 1936. Soon after, as he was recovering from a hernia operation, Jack was offloaded to Bournemouth altogether. It was possibly Major Buckley's biggest footballing regret.

Pick of the Cherries

There is one or two things you need to know about Bournemouth. To start with, that was just the lazy way of referring to them. Their full name was Bournemouth and Boscombe Athletic Football Club, who played at Dean Court. For forty-three straight years this ground hosted Third Division football, and that could partially be due to the club's nickname. Obviously they did not put much thought into picking "The Cherries", which to opposing teams seemed less an intimidating presence more an appetizing one. And most importantly – as far as Jack Rowley was concerned – they had reluctantly assumed the mantle of being the place where Wolverhampton Wanderers dumped their rejects. Indeed, as many as ten of Wolves' 1930s league players were transferred directly to the south coast club.

Jack had not even been given one opportunity to play a competitive match for Wolves before being discarded by Major Buckley. However, coming from a big First Division side, he was poised to finally launch his career and display his qualities of speed, finishing, and – after his first match – strength. Jack made his league debut at the age of 18 on February 27th, 1937, when he was selected at outside-left against his father's old team, Walsall. Alec Shorrocks' classic book, 'Winners and Champions', contains a host of personal quotes from Jack, including the admission that his league bow was a memorable one.

Facing Jack at right-back that day was an old West Brom veteran who Jack thought nothing of skinning time and time again. Finally fed up, the humiliated fullback waited for the next time Jack hared past him and he slammed him to the wall that ran alongside Walsall's touchline! At halftime Jack's father, who was watching from the stands, approached him with some advice that stuck with him for the rest of his career: "Son, hit him back. He won't hit you again anymore if you hit him back". That was all Jack needed to hear to embark on a career of aggression. Controlled aggression, I hasten to add, for he never went out to hurt anyone, just to protect himself, especially as he was a young and inexperienced player entering professional football at a time when on-pitch violence was the reason of existence for most defenders. Not that the fans in the stands minded. To the contrary, they were always quick to roar their approval whenever Jack flattened an opponent or two on the way to goal.

That match ended in a 1-1 draw. A week later, on his home debut, Jack scored his first league goal as the Cherries beat Luton Town 2-1 to record their first victory in eight matches. Jack struck the following week at Cardiff City then added a brace in a 3-1 defeat of Crystal Palace. His burst of goals was just the tonic Bournemouth needed as they started to climb up the table. Despite operating on the flanks, Jack kept tucking them away, including a couple at Queens Park Rangers, to finish the first season of his career with ten goals in 12 outings. And Bournemouth benefitted too, rising from mid-table to claim a joint-fourth spot, though sixth on goal average. Still, this was the Cherries' highest ever placing up to then, thanks largely to the introduction of Jack Rowley on the wing.

A Devil in Red

Following his exploits in his first dozen matches, there was little chance that Jack was going to remain a Third Division footballer for much longer. In fact, he would not even see out the first two months of 1937-38. His high strike rate had temporarily eluded him at the start of the season but his skill still shone through on the flanks. When he netted in a 2-1 win at Notts County on October 16th, it was only his second goal in 11 matches in this campaign so far. It was also his last for Bournemouth. Jack Rowley had been discovered. He would make just one more appearance for the Cherries… in the Netherlands, of all places.

Bournemouth's record sixth-place finish of last season did not qualify them for any European competition, but it so impressed their manager Charlie Bell that he rewarded the players with a mid-week hop on the ferry to the continent. The tour included a friendly game against the Dutch national side, no less. Of course this was long before the *Oranje* selection entered their 'Total Football' phase and they were only able to register a 1-0 win over their Third Division guests. The glamorous encounter obviously whetted Jack's appetite for the big time. The team did not get back home until the early hours of Friday yet the next day he was playing in a higher division.

There had already been interest shown from several clubs, such as champions-elect Arsenal. Some teams had sent their scouts over to Dean Court while others commissioned their managers to run the rule over this young prodigy. But Second Division Manchester United adopted a novel approach: they left it to the chairman of the club to unearth Jack! James Gibson was the wealthy man who solved United's financial crisis of the early thirties. He also happened to own a house in Bournemouth where he would often attend matches at Dean Court. As a result, he was able to witness at first hand Jack's progress, and he was now ready to pounce. Manchester United may have occupied 14th place in Division Two but an enormous £3,000 cheque made Bournemouth all too eager to do business.

Rowley was shell-shocked. Having just turned nineteen a fortnight earlier, he did not even have any idea where Manchester was. But he was about to find out very soon. United manager Scott Duncan was on hand to accompany him that same Friday morning on the train ride up to his new home where he would stay for the next eighteen years. The very next day, October 23rd, 1937, Jack was put straight into the line-up for the visit of Sheffield Wednesday to Old Trafford. The new recruit began brightly but the match was barely ten minutes old when his wing partner, inside-left Ron Ferrier, had to be carried off injured. Good thing he got the only goal of the game before trudging off. For the rest of the match, however, Jack had to do the work of two players and, not surprisingly, especially considering all the travelling of the last few days, he faded in the second half.

It was an all too overwhelming week for Jack. Showing a wise head for someone so young, he subsequently asked for some time away from the spotlight, not only to swing back by Bournemouth and bring his belongings, but also so he could adapt to being a Manchester United player. This was definitely a big step up from the eight months he spent at Dean Court to a once major club that could now be kindly categorized as a sleeping giant. There had been glory days at United but these were confined to a golden period from 1908 to 1911 when two league championships and the FA Cup were won. It was after that that the giant took a nap which dragged on comfortably for nearly three decades. Manager Scott Duncan promised United a return to the First Division but he only offered a glimpse: one season in the top flight in 1936-37 ended with a quick return to where they came from.

This was the state of affairs when Jack arrived at Old Trafford with United tamely sitting in the bottom half of the Second Division table. Yet in his first few weeks in Manchester a lot of changes occurred. Barely 17 days after signing him, Duncan resigned from the hot seat, the reasons believed to be politics within the club. Instead of finding a replacement, United decided they could manage without a manager. Secretary Walter Crickmer was tasked with minding the playing side of things for a while, and later an unheralded chap called Jimmy Porter came in to help. This was November 1937, and the Reds opted to remain without an official manager until February 1945 when they hired a man named Matt Busby to see what he could do.

Incredibly, United seemed to flourish in their gaffer-less predicament and started winning games again. Jack was now ready and eager for a second try with the first team. Six weeks after his debut he was recalled on December 4th for Swansea's visit to Old Trafford. How they wished they had never stopped by: Outside-left Jack Rowley banged four goals in a 5-1 mauling! At nineteen years and 58 days, he became what is considered Manchester United's youngest ever hat-trick scorer in league action. In one afternoon he announced to the Old Trafford masses what a star they had acquired.

Around the same time Jack arrived in Manchester, two other players were introduced into the first team, and all three would develop into Manchester United legends over the next decade and a half. The first was an Irishman by the name of Johnny Carey who was good in nearly any position but great at right-back. In time he would become Jack's captain. The second would become his long-lasting attacking partner, a local lad called Stanley Pearson. The two

Jack (top right) guesting for Walsall in 1940-41.

would form arguably the greatest forward partnership in United's history, and I am basing that on duration, prolificacy, and understanding. They complemented each other perfectly: Stan had the finesse and creativity to make openings for Jack, who in turn had the directness and power to provide the knockdowns for Stan. They led United to trophies together, represented England together, and all this time they were scoring. Over the next 17 years they plundered nearly 600 goals in the name of Manchester United, including of course war games and friendlies.

Jack's presence on the left wing had a positive impact on United's play. Either by him creating or converting, the goals flowed. Of his first 16 league appearances for the Reds, 11 were won and only one lost. United climbed up the table unstoppably to end the season in second place and secure promotion to the First Division. With 25 league appearances and nine goals, Jack had delivered success at the first attempt.

The last two times Manchester United had competed in the top flight they had been relegated: in 1931 and 1937. But now equipped with a Jack Rowley the Reds fared much better in 1938-39 to attain 14th place. You could call that mediocre… unless it was your highest finish for 10 years. They were now here to stay. Jack's Division One debut had been on August 27th at Middlesbrough though a game he really looked forward to came in November when he faced his old employers, Wolverhampton. He made sure of scoring in that outing but, as Wolves triumphed 3-1, Major Buckley did not feel too much regret… for now. Jack went on to establish himself as a mainstay of the first team, missing just four matches during the campaign. He played mostly on the left wing but would switch to the opposite flank whenever Billy Bryant was unavailable.

His goal return was a modest 10 goals, but you have to remember that he was operating on the wing and was still a youngster trying to adapt to the highest standards. Besides, those ten goals would have seen him finish as the club's top scorer for the season had he not been overtaken by Johnny Hanlon on the last day. And he was doing a splendid job on the wing, to be fair, an article of the day praising "his fleetness and daring raids, and the 'guts' he has for the job at hand". However, just as Jack thought he had acclimatized to the world of First Division football, the whole world itself changed, and Jack would not appear for United in a competitive match again for seven years.

Shooting

Jack was injured at the beginning of 1939-40. Privately, he may have wished the season did not start without him and, if he did, he certainly got his wish on September 3rd: football stopped! Only a world war could bring this universal game to a halt, and Hitler's Germany obliged when it decided to turn the world Nazi. Thus, by a chain of events thousands of miles away, Jack's life was flipped upside down.

Most of us can only imagine what it must have felt like for a young prodigy, not even twenty-one years of age yet, having to put his promising career on hold till God knows when, and to go fight in a war he might never return from alive. However, there were greater issues at stake now than a footballer's career, and the FA accordingly cancelled all official matches. A few weeks later there was another twist – football was back... but only in regional leagues of non-competitive nature, to keep the people's spirits up. Footballers were now entertainers in the purest form.

Only Jack was no longer around to entertain Mancunians. As soon as hostilities broke out, he joined the army and was posted to the South Staffordshire Regiment in Worcester, close to his hometown of Wolverhampton. It could have been worse – he could have been shipped to the war front right from the start – but, luckily for him, he did not see any dangerous combat until a few years into the war. His particular area of expertise, appropriately enough, was as an anti-tank gunner. And why not? With no on-field opponent to shoulder-charge or climb all over, this was the next best method for him to channel his aggression.

As footballers were posted to all corners of the land, the FA sensibly re-launched the concept of 'guesting' that was originally implemented during World War I. Depending on where they were stationed, players could represent nearby sides instead of their actual clubs. As a result, throughout the war, Jack Rowley travelled the land in search of goals. Just mapping his war path is a thankless task but it is worth the effort if only to reveal how prolific he could have been throughout his twenties. If only...

As at first he was posted to Worcester, his superiors could not believe their luck in having a First Division sharpshooter in their ranks, and they would not let him go anywhere - he *had* to represent the depot outfit every Saturday. But Jack could no longer be held back. When the 1940-41 campaign began, Jack was able to guest for Walsall where they still talk about his exploits to this day. At least the statisticians do, especially when they gawk at the club record he set in the autumn of 1940 of thumping four goals in one game... on four separate occasions!

His fans back in Manchester had not been accustomed to such feats from his two seasons with United but, in February 1941, they finally got the chance to witness them with their own eyes. Jack had been granted permission to return to Lancashire for the odd match, so he made his comeback for the Reds in a War Cup tie against Everton. Naturally he scored - pouncing on a dodgy clearance from the keeper to ram the ball home – and did so again in the replay. A fortnight later he turned out at Old Trafford again to face Bury and bury a hat-trick past them. It was March 8th, 1941, and it proved to be a historic match.

A mere four days later a local newspaper report on German plane bombings of the area contained the following chilling words: "Slight outbreaks of fire were reported from a football ground and a training institute". It was the paper's not too revealing way of saying that Old Trafford, the Theatre of Dreams itself, had been hit. And it was a bad hit too, the damage to the stands rendering the stadium unsuitable for matches. Jack would not play, or score, at Old Trafford again for another eight years!

Intriguingly, this was the second attempt to burn down Old Trafford. The Nazis succeeded where the IRA had failed. Back in 1921, on March 22nd, to be exact, a man named Patrick Fennell tried to set the ground on fire as part of a series of IRA attacks around the city. Luckily he was halted in time and slapped with a seven-year sentence for his troubles.

Now the homeless Reds would rather have led a nomadic existence than share Maine Road with Manchester City but the harsh war already provided the club with enough enemies from abroad. So ground-sharing it was for the ensuing eight years. Not that it bothered Jack much – Maine Road for him was as good a venue as any in which to score – and he started off like he meant to continue. On April 14th United showed their new landlords their gratitude by thumping City 7-1, which is better than a 6-1 scoreline. Jack's haul was four goals – an impressive haul surely, but not as impressive as the five he hammered past Chester in the next match. By the end of the season he had managed 13 matches for United and struck 19 goals! His legend was starting to grow. He was also able to blag a medal when he helped the Reds beat Burnley 1-0 in the Lancashire Senior Cup final.

The six months that followed the start of the 1941-42 season were to become the most magical, enchanted, and fruitful spell that a Manchester United footballer ever experienced. Jack Rowley was constantly able to turn out for the Reds and it seemed he just needed to wink at the ball and it would ripple the opposition's net. It helped that he never said 'no' to a shooting opportunity, even if he was stood by the goal-line while a teammate or two were better placed. Take the opening day of the season as a prime example when New Brighton – still a League team at the time – innocently stopped by at Maine Road. United proceeded to cream them 13-1 to record the biggest win in their history, apart from a 14-0 victory that was declared null in 1895. Of the 13 goals, one selfish Jack Rowley claimed more than half! For the mathematically challenged, that was a staggering seven goals. No United player before him had reached such a haul and no one other than him has done so since. It had only taken him 12 minutes to flash a hat-trick and the newspaper understatedly described him as "ludicrously dominant".

Jack remained ludicrously dominant thereafter, alternating between outside-left, inside-left, and centre-forward. On consecutive weekends in September he blasted four goals past Stockport County. Another quartet was reserved for Chester City in October, while Tranmere Rovers were privy to five Rowley rockets in November, just for being Scouse. Rationing may have been in effect during the war but obviously they had forgotten to tell Jack there was a ration on goals too. By the time he signed off at the end of February he had tallied 42 goals in 23 matches! More impressively, he had completed a full year of wartime action for United and netted 61 goals in 36 outings. It made you wonder whether he attended any army function at all because it seemed all he did was eat, sleep, and score. The Red masses had observed what a star he had become and they were now willing Winston Churchill to win the war if only to see what Jack could do in competitive football.

It would be a few years, of course, before Churchill saw to their wishes. In the meantime Jack was being moved overseas... to Northern Ireland. He would spend about a year there from March 1942. Before he went there, however, he guested for his first club, Wolverhampton, on March 7th and rifled five goals past Everton! A couple of months later, on leave back home for a few days, he turned out for Wolves again on May 30th. They were facing Sunderland in the War League Cup final and, just for the occasion, Jack struck a brace to lead Wolves to a 4-1 win and earn himself the medal that went with it.

Not that Rowley abstained from football when he was in Ireland. The Emerald Isle is famous for producing numerous Manchester United stars down the years, and Jack probably felt he could give something back while he was stationed there. So he hooked up with Distillery in Belfast, making his debut on March 28th and scoring, naturally. In total, he donned Distillery's white shirt 29 times and tallied 26 goals. Jack was one of hundreds of servicemen who guested for Irish clubs during this time. In fact, on September 14th, 1942, a match took place between the British Army and the Army-in-Ulster with Jack representing the latter. His name again was on the scoresheet but his team lost 3-5.

Jack spent only one year in Belfast but continued to be fondly remembered by the folks at Distillery. Over a decade later, after peacetime football had long been back and Jack had achieved all there was to achieve, he was invited to guest for Distillery again, this time for a special occasion. On October 4th, 1954, the club installed the first floodlighting system in Northern Ireland at their Grosvenor Park ground. Swiss club Servette provided the opposition and the fodder – they were trounced 4-1 including a goal from old man Jack.

There was more action for Jack during 1942-43. On another short leave to Wolverhampton, he represented the Wanderers on November 21st against Derby County and rammed eight goals down their throats. Just how do you score eight in one match? Only Jack knows! He was also nice enough to appear for his parent club, Manchester United, on seven occasions during the campaign, tucking in eight goals. Three of them came over two legs in what arguably was the best thing the Reds did during the war – defeat Liverpool 6-4 on aggregate in the Lancashire Cup final in May. Incidentally, as his wartime exploits became legendary, his presence in or absence from United's teamsheet became a source of weekly discussion in the club programme, which reported on his whereabouts and availability to the eager Reds fans.

Before 1942-43 was over, Jack made one appearance for Tottenham. It was in April 1943 and his war experience was taking a serious turn. He had been moved from Ireland to Folkestone for invasion training. The Allies were planning a counterattack on their enemies and, luckily for Jack, he would be part of it! His new base was close to London, of course. One of his mates in the regiment was an inside-forward named Les Bennett who had played alongside him at Distillery. Bennett was on Tottenham's books, however, and he invited Jack to come play at White Hart Lane. It was a masterstroke by Bennett: Jack spent most of 1943-44 with Spurs and, averaging more than a goal a game, led them to the Football League South championship as top scorer with 22 goals. He also made sure to create a record for the club when Luton Town stopped by on February 12th, 1944. He decided to live a little so he walloped seven goals in an 8-1 victory to match his previous outrageous feats with both Manchester United and Wolverhampton.

Speaking of the Devils, Jack was considerate enough to check on his parent club in late winter and early spring, registering six goals in five appearances. And speaking of Wolves, he struck one for them too in three matches. Putting it all together meant that Jack Rowley was garnering a name in footballing circles as a marksman of the highest repute. What else did he expect after his scoring exploits? Few are the strikers who can go through their entire careers and claim to have had that one afternoon when they notched more goals than they ever could have dreamt. Yet Jack had reached at least seven strikes in a game on three occasions in two and a half years!

The upshot of Jack's feats was that he was in demand by representative sides, gaining dual recognition in the latter part of 1943-44. On March 11th he was selected at inside-left for the Army in a tussle with a strong FA XI that included Stanley Mathews. The soldiers stormed to a 5-2 victory with a one-goal contribution from the Gunner himself. And better was to come on May 6th when he was chosen for the England national side for the wartime international against Wales at Ninian Park, Cardiff. Jack was a very late addition to the line-up, not that it mattered to him. He proudly took his place at inside-left alongside the likes of Tommy Lawton, Joe Mercer, and Captain Stan Cullis. This was England's 24th match of WWII yet it was the first occasion that a Manchester United player had been called up. Later on, United fullback Joe Walton would be selected too but Jack retains the honour to this day of being the only Red to be capped by England both in wartime and full internationals.

For once Jack did not score in that match in Cardiff but he played his part in a 2-0 victory over the Welsh.

Playing for England and running about in front of 50,000 spectators! Jack must have been thinking about that exactly a month later and probably even wondering if he would play football again. The date was June 6th, 1944, which has gone down in the annals of history as D-Day: the invasion of Normandy. It is what Jack had been training for since the previous year. If you have ever watched the opening scene of Saving Private Ryan you will know how it was like for Jack that day. If he was not necessarily in the midst of it then he was not that far behind. That day he was finally exposed to the full horror of the war. All the goals he ever scored meant nothing on the battlefield. Here a flying piece of shrapnel or a stray bullet separated life from death. This was Jack Rowley's reality from now until the end of the war. There was hardly any time for football and indeed only on the odd leave was he able to squeeze in a game back home during 1944-45, tallying a mere half a dozen outings for United, Spurs, and Wolves combined.

For once Jack had to give up his role as the Red Devils' main goal machine, leaving that task to one Jack Smith – the only United player to outscore him in the war. Here was a man who the Germans really did for with that war of theirs. Smith never even gets a mention when United's prominent strikers in history are discussed, mainly because the record books show that his contribution was a paltry 15 goals. Yet during the war years he turned out for the club in 201 outings and thumped 160 goals! If anybody's Old Trafford sojourn was obliterated by the war then it was Smith.

Born in Yorkshire in February 1915, Smith began his career in 1932-33 with Huddersfield who were then giants of the game. After 24 goals in 45 appearances he was signed by Newcastle United. For three seasons he was leading scorer for the Magpies. On January 1st, 1938, he grabbed a brace in a 2-2 draw with Manchester United, for whom Rowley scored. Just one month later Rowley and Smith both scored for the Reds in a similar draw with Barnsley. The latter had been signed by United for a club record £6,500 fee, much to Newcastle's fans' ire. Their reasons were obvious – Smith's eight goals in 17 matches propelled the Mancunians to the top flight within three months. Subsequently, of course, the war saw to it that his staggering tally of 185 goals in the red shirt (including war and friendly matches) remains a secret to most of the club's fans.

The Centre-Forward

On May 7th, 1945, the Germans signed their unconditional surrender to the Allies. It was considerate of them, for Jack Rowley could now get back to normal life. He may have put his rifle away but there was no competitive soccer to satiate him yet. The football authorities had taken into account that too many players were still stationed abroad and sensibly decided that 1945-46 would be branded as the final season of wartime football.

Jack himself may still have been in uniform but his mission still consisted of playing football! Shortly after Germany's surrender he was instructed to represent the British Army on a tour to entertain the troops. Matt Busby, who three months earlier had signed on the dotted line to become Manchester United's first manager in eight years, had personally selected Jack for the Army team to play in Italy, Egypt, and Greece. It was a tour that made Jack sick, though that should not reflect on Busby in any way. Rowley was rather taken ill in Naples and the big fellow had to concede to the little bugs for two weeks of the tour!

By September 1945, Jack was back in Manchester for good (bar one more guest appearance for Wolverhampton). War had changed life beyond recognition. A damaged Old Trafford had gradually developed into a Theatre of Weed, if you like. Jack had lost half a dozen years of his career. Whether he had been shot at, or he had shot at someone, Jack never discussed publicly. It was time to leave all that behind and move on. At least he was back. A long-time teammate, right-back Bert Redwood, had passed away during the hostilities. So had reserve players Ben Carpenter and George Curless. Others had been wounded (Allenby Chilton) or taken prisoner (Johnny Hanlon), so Jack could consider himself fortunate – in the circumstances – to resume his career. He may have only had two seasons of first-class football but he had as much experience as a twenty-six year old, which, in reality, he was. All those years fighting for his country and guesting for various clubs (he had also briefly turned out for Aldershot, Shrewsbury Town, and Folkestone) had seen him grow as a player and a man. Add to this the fact that a lot of Manchester United players failed to carry their careers across the war, it all meant that Jack had become one of the club's senior members.

Which brought new issues to the fore. Jack now had the confidence and the dressing-room rank to express himself. The problem was that how he played on the field was exactly how he lived his life. For aggression and power, read abrasiveness and a fiery temper. He was a practical person who never sought publicity and accordingly he had no time for those who did. Sometimes he could be blunt and would tell it like it is without a care whether he offended others. That is how he was and, if that perhaps did not sometimes make him the most popular fellow in the dressing room, it was a small price to pay for the adulation it brought him from the terraces.

When Matt Busby first assumed his duties as Manchester United boss he was warned about Jack. He was hard to control, Matt was told. But years later the great manager admitted: "I never had one moment's trouble with Jack".

That was not entirely true. Jack had his 'moments' but Busby was wise enough to turn a blind eye. The reason was simple: he knew how good Jack was and that, if he was going to bring success to United, he needed the goals and effect of the fiery gunner. So he treated him at times with kid gloves, much like the approach he adopted with George Best a couple of decades later, or how Sir Alex handled Eric Cantona in the nineties.

A perfect example can be found in Dennis Viollet's biography, 'Viollet', by Hughes and Cavanagh. One day after training Busby rushed into the dressing room after hearing a lot of commotion. The first thing he saw was Rowley's hands wrapped around reserve player Brian Birch's throat. Jack was fuming with rage at the youngster's ongoing wisecracking and only the swift interception of several teammates prevented Jack from choking him! Busby knew what to do: he used wise words to calm his irate striker down while Birch was sold off not long after.

Jack, on the other hand, stayed at Old Trafford for many years. Busby had plans for his star striker. Jack's goals during the war had come either from the outside-left or the centre-forward positions, but Busby recognized where Jack would operate best. The manager had a knack for identifying a player's optimal position, moving around several United players for the better. And with Jack it was simple: Busby switched him from the left flank to the middle where he would go on to establish himself as United's greatest centre-forward up to then. In fact, even to this day, the only other player who could rival him as a superior centre-forward – in the position's pure, old-fashioned sense – is Tommy Taylor. And Taylor, incidentally, spent his first two years at Old Trafford mastering his skills under Jack's guidance.

Not that Jack never ventured to the wing – or put his aggressive streak to good use, as the following anecdote demonstrates. A long-standing Reds fan named Jimmy Billington remembered Jack well in the book 'Take Me Home, United Road': "They were playing Middlesbrough and there was a bloke who kept having a go at Charlie Mitten. Rowley told Mitten to go into the centre. Five minutes later this bloke was on the deck and, after that, Rowley told Mitten to go back on the wing! He was a tough lad, Rowley. They say that to practice he used to stand two bricks on the ground, put the ball on top, and hit it as hard as he could!"

Gradually, Busby's masterstroke paid dividends. During 1945-46, as the game prepared for the return of competitive football, Jack established himself in his new position and – much like the salivating fans had hoped – proved that he could translate his wartime potential onto the higher standards of the First Division. At least whenever he could get leave and rush to Manchester. And let's not forget the time he missed the train from Wolverhampton! But soon the goals began to flow in peacetime football, sometimes at a rate of three goals

Jack (extreme left) heads the 2nd of his 4 goals past Northern Ireland.

in nine minutes, much to Blackburn's bemusement on March 9th. By the end of the campaign, out of United's 46 league and cup fixtures, Jack had appeared in 32 and notched 22 goals to finish as the club's leading marksman. It was an illustration of what was to come from him over the next half a dozen years. And to finally put the war years to rest, Jack struck the only goal of the match on May 11th as Manchester United defeated Burnley to win the Lancashire Senior Cup.

Record Breaker Jack

If soccer fans were happy when League football finally resumed on August 31st, 1946, they were extra happy at Maine Road where they were witnessing the best football being played in the land. Not by Manchester City – they were putting in another stint in Division Two – but by the team in red who were renting the venue at £3,000 a year. Foremost among them was Jack Rowley. In Matt Busby's first league match in charge of Manchester United, it was Rowley who rose high to head in the winner against Grimsby Town with 20 minutes to go.

It seemed Jack had made a resolution to score in every League match under Busby – he kept the resolution running for five games. All ended in victories and United were top of the table. The *First Division* table! It was a pleasant surprise to Reds who had not seen this before, or at least anyone under fifty. United were playing the best brand of football around, especially the five-man forward line. All five would gain international recognition. Outside-left Jimmy

Delaney represented Scotland; the middle trio of Johnny Morris, Jack Rowley, and Stan Pearson gained England caps; and outside-left Charlie Mitten turned out for Colombia, oddly enough, but that is another story.

When they attacked as a unit, their interchange was mesmerizing, with an array of one-touch passes, hanging crosses and lovely finishes. It was almost telepathic. Around the same time in the forties but in South America, a team called River Plate was dominating the Argentine League with a similar forward line that became famous for the precision passing and perfect understanding. That attack was nicknamed 'La Maquina' – The Machine – and the same label could have been applied to United's five forwards. They knew instinctively where everyone was and what they were going to do next. The result was thrilling forward forays that bought joy to Reds raised on the tedium of the previous 35 years.

Former Liverpool manager Bob Paisley faced various Manchester United sides down the decades, both on the pitch and from the dugout. After playing against United's forties team once and getting absolutely creamed 0-3, he formed an opinion that he expressed decades later: "For my money, they had then as good a team as they've ever had". And leading this team from the front was the Gunner himself, Jack Rowley. If you make a habit of looking at general team photos from the forties and fifties, you could usually tell with ease who the centre-forward was. He is mostly sat in the middle of the front row with a slight smile on his face and a confident, knowing look that he is about to savage the opposition defence. In United's pre-match snapshots, that is exactly how Rowley is identifiable. A word of caution, mind: his smile may have been free but his goals cost you.

His selfishness and directness, we have already discussed, but Jack excelled at the link-up play too. He was in tune with all his fellow attackers and would effortlessly bring them into play or set them up for scoring for a change. His long-time strike partner Stan Pearson commented in 'Winners and Champions': "Jack could play anywhere in the front line and give you a good match". He also remembered one occasion the day before a tussle with Preston North End when Jack was getting criticized by his teammates in the dressing room: "On the day of the match, Jack just rolled up his sleeves and slaughtered them all on his own, including two goals in the first 20 minutes". Jack was a handful, and there was no use for defenders to double up on him. He would instead drift all over, pulling them with him and creating gaps for the rest of the forwards.

The best bit for the fans was that Jack seemed to have fulfilled in competitive action all the rich potential he showed during wartime football. He was scoring goals like no one they could recall seeing at the club. In December he rattled a hat-trick versus Brentford. Then in April, facing his old club Wolves, he got hold of the ball in the centre circle, charged two opponents off, raced to the edge of the area, and simply thumped it into the net. He got a brace that day in a 3-1 win that helped United pip Wolves on goal average come the season's end... but not to first place. With four matches to go, United travelled to Liverpool, a team they had plastered 5-0 earlier in the campaign. But on May 3rd Liverpool took a 12th minute lead then defended for their lives for the victory. When the final table became clear a few weeks later, the Scousers had finished in first place ahead of United by a single point!

Yet it did not seem too calamitous at the time. For Manchester United to finish as runners-up in the First Division was a fantastic achievement as far as their fans were concerned. It was easily the club's highest placing for 36 years. A big part of it was thanks to the leader of the front line, Jack the Gunner, who slammed 26 league goals. Of course, the days of smashing forty-plus goals in a year in regional wartime football were over, and those 26 strikes were so impressive they enabled him to break the club's scoring record of 25 held by Sandy Turnbull since 1908. Jack was on 23 goals with one fixture left of the 1946-47 campaign but a timely treble against Sheffield United inscribed his name into the history books.

One Sunny Day at Wembley

It is one thing getting your name into the record books, but to have it emblazoned in gold, you had to lead Manchester United to glory of one kind or another. At the time nothing was more glorious than the FA Cup. Sadly, up to then, United's story in the old cup tournament was a book that you *could* actually read by its cover. Go back to 1926 – that was when United last reached the semi-final. Go back further to 1909 – that was the only time the Reds had won the trophy. The End.

So in January 1948, a resurgent Manchester United embarked on a determined assault on the FA Cup, their plan for world domination consisting of kicking off at Villa Park a goal down! Aston Villa had started the match 13 seconds earlier and promptly taken the lead. But six minutes later Rowley headed in an equalizer to set United on their way to a surreal 6-4 victory. He also netted in the next tie, a straightforward 3-0 drubbing of Liverpool. And when the holders, Charlton Athletic, were knocked out in the fifth round, United became hot favourites for the Cup.

The hysteria even spread into the League programme. When United entertained table-toppers Arsenal at Maine Road, 81,962 spectators turned up to create the record attendance in Football League history. The match finished 1-1 with Jack notching United's goal, and when he did, it was greeted by possibly the loudest cheer ever heard in English League football.

Back in the FA Cup, Jack was effervescent in the 4-1 stuffing of Preston North End in the quarter-final. He scored with one shot, sent an opposition

Fun with the phone - Aston, Downie, Rowley, Carey and Crompton

player pole-axed with another, and exchanged places with right winger Jimmy Delaney so effortlessly and at will that Preston's defence was shredded to pieces. All of United's opponents had been decent First Division teams and they had all been outclassed with at least a two-goal margin. And there was more of the same in the semi-final again when Derby County were swept away 3-1. For once Jack was upstaged by his partner-in-crime Stan Pearson who claimed a hat-trick, bringing his tally to seven goals in the cup so far. But Jack had set up several of Stan's goals during this run, some with backheels, others with overhead kicks, believe it or not!

So Manchester United were back in the FA Cup final after a wait of nearly forty years. As a matter of fact, this would be their – and Jack's – first visit to Wembley. The date was April 24th, 1948, the opponents Blackpool. Ninth-placed, the Seasiders may have been considered underdogs to runners-up Manchester United but, in Stanley Matthews and Stan Mortenson, they possessed England's default right-wing partnership of the late forties. Not that United's preparations were plain sailing either. Jack himself received an untimely knock to his leg the week before the final and had to leave the field early in the second half. For a few days his presence in the final was in doubt, a coy Matt Busby teasing the press by stating: "We shall wait and see".

There was another personal issue facing Jack. His wife (Violet Ward, whom he had wed in early 1942) was a week overdue with their second child. Even at the last minute she was preying on his mind, as he confided to Shorrocks in 'Winners and Champions': "I had phoned her up before the kickoff and nothing had happened, and even while I was getting changed, my thoughts were back home. Was everything OK… she is missing all this". But perhaps Jack ought to have taken his priorities into consideration some nine months earlier! Now there was an FA Cup final to win, and he strode onto the Wembley pitch along with his teammates: Crompton; Carey, Aston; Anderson, Chilton, Cockburn; Delaney, Morris, Rowley, Pearson, and Mitten.

This was the famous five – 'The Machine' – who had terrified defences all season long but, on this occasion, they seemed to start sluggishly. Perhaps the Wembley nerves affected them or Blackpool's defensive plan. Jack was the exception, however, playing to his usual standards as if beckoned by destiny. Twice he went close with typical headers only to be thwarted by keeper or fullback. Eventually Blackpool took the lead from a penalty kick and held on till the half-hour mark.

Then United's right winger, Jimmy Delaney, sent a deep high ball towards Blackpool's penalty area. Two defenders and the keeper converged to snuff out the danger… then stood there as if mesmerized by the ball's bounce. In a flash Jack appeared from nowhere and had the presence of mind to nudge the ball above the keeper's head. He ran past him and tapped it into the empty net with the nonchalance of a lad knocking a beach ball around on the sand rather than in front of nearly 100,000 spectators at Wembley. He even used his right foot to score, which generally had a ceremonial function, so it was appropriate he only brought it out for the cup final.

As easy as that goal seemed, it was not entirely so, at least in Jack's mind. Years later he admitted in David Meek's book, 'Legends of United': "I went round the goalie and then seemed to wait hours for the ball to come down. Eventually it did and I just had to side-foot it into the net".

The Seasiders again grasped the lead and even threatened to extend it. The Reds were flagging, but Rowley remained bullish as the seventieth-minute mark approached. Johnny Morris earned a free-kick out on the right flank which he quickly centred towards the six-yard box. The Blackpool defenders were again accommodating, several of them still having their backs turned to the action while the ball was in flight. For Jack, it was a gesture of convenience unmatched since the invention of the zip, and he could not turn it down. Instead, he leapt high at the left side of the small box and headed the ball diagonally back to the right side of the goal, above the stranded keeper and into the net.

United again had parity as well as from now on the momentum. Stan Pearson, the other forward who had made his debut eleven years earlier like Jack, put the Reds ahead, and halfback Anderson added a fourth goal to make

Rowley powers a goal in a 2-1 win against Spurs in January 1951

sure. Manchester United strode on to win 4-2 in what everyone considered one of the best FA Cup finals of all time. Twice they came from behind and it was thanks to Jack. When people talk about the 'Matthews Final' of 1953 when Sir Stan finally earned a winners' medal, it was because of Jack Rowley and his game-saving brace of 1948. More importantly, he led United to glory at long last. You can forget the 26-year title wait that came to an end in 1993. At least during that time United won the European Cup, European Cup-winners' Cup, the League Cup, and four FA Cups. When Jack led United to the FA Cup in 1948, it was the first major trophy the fans had seen for 37 years.

Rowley Recognized

He had a combative and confrontational nature and was outspoken in his views. They were an uptight, self-aggrandizing organization who disdainfully looked down through their noses on any 'characters' in the game. He was a prolific marksman who combined well with his forward line. They were a petty, spiteful international selection committee that only took into consideration players from the 'goodie-two-shoes' category, preferably 'goodie-three-shoes' even. He was the toast of the town following a brace of goals in the cup final at Wembley. They were reluctantly forced to select him for England at long last.

It is not a hidden secret why Jack Rowley did not enjoy a lengthy international career. England's manager, Walter Winterbottom, was an ex-teammate of Jack, but he had no say in capping players. That was done on a whim by the Selection Committee, and that lot made it their default setting to dislike Rowley's nature. It is true that England were well endowed with excellent centre-forwards at the time, but Jack was more prolific than most and played for the hottest team in the land. Red Devils like Aston, Cockburn, and Pearson had collected dozens of England caps since the war, yet Jack was the best of the lot and he was made to wait till he was thirty before earning his first.

By the end of 1947-48 his displays had finally forced their hand. He starred in the cup final, of course, but he also dazzled in the League. He may not have broken United's scoring record again but he created a separate one which he maintains to this day: becoming the only player in United's history to score four goals in a competitive game twice in the same season. So, on December 2nd, 1948, Jack belatedly launched his England career which the Selection Committee, pettiness their hallmark, limited to just six caps over a five-year period when he was at his best with United. And even then, they contrived to place him almost anywhere but at centre-forward.

Take his debut against Switzerland, for instance, when he was selected at inside-right, a position he had never appeared in for United in competitive action. Regardless, Jack donned the England jersey with pride and honour and did what he did best whenever called upon. In his six matches for England he notched six goals, and all six have been captured on Pathé videos. The first one, which helped roll the Swiss 6-0 on his debut, possibly advocated the introduction of slow-motion action replays. He picked the ball up fully 35 yards from goal and sent an absolute screamer rocketing into the net.

It was hailed as a 'masterpiece' in the papers, but Jack was dropped for the next match. He did get called up for an end-of-season tour of the continent, playing against Sweden and France in May 1949. In Paris he was the star. England recovered from a first-minute deficit to triumph 3-1. Although Jack did not score, he assisted the first two goals and helped create the third.

Perhaps he was saving his goals for a particular occasion. If you want an idea of how good Jack could have been for England, look no further than on November 16th, 1949 – the date of a World Cup qualifier against Northern Ireland. Everything was set up right: the venue was Maine Road where Jack had played for eight years with Manchester United; he was selected in his preferred slot at the focal point of attack; and he was partnered up front with a familiar-looking chap – club mate Stan Pearson. And when everything is set up right, you know what inevitably happens – Jack Rowley scores four goals! Pearson helped himself to a couple also, and England thumped the Ulstermen 9-2 to record their biggest win against a Home Nation in the 20th century.

This created an irritating dilemma for the selectors. The only reason Rowley was originally picked was to deputize for their beloved Jackie Milburn who was out injured. Milburn was fit a fortnight later for the visit of World Champions Italy but the committee grudgingly elected to persist with the four-goal Gunner. Again present at centre-forward, Jack on this occasion took his time. The game was goalless till the 76th minute when he pounced on a ball inside the area and sent a sizzler into the top right-hand corner of the

The famous left foot.

net. It was a shot for which the Italian keeper adopted a look-but-don't-touch approach that was of utmost benefit for his safety if not his self-esteem. England went on to win by a 2-0 scoreline, the second goal completely a fluke – Billy Wright randomly lumped the ball forward from midfield and it sailed all the way in.

Jack was the hero again but his reward from the committee was cruel – he was shoved into the international wilderness for two and a half years! Even when the World Cup came around in the summer of 1950, he did not get a look in. Perversely, his four goals in his solitary qualifying appearance against Northern Ireland had made him England's top scorer in the qualifying campaign. Of course, it was their loss, and the footballers taken at his expense did not exactly cover themselves with glory in Brazil, especially the day they lost 0-1 to a team hastily cobbled together and tasked with representing USA.

Jack earned just one more cap after that… in April 1952 at the age of 33. He was creating all manner of scoring records for Manchester United, so England did the sensible thing and posted him on the left wing! He did not score against Scotland but played his part in a 2-1 victory that earned England the British Championship for the season. It is a shame that his international career was limited to just half a dozen outings, but he had stiff competition on the field as well as, tellingly, in the FA corridors. Still, he managed to put together an impressive CV with six goals and a personal claim to fame: he remains the only post-war footballer with four or more England caps to average a goal per game.

Aside from his England caps, over the years Rowley played for several representative sides that smartly followed the maxim 'pick him and he will score'. Jack never disappointed when called upon. He once appeared for the England B team in May 1949 when they faced Holland's full selection in front of 60,000 fans in Amsterdam. He walloped a second-half hat-trick in a 4-0 win. Twice he turned out for the Football League selection. The first time was in October 1941 when he notched a late winner against the Scottish League. The last time was in April 1948. It was 10 days before his appearance in the cup final and he practiced for that by netting twice in a 4-0 thumping of the League of Ireland.

Speaking of the Irish, Ulster and Eire decided to form an All-Ireland XI on May 9th, 1955, and they invited an England International XI over. It was made up of a bunch of old timers – Jack was 36 himself. The Irishmen scored five times but the old timers scored six, with one goal from Rowley deciding the outcome. It seemed no matter the representative side nor his age, the old maxim held true: if you pick Jack, he would score.

The Golden Age of Rowley

Cups and caps, he had them all now. What Jack was still missing was the big one: a League championship medal. In the first two seasons after the war Manchester United finished as runners-up and, in 1948-49, they contrived to pull off the same trick for the third year running. United had maintained their consistently high standards but Portsmouth came out of nowhere to pip them to the title. However, you could not fault Jack for any of that. By the end of the campaign he had conjured another record: the first Manchester United player to reach 30 competitive goals in one season.

He could not have done it without the help of little non-League Yeovil Town. United had met Yeovil in an FA Cup tie just before the war and under 50,000 spectators attended. But in 1949, now that United were one of the finest outfits in the land and Yeovil had caused a few upsets during their run, 81,565 souls clamoured into Maine Road! In the fifth round! It is also worth noting that United's fourth round tussle with Bradford Park Avenue had attracted a 213,205 attendance... over three ties, mind. Anyway, the large crowd meant that there are over 81,000 people around who were there the day Jack Rowley scored five goals in an 8-0 slaughtering of the non-League minnows. Of course Jack already held the club record of seven goals from the war days, but now he had the peacetime record for a cup tie too. Only one man has ever been able to better him since – George Best.

That was a memorable match for Jack, and another one came a month later at St. Andrews. A fearless Jack went head first into a Birmingham player's boot, the outcome being a stream of blood gushing from said head. But they did not call Jack tough for nothing. He was soon back on the pitch with a big plaster wrapped around his noggin. Then there was the time United's keeper, Reg Allen, went off injured against Bolton. Jack took a break from scoring goals to concentrate on stopping them instead as he went between the posts for the last ten minutes. Bolton threw everything at him but Jack blocked it all – ball and kitchen sink – to preserve United's one-goal lead.

On August 24th, 1949, Bolton were again the visitors, this time for a special day: the reopening of Old Trafford at long last after the war. Jack had played – and scored a hat-trick – in the last match before the German bombs of March 1941. Eight years later he was on the teamsheet and scoresheet again as the Wanderers were beaten 3-0. It was as if he had never been away.

In 1949-50, United finally relinquished their stranglehold on the runners-up spot to drop to fourth. Ironically, this was their best shot at the title of all the immediate post-war years. With ten matches to go, United had a four-point lead at the top but, after only adding six more, ended the season three points behind Portsmouth again. Jack, with 23 goals, was top scorer for the fourth year in a row, and that is a record he holds for the entire history of Manchester United. Even then, Jack was a legend.

Some of his own teammates at Old Trafford were in awe of him too. Tony Waddington, Stoke City's long-standing manager of the sixties and seventies, spent his youth days with Manchester United. His debut was in that wartime match versus New Brighton when Rowley hammered seven goals. Years later he remembered Jack affectionately in the 'Manchester United Story' by Derek Hodgson:

"My proudest moment came when Jack Rowley discovered I had the same size of foot as himself and gave me the job of wearing in a pair of boots for him. I can still see that left foot of his, hitting them from as far out as 40 yards. But for the war Jack would have been remembered as one of the greatest centre-forwards who ever lived".

You could lay some of the blame on the 'flu too. In December 1950 Jack caught the bug and was laid low for several weeks. In his absence, Matt Busby came up with an original idea: he moved England's left-back, Johnny Aston, to centre-forward. Johnny went and scored twice in his first three matches up front, thus convincing Busby of his worth. When Jack returned from illness, Busby had another idea, though not an original one. He moved Jack back to the left wing berth that had been vacated by Charlie Mitten, who had departed to Colombia. The last time Jack spent an extended run at outside-left had been in 1939, but he reluctantly gave it another go, all the way till the end of the season. Although he still scored seven times in 19 matches on the flank, it was understandably not enough for him to be leading marksman again. For the converted Johnny Aston, the sacrifice was bigger. He was never picked for England again.

Champions at Last

By the end of 1950-51 Manchester United had reclaimed the runners-up spot in the League for the fourth time in five years. It was Tottenham's turn this time to come out of the blue and clinch the title. Consistency is one thing but did United want to be the bridesmaids forever? For once Jack longed to be the bride. It was now forty years since United won the championship and, not only was the joke getting old now, so were the players. Jack was 32, as were Pearson, Carey and Chilton. In other words, they were running out of time if they really wanted to be remembered as Sir Matt Busby's first great team rather than the half decent one.

One Jack Rowley decided to take matters into his own hands. Or, to be more precise, his feet and occasionally his head. In the opening fixture of the 1951-52 season, he claimed a hat-trick against West Brom. In midweek United entertained Middlesbrough. Whether they wanted to see the same act as West Brom, he did not check. He banged in another hat-trick regardless. In the subsequent four matches, he added five more goals. And when Stoke City turned up at Old Trafford next, Jack stretched his tally to a staggering 14 goals in seven matches by thumping yet another hat-trick! The season was a mere 21 days old yet this was his third of the kind. Forget Manchester United, the entire top flight had not seen anything like this, before or since.

Clearly the man was on a mission: Operation League Championship. Yet he was not alone. Stan Pearson was as determined. Of the famous five forwards who thrilled the crowds in the late forties, only those two were still around. And, if Jack was playing like a man possessed, Stan was the man obsessed, and they pressed towards glory. Jack's meteoric scoring rate understandably decreased during the season, especially as he trudged out on nearly a dozen occasions on the left flank out of necessity because Matt Busby asked him to. Still, the Reds marched on.

With one match left United could almost touch the title. At a time when a victory was still worth two points, they held a two-point lead over Arsenal. Bizarrely, the last fixture was against Arsenal, who could still pip United. All the Londoners had to do was come to Old Trafford and win by seven goals! Impractical? Perhaps, but Jack had seen enough flavour-of-the-season teams pop up temporarily like fruit flies and take turns at pipping United. He was not taking any chances as he took to the field on April 26th, 1952. Indeed, leaving his entire career aside, Jack should be considered a United legend purely for his feats on that afternoon alone.

In only the eighth minute Carey lobbed the ball forward and here Jack himself picks up the commentary: "I scored from inside the penalty area with my right foot and it screamed in. In some of the reports the next day the press wrote 'So Rowley *can* kick with his right foot'!"

On 25 minutes he let his left foot do the damage. You may be familiar with the term 'hospital pass' but Jack here unleashed what could be labelled a 'hospital shot' – a strike so violent it broke Arsenal centre-half Shaw's wrist! He was out of this match as well as the following weekend's FA Cup final.

After Pearson had doubled the lead Jack hit the crossbar then focused on creating 'one of the most brilliant goals of the season', as far as the *Sunday Dispatch* were concerned. He ran at the Arsenal defence, dribbled past two, three men, all this time tightly keeping the ball from crossing the byline, then set Roger Byrne up for a goal the left winger would have been impolite to turn down.

In the second half Jack lobbed the keeper Swindin to make it 4-0. Although Arsenal immediately pulled one back, the stadium's atmosphere was turning into celebratory mode as the fans could finally sense the title. Even Jack was brimming with confidence now. When United earned an 80th minute penalty he stepped up to take it with a daredevil attitude: "I had the cheek to take it with my right foot again. I always remember George Swindin saying 'You bloody thing Jack… I didn't know you could kick with your right foot!'"

He could centre too, as he did in the last minute for Pearson to flash in another. Manchester United had destroyed their nearest rivals 6-1 with three goals and two assists from Jack. Most importantly, he had performed superhuman deeds all season long to finally bring the championship to Old Trafford. It had only been a 41-year gap, so said the few old fans who had remained loyal enough to wait around that long.

Yet spare a moment for poor Stan Pearson, the scorer of 22 League goals in 1951-52. It was his personal career best tally, but it was a tally that left him trailing Jack and only bestowed upon him a dubious honour: the scorer of most league goals in a single season without ending as Manchester United's leading marksman. It needed a spectacular feat to eclipse such an accolade, and

Jack Rowley duly obliged. Already he held the club record for highest scorer in a season with 26 goals in 1946–47, and he was able to break that with two matches to spare. So, when he flashed his fourth hat-trick of the season past Arsenal on the final day, he took his figure to 30 League goals! When it comes to Manchester United league scoring records, that is nearly as good as it gets. Only two men have bettered it since and only just: Dennis Viollet with 32 and Ronaldo with 31.

Friendly Fire

A week or so after the end of the 1951–52 domestic campaign, the Manchester United players were off to the United States. It was not necessarily a reward for winning the championship because, a couple of years earlier, the Reds had finished fourth yet still toured the USA afterwards. That trip back in 1950 was in fact the first occasion that Manchester United had ventured outside Europe. Apparently they enjoyed it so much that they returned barely two years later. What is not to love in the New World? It was the land of ration-free, huge portions, Hollywood movie stars… and substandard defences. Just a glance at the club's results validates the last statement. Americans love big scores in their sports and United duly obliged. In the first tour, the club played a dozen games and accumulated 47 goals. The second time around, in the same number of fixtures, United struck 57 times!

And you know who was up bright and early whenever there were goals to be scored: Jack Rowley was a man who took every game – any game – seriously and played to win. In a sense, Manchester United were lucky to have had such a footballer in their ranks. There are millions of fans out there who would dream of playing for United. Even if it was some solitary friendly, we would try our best in the name of United. Similarly, Jack's attitude made each outing in red a meaningful one.

In fact, sometimes he took exhibition matches too seriously! The 1952 tour included back-to-back encounters with the Mexican outfit Atlas in Los Angeles. The first meeting was enough to provide Jack with 'form' with some of their players, cranking up the heat for the rematch. Midway through the first half, when Jack rose to nod the ball down for Pearson to open the scoring, an opponent collided into him, hurting his neck. Whether it was intentional or not, Jack opted to go with 'intentional'. For a good hour afterwards, he adopted the motto that 'if it is a Mexican it is a piñata' and he bashed them at will, only relenting after a stern talking to from his captain, Johnny Carey.

This unfriendly friendly apart, Jack generally used orthodox means to hurt the opposition, and it involved what he did best. In the six matches that preceded the Atlas double-header, Jack walloped an astonishing 18 goals! The highlight came on May 21st in Massachusetts when United met an American

Soccer League team called Fall River and trounced them 11-1. There were enough goals theoretically for every United player to score once but in reality just two got their names on the scoresheet. John Downie notched a hat-trick but Jack Rowley claimed seven! The last goal was put through his own net by an opponent for lack of a better option. It was the second instance of his career that Jack had plundered seven goals in one match for United following that fruitful wartime outing in 1941 and, to this day, he remains the only Red to have ever reached such an outrageous figure.

There was another record he attached to his name in 1951-52. Already he had amassed an unprecedented 30 League goals, a further 21 strikes in friendlies took his tally to 51 goals in all matches. It was a total that stood unmatched for half a century until Ruud Van Nistelrooy squeezed in 52 strikes in 2002-03.

Another memorable exhibition match took place in May 1953 when United participated in the Coronation Cup. It was an eight-team knock-out tournament held in Glasgow between English and Scottish crack outfits. In the quarter-final United defeated Rangers 2-1 at Hampden Park with Rowley flashing the winner. The shot was captured on Pathé Video and the Rangers goalkeeper did not bother to move because there was no point. After beating the Scottish champions, Jack went on to score in the semi-final too, only for United to lose 1-2 to Celtic, who had endured a miserable season and only evaded relegation by four points. Obviously the Hoops roused themselves for this competition for they proceeded to beat Hibs in the final in front of 117,000 spectators.

In all, Jack played 50 friendlies for the Reds notching 47 goals. It is an impressive goal-a-game ratio that slightly faded in his last couple of seasons when he reverted to operating on the wing. Still, those 47 strikes make him United's all-time leading marksman in friendly outings, as if he needed any more accolades.

Jack and the Babes

League championship: won it. FA Cup: that too. Lancashire Senior Cup: ditto. Promotion: achieved. England caps: earned them in peace and war. 'B' caps: got one of these as well. Football League: represented them. When Jack sat down to assess his checklist of achievements at the start of the 1952-53 season, there was only one more medal missing from the complete set that he could have won at the time – the Charity Shield. Conveniently, closure was just around the corner as Champions Manchester United faced FA Cup winners Newcastle United in September. The Reds triumphed 4-2 and Rowley's take out of it was two goals and a kick in the head.

Early in this season, however, something was becoming clear about United: the most consistent team of the post-war era was now over the hill. And Matt

Jack in his days as Ajax manager.

Busby had anticipated that the players were ageing, and he was grooming a new team that could climb over a bigger hill – The 'Busby Babes' were being born. Starting now and over the next couple of years, the young men gradually replaced the older ones.

For Jack, 1952-53 was a disappointing season but for a different reason. In late October an injury presented him with the longest spell out of his career. He would not kick a ball again until February. Then a month later Matt Busby spent all the club's money to purchase a new centre-forward named Tommy Taylor. From now on, Rowley hardly ever wore United's Number 9 shirt again. The Number 8 top was handed to him for a while as he moved aside to make way for Taylor, but eventually he was shunted to the left wing and asked to stay there. Outside-left was where he began his career and it would be where he would spend his last year and a half at Old Trafford.

Of course Jack's goal return diminished thereafter as you would expect from someone in his mid-thirties operating on the flank. While he had amassed 30 league goals in 1951-52, it would take him 84 matches over the next three seasons to replicate that figure. However, his influence was not purely judged by goals now. Matt Busby had entrusted him with a different role. Back in 1948, when Busby was tasked with taking a Great Britain team to the Olympics, he called upon Jack along with Stan Pearson and Johnny Carey to help him out. Fresh from scoring a brace in the FA Cup final at Wembley, Jack spent part of the summer whipping this collection of amateurs into shape at a derelict Old Trafford.

Busby had seen Jack's educational potential and wanted him to do the same with the Babes now. After all, in October 1954, after exactly 17 years at Old Trafford, Rowley had become the club's longest-serving player when Carey and Pearson had left. Accordingly, as most of the ageing players moved on and the Babes filtered in, Jack stayed on in attack to guide all those youngsters haring about. The likes of Taylor, Viollet, Webster, and Blanchflower looked up to him for advice and inspiration.

Jack's helpful part in the development of the Babes should not be underestimated. Matt Busby certainly did not. In his first decade in charge of Manchester United, he won three trophies, and they were all thanks to Rowley. The Gunner had netted twice as the FA Cup was won in 1948, led the scoring with 30 strikes to seal the title in 1952, and then grabbed a brace to beat Newcastle in the Charity Shield. These trophies bought the manager time to slowly produce the Babes team to which Jack helped apply the finishing touches. In retrospect, were it not for Rowley, Sir Matt would have possibly gone down in history as plain Matt Busby, the former Manchester City half-back.

Instead, the Babes progressed to twice become Champions of England before their sad demise at Munich in 1958. Jack was long gone by then, having become a manager himself at Plymouth Argyle, but the tragedy affected him greatly. After all, most of the players had been his teammates. Upon hearing of the crash he approached the Plymouth board, as he recalled in 'Winners and Champions': "I said to them 'Look, I call Manchester United my home... so I would like to go back and see what I can do for them'. I was up here for about two weeks helping out. I went to as many funerals as I could get to because I knew these lads. I still say it... to me this would have been the greatest team ever".

Jack played his last match with the Babes - and for Manchester United - on January 29th, 1955, in an FA Cup tie against Manchester City. The video highlights of the match still exist and you could see that Jack had kept himself in slim shape till the very end. The speed may have gone but the accomplishments were there for eternity. In 380 league matches Jack netted a club record 182 goals. Only Bobby Charlton has since topped that. In 422 competitive matches in all competitions, Jack's tally was 208 goals – another record at the time and only surpassed by Charlton and Denis Law. His 30 league goals in 1951-52 made him the club's highest scorer in one season – only Dennis Viollet and Cristiano Ronaldo have bettered that. And he had the longest spell at the club of 18 years from 1937 to 1955, a record that Ryan Giggs had to grow grey hair to be able to improve on just recently. Charlton, Law, Ronaldo and Giggs – you had to be a true great to outshine Jack Rowley.

In Green and Suit

On Tuesday, February 15th, 1955, Jack was down in London. Arsenal defenders rushed their children in and locked the doors. They need not have worried – Jack was dressed in suit and tie and was being interviewed by the Plymouth Argyle officials for a managerial job. Jack 'combustible on the field and volatile off it' Rowley? He was made for management! He was actually on a shortlist of five men but three days later came the announcement: Jack was appointed player-manager at Plymouth till the end of the current 1954-55 campaign, with the option to continue his dual role in the following one, before turning into fulltime management in 1956-57.

A star for Manchester United and England he may have been but Rowley had not a day's experience as manager. At first that would make you wonder why any League side would appoint him. However, Jack had ample experience at football's highest level; he had the 'name' and stature to command respect; and his connections could come in handy when wheeling and dealing for players. Besides, it was not as if Plymouth were offering the ultimate job in football. To find their position in the sports pages you had to skip past the First Division table, go to the Second Division one, and look just above bottom-placed Ipswich Town. That was where Plymouth were sitting, in the relegation zone, and playing the type of football that was worth the entry fee… only for those with complimentary tickets. They were as far removed from Manchester United as possible, not just geographically but in status too. Indeed, the two clubs had only one thing in common: Argyle's home ground – uncomplicatedly named 'Home Park' – had also been blitzed by the Nazis during the war.

So Jack's first gig as manager was not going to be an easy one, though it did bring his footballing life full circle. He had begun his playing career on the south coast with Bournemouth, spent 18 years with United, and now, at 36 years of age, he was embarking on a managerial journey on the south coast again. The 'Gunner' had become a 'Pilgrim'. At least his first decision was a smart one: he selected himself at inside-left for Argyle's match at Fulham on February 19th, 1955. Fulham's left winger was a chap named Charlie Mitten, but the Pilgrims were out to impress their new player-manager, and they finally earned their first away win of the season.

The next match was away at Hull and they won that too, on the day Rowley notched his first goal in green. His introduction had certainly stirred the place up. When he finally made his Home Park debut on March 5th, nearly 26,000 fans turned up to register the biggest league gate since the opening day of the season. Just to please them, Rowley won his third match in charge. He was actually operating in a more withdrawn role, closer to midfield where he could better influence the play. By the end of the season he had appeared in all 13 matches since his arrival, though he only managed two goals. More pertinently, however, he had steered Argyle to safety at the first ask.

Just don't mention the second ask. Jack may have thought this management gig was all too easy... until Plymouth eased into relegation in 1955-56. You can blame it on the Second Season Syndrome; or the fact that Argyle had been a weak team for years now; or the other fact that Jack had been overhauling the squad with young players who needed time to improve. As a matter of fact, by the summer of 1956, 30 of the 39 players on the club's books were youngsters with no previous experience at other professional teams. Alternatively, you could lay the blame on the fact that Jack – as a player – endured his worst season up to now.

He had actually taken the option to continue playing in 1955-56, and that seemed a great idea, up until October 22nd, at least. On that afternoon he took his tally to six goals for the campaign, which put the 37-year-old on top of the club's scoring charts. After that, however, he struggled to stay fit, and he was only able to put in three more appearances throughout the remainder of the campaign. Correspondingly, Plymouth struggled and slid towards the Division Three South trapdoor, with only Neil Langman able to match or exceed Jack's six goals.

That October 22nd afternoon turned out to be the highlight of Jack's season... for another reason. By netting twice at Barnsley he took his league goals total past the 200 mark – not bad for a player who lost seven years to the war. Incredibly, on the same afternoon, also playing a Second Division away match (at Fulham), Jack's brother Arthur score twice for Leicester to take *his* league tally to 200 also! It was a tremendous day in the Rowley household: not only did Jack and Arthur become the first – and so far only – brothers to reach this milestone in English football, but they also achieved it within nine minutes of each other... with young Arthur being the quicker Rowley.

Arthur loomed large in Jack's picture in 1955-56, when the siblings were present on the same pitch for the last time. Not that this occurred often. There were one or two occasions during the war when they formed Manchester United's left-wing partnership. In 1949-50, when Arthur was a Fulham player, the two shared the gloating rights over two games. Jack got a goal and a victory with United against relegation-bound Leicester early in 1954-55. But Arthur had the last laugh this season when he claimed the only goal of the match between Plymouth and Leicester in September.

The original deal was that Jack would hang up his boots by the summer of 1956, if not earlier, but he came to a decision instead that he could manage best from the pitch. After all, here was a host of Third Division defenders he had yet to terrorize. So, during 1956-57 he took to the field to uphold his reputation. He may have been 38 by now but he still could handle himself, not to mention score. He appeared in 26 league matches and grabbed six goals, and he added another in the FA Cup for old times' sake. His last match was on April 13th, 1957, when he led Plymouth to a 2-0 victory over Gillingham. It had been a good 20 years since his debut for Bournemouth, also in Division Three South. Since then he had amassed 238 goals in 504 League and Cup outings. Much to the relief of defenders – and statisticians – nationwide, it was time to put the boots away for good.

It was suit and tie for Jack Rowley from now on. Going into management fulltime, he decided to put into it the same qualities of seriousness and determination that he had during his playing days. Plymouth may not have boasted the stature or tradition but Jack had the connections. And it was time to use them. One First Division player after another started arriving at Home Park, eager to impress the great Jack Rowley. Some included the likes of Wilf Carter and Johnny Newman who went on to become club legends. By the end of 1957-58 promotion was nearly attained. At a time when only the division champions went up, Argyle finished two points behind Brighton. The club appreciated all that Jack was doing and they honoured him with a testimonial match on April 28th when top flight Sunderland were dispatched 3-0.

Jack's hard work was finally rewarded in 1958-59 as he led Argyle to promotion. This was the first season that Third Division North and South had been re-arranged into Division Three and Four, and Argyle deemed it the perfect time to become inaugural champions of Division Three. It was Jack's first success as manager, and possibly the first time he had won at football without having to personally thump a load of goals. Unfortunately, success made the Plymouth directors too big for their boots. When the team did not immediately set the Second Division alight in 1959-60, the board eschewed reason for impatience. There was also a hint of egos bruised by the forthright gaffer. Jack opened the *Western Evening Herald* one day to find out that he had been sacked! By resurrecting the club, he had dug his own grave.

In truth, it was a tough division that year, with the likes of Aston Villa, Liverpool, and Sunderland. The Home Park fans could only wonder what might have been had Rowley been afforded more time to adapt to the higher division. After all, he had put together a decent outfit that would continue to develop – Plymouth would keep their place for years in the Second Division. For Jack, the only consolation was that he had lasted five years in the Plymouth hot seat. No other manager has survived that long since then, and God knows thirty-six have had a try.

The Nomadic Gaffer

They called them the Swinging Sixties and one look at Jack Rowley's managerial track record during the decade would tell you why. Gone was the stability of 23 years spent with just Manchester United and Plymouth. Instead, Jack opted to put in five separate managerial spells before the decade was out.

And where better to start than at the very bottom? To be fair, Oldham Athletic were not the worst Football League team in the land – Hartlepool United were... by one point! But the Latics were heading down fast and one can only guess how many more re-election applications they could have survived. Somehow for Jack, Boundary Park was his ideal calling. He arrived in the summer of 1960 and immediately started to construct an attacking side. It was not a smooth transition, at least judging by the nine defeats in the opening dozen matches. In October, however, Jack put his reputation to good use.

Bobby Johnstone had been a legend at Hibernian, one of the 'Famous Five' players who led the club to two Scottish League titles. He had also enjoyed a spell at Manchester City where he became the first player to score in two consecutive FA Cup finals. He had been capped and lauded yet, in October 1960, he signed for bottom-of-the-league Oldham Athletic. Only one man could have lured such a big name into the lower reaches – Jack Rowley. And he was not done yet. Johnstone was a creator of goals, so Jack bought Bert Lister from City to finish them.

The impact was sudden. Eight consecutive victories propelled the Latics to ninth, and they ended the campaign comfortably in mid-table. 1961-62 was another season of consolidation as Jack brought in more astute signings to the club. The average home gate jumped from 4,000 to 15,000. By 1962-63, the transformation was complete: from utter shambles, Oldham had gained promotion to Division Three. By his steely determination and straightforward style Jack had achieved success again.

Yet it was these same qualities that brought about his demise. Much like at Plymouth, certain directors were irked by his blunt honesty. It seemed the club's fortunes came second to their personal pride. Even as the Latics were celebrating promotion, a split board of directors voted him out! He was not even able to enjoy his achievement. Instead, he ruefully reflected: "Some seem to think I'm too tough a boss. Well, I call a spade a spade and do some straight talking".

Why bother with the Third Division when you can manage in the Dutch top flight! And with Ajax Amsterdam, to boot. Twenty-six years after touring Holland with Bournemouth, Jack Rowley was back for a more permanent visit. Admittedly, this was before Johan Cruyff emerged to transform Ajax into a European superpower, but this job was an exciting challenge that Jack was eager to take on. As always he was candid with them when they approached him: "Before we go any further, I won't have anything to do with defensive football. If you want that, you're wasting your time with me".

So Ajax attacked in 1963–64 and averaged more than two goals per game but, ironically, this was their lowest return in six years. Although they had been runners-up before Jack took over, this was an ageing Ajax side. Jack did well to guide them to fifth. Johan Cruyff's introduction was one season away and it was incidentally a season in which the team dropped to 13th. Jack had left by then, his contract not renewed in the summer of 1964, possibly due to more personality clashes. Had Jack mastered bluntness in Dutch? In reality, the club had decided to adopt a different approach to playing the game. Rowley was not Ajax's first English boss. In fact, in only 11 of the previous 54 years did the club not employ a British manager. However, they were now looking to dabble with a new concept called 'Total Football'.

For Jack it was time to embark on a period of total relaxation instead. For a year and a half he had nothing to do with football. Then, in January 1966, he glanced at the bottom of the Fourth Division table and decided he fancied the Wrexham job. He was back in the game and at the same level he had been before heading to Holland. You could tell his first team-talk was about attacking football because Wrexham went out and battered Barnsley 6-3! Results rapidly improved, the team rising to 16th out of 24 with ten matches to go. At this point, an over-confident Jack tempted fate by promising his players that, if they avoided the re-election zone, he would throw 'the biggest party Wrexham had ever seen'. Unfortunately, his pledge backfired – the players lost their focus and picked up a mere four points thereafter to plummet to bottom spot!

No further such promises were thus made for 1966-67. Instead, with renewed drive, Jack guided the Robins towards the top of the table. By the end of November they had gone 16 league matches without defeat to set a new club record that lasted for 37 years. But the momentum stalled and Wrexham dropped out of the promotion zone. Jack became disillusioned and, on April 2nd, he unexpectedly left the club to take over at Bradford Park Avenue instead. It must have been Bradford's position of 22nd that attracted him!

There is no telling whether Jack had run into more board politics at Wrexham, but his short stint at the Racecourse Ground was fondly remembered. At least by Steve Stacey, a former defender who served under him at the time: "Jack Rowley was a likeable chap and the players respected him immensely. He was an inspiration when he spoke and, had he stayed, I think things would have improved greatly. I was quite surprised when he quit and went to Bradford".

It was surprising then and it remains surprising now. Jack had been steering Wrexham upwards whereas Bradford were heading in the other direction at twice the speed. Perhaps he still had an image of Bradford from 20 years earlier when they had some exciting cup tussles with Manchester United. But those days were long gone as was any money the club had. Even their captain was on loan from another team. Park Avenue were the worst League team around... officially: for the next three seasons they kept scraping the bottom of the Football League until they made a hole in it and dropped out.

Jack had long gone by then, having found yet another thankless task to take on. It was a strange trait of Jack's, this. All the glory he sought as a player was inversely mirrored by the misery he seemed to chase as a manager. And his new position was at a club he never thought he would return to: Oldham Athletic. Apparently, the board that had sacked him back in 1963 had since been ousted by a new owner, name of Ken Bates – the one and only – minus the white beard and with a shock of brown hair. So Jack headed back to Boundary Park in late September 1968 for some "unfinished business". What he had let himself into, however, was some monkey business. Bates had been running Oldham all the way from the Caribbean where he was living at the time and, subsequently, all the good work Rowley had achieved in his first spell had been undone. The Latics were bottom of Division Three (surprise, surprise) with just nine points from 21 matches, but Jack was nonetheless optimistic: "I am very pleased indeed to be back with Oldham. I realise, of course, that it will be a struggle, but it cannot be any worse than it has been".

Indeed, with Jack back at the helm, performances improved, with Oldham averaging a point a game thereafter. It was mid-table form but, due to their predicament before his arrival, not enough to save them from relegation. A rueful Jack concluded: "The lads have done a tremendous job since Christmas, and it is a great pity they did not have a better start to the season". It was also a great pity they did not have a better start the following season either. When Bates sold up in December 1969, the new chairman came in and immediately let Jack go. It proved to be his last job in football.

In truth, he had had enough. The 20 years he spent as a footballer were a thrill a minute, but the fifteen as a manager would in time turn him off. He may not have been as successful from the dugout but he certainly was not a failure – otherwise, why did they keep hiring him? However, it was his straightforward personality that tended to get him into conflicts with those who hired and fired. And the frank truth was that he was never afraid to lose his job. Results were secondary to him, a distant second in fact to what he loved to do most, going back to when he was a player: to entertain.

So, as football moved toward a defensive, 'win at all costs' philosophy, Jack drifted away from it. It was not hard for him to find affection for other sports – already he was a keen golfer and cricketer – and, as the years passed, he took to watching rugby instead where "they take the knocks, shake them off and then later are the best of pals at the bar", as he confessed in 'Legends of United'.

During the 1970s, Jack Rowley mellowed, believe it or not. His new job helped – he ran a newsagents and sub-post office in the Shaw district of Oldham where he continued to live. His wife Violet assisted him too when she was not busy raising their three children. By 1980 he was working for a local mail order firm until retiring in 1983. He was 65 years old by then, it was time to relax, and who was going to tell him 'no'?

Three Hundred Sixty Something

This is a book about Manchester United's legends of the past. So, forget about Jack Rowley's time with the likes of Bournemouth and Plymouth, and do not bother with his various spells in management. Just look at the era he spent at Old Trafford and you will see that he ought to rank among the greatest of all Manchester United legends.

Nowadays we marvel in amazement whenever a striker manages to put the ball in the back of the net, and the striker himself laps up the adulation, a month's work fulfilled. Yet, for 18 years from 1937 to 1955, Jack Rowley never seemed to run out of goals. He would smash a hat-trick one weekend and you would think that he was done for now, but he would always come back to belt in more the next time out.

There were spells, such as in the autumns of 1941 and 1951, when he attained a level of finishing nirvana that if you gave him one pass he would get you two goals, or so it seemed. We could dwell for days about a past player's merits but just look at Rowley's numbers. In the Football League alone, he rattled in 182 goals for United. Twenty-nine more came in the FA Cup and Charity Shield to take his competitive total to 211. Jack slammed a further 104 strikes during the war years, be it in the regional leagues, the Lancashire Cup, or the Manchester Senior Cup. And he topped that off with another 47 strikes in friendly matches, taking his overall tally to a bewildering 362 goals for United! Not that I was keeping track. You can hail the Charltons, Laws or Rooneys to the heavens all day long, but no one comes remotely close to Jack's achievement.

Some might criticize Jack's figures, arguing that a big chunk of it came in the undistinguished arenas of wartime football and friendlies. But when it comes to goals, Manchester United fans do not discriminate. Us true Reds may chatter excitedly about new signings or gasp at a brief display of artistry, but the basic essence of our existence - what we crave and the specific reason we watch United - is those precise moments when the team scores. That is when we spontaneously explode in celebration of a goal. And Jack Rowley personally made United fans burst with joy over 360 times! Besides, the reason Jack netted so many wartime goals was because he lost seven years of his competitive career when he was busy saving the country. Try taking seven years away from Charlton or Law's careers and see where that leaves them.

A statistical breakdown may be tedious but this really *is* the place for a brief sideways look at Jack's startling tally, if only to highlight one specific phenomenon: the hat-trick. Out of 362 goals, there are bound to be a few: indeed, during his time with United, Jack blasted a stunning total of 28 hat-tricks! Eleven came in the League, one in the FA Cup, a dozen during the war, and four in friendlies. And only 16 of the 28 were pure hat-tricks in the simplest definition of the term. There were seven occasions when Jack went one better and fired four goals per outing. Then there were three separate instances when that was not enough and he would not be satisfied until he grabbed five. And that leaves two unforgettable occasions when he exceeded all Reds before him or after by powering seven goals in single matches!

The next time you are asked to compile a list of Manchester United's greatest players, it is probably best to put Jack Rowley in first then proceed to fill in the rest of the names. He brought trophies to the club when we did not know what they looked like, and he provided a continuous supply of goals as if they were the only substance that kept us alive.

Jack passed away on June 28th, 1998, aged 79 and based in a nursing home, suffering from dementia. The fear remains that, in his old age, he might have forgotten some of his achievements. Let us hope that we don't.

Jack Rowley

Born: 7.10.20 in Wolverhampton
MU debut: 23.10.37
England: 6/6

		LEAGUE		FA CUP	
Season	Club	Apps	Goals	Apps	Goals
1936–37	BOURNEMOUTH	12	10	–	–
1937–38	BOURNEMOUTH	11	2	–	–
1937–38	MANCHESTER UNITED	25	9	4	–
1938–39	MANCHESTER UNITED	38	10	1	–
1945–46	MANCHESTER UNITED	–	–	4	2
1946–47	MANCHESTER UNITED	37	26	2	2
1947–48	MANCHESTER UNITED	39	23	6	5
1948–49	MANCHESTER UNITED	39	20	9	10
1949–50	MANCHESTER UNITED	39	20	5	3
1950–51	MANCHESTER UNITED	39	14	3	1
1951–52	MANCHESTER UNITED	40	30	1	–
1952–53	MANCHESTER UNITED	32	1	5	–
1953–54	MANCHESTER UNITED	36	12	1	–
1954–55	MANCHESTER UNITED	22	7	3	1
1955–56	PLYMOUTH ARGYLE	13	2	–	–
1956–57	PLYMOUTH ARGYLE	16	6	–	–
1957–58	PLYMOUTH ARGYLE	26	6	2	1
TOTAL		458	208	46	30

BIBLIOGRAPHY

Blundell, Justin. "Back from the Brink". Empire, Manchester. 2006

Busby, Matt. "Soccer at the Top – my life in Football". Weidenfeld & Nicholson, London. 1973.

Busby, Matt with David Jack. "My Story". Souvenir Press, London. 1957.

Cavanagh, Roy and Brian Hughes MBE. "Dennis Viollet – the life of a legendary goalscorer" – Empire, Manchester. 2001.

Crompton, Jack with Cliff Butler. "From Goalline to Touchline". Empire, Manchester. 2008.

Doherty, John and Ivan Ponting. "The insiders guide to Manchester United" – Empire, Manchester. 2005.

Dunphy, Eamon. "A strange kind of glory". William Hienemann, London. 1991.

Dykes, Garth. "The United Alphabet". ACL & Polar, Leicester. 1994.

Foulkes, Bill and Ivan Ponting. "Manchester United & Beyond". The Bluecoat Press, Liverpool. 2003.

Giles, John. "John Giles – a football man". Hachette Books, Dublin. 2010.

Glanville, Rick. "Sir Matt Busby – a Tribute". Manchester United plc, Manchester. 1994.

Green, Geoffrey. "There's only one United". Hodd and Stoughton, London. 1978.

Harding, John. "Football Wizard". Robson Books, London. 1998.

Hughes, Brian MBE. "Starmaker – the Story of Jimmy Murphy". Empire Publications, Manchester. 2002.

Kelly, Stephen. " Backpage United". Queen Anne Press, London. 1990.

Liversedge, Stan. "Epitaph to a Legend". Soccer Book Publications Ltd, South Humbershire. 1994.

Matthews, Stanley. " The Way it Was". Headline Book Publishers, London. 2000.

McColl, Graham. "Take Me Home, United Road". Manchester United plc, Manchester. 2005.

McGuinness, Wilf with Ivan Ponting. "Manchester United – Man and Babe". Know the Score, Warwickshire. 2008.

Meek, David. "Legends of United". Orion Books, London. 1988.

Meek, David. "Manchester United – 100 Greatest Players". Manchester United plc, Manchester, 2001.

Miller, David. " Father of Football". Stanley Paul, London. 1970.

Murphy, Jimmy. "Matt, United and Me". Souvenir Press, London. 1968.

Shorrocks, Alec. "Winners and Champions ". Arthur Baker limited, London. 1985.

Taw, Thomas. "Manchester United's Golden Age". Desert Island, Essex. 2004.

Thornton, Eric. "Barson to Busby".

White, Jim. "Manchester United – the Biography". Sphere, London. 2008.